DREAMERS AND

True Stories of the Heroes

WRITERS:
Jack Henderson, Matt Latimer, Keith Urbahn

CONTRIBUTORS, RESEARCHERS & EDITORS:
Kate Albers, Stephanie Clarke, Victoria Cox,
Maggie Crawford, Kevin Smith

WRITTEN & EDITED BY:

GLENN BECK

WITH KEVIN BALFE

DECEIVERS

and Villains Who Made America

Threshold Editions   Mercury Radio Arts

New York London Toronto Sydney New Delhi

Threshold Editions/ Mercury Radio Arts
A Division of Simon & Schuster, Inc.
1230 Avenue of the Americas
New York, NY 10020

First Threshold Editions/Mercury Radio Arts paperback edition August 2015

THRESHOLD EDITIONS and colophon are trademarks
of Simon & Schuster, Inc.

GLENN BECK is a trademark of Mercury Radio Arts, Inc.

For information about special discounts for bulk purchases,
please contact Simon & Schuster Special Sales at
1–866–506–1949 or business@simonandschuster.com.

The Simon & Schuster Speakers Bureau can bring authors to your live event. For more information or to book an event, contact the Simon & Schuster Speakers Bureau at 866–248–3049 or visit our website at www.simonspeakers.com.

Interior design by Robert Ettlin
Jacket illustration by Joel West

Manufactured in the United States of America

10   9   8   7   6   5   4   3   2   1

Library of Congress Cataloging-in-Publication Data

Beck, Glenn.
   Dreamers and deceivers : true stories of the heroes and villains who made America / Glenn Beck.
      pages   cm
   Summary: "Glenn Beck provides stories of the people who built America and the people who sought to destroy it"—Provided by publisher.
   1. Heroes—United States.   2. Villains in popular culture—United States.
3. United States—Biography.   I. Title.
   E176.B384   2014
   305.9'06920973—dc23   2014032810

ISBN 978-1-4767-8390-1
ISBN 978-1-4767-8715-2 (ebook)

Dedication

To Brent Ashworth, Harlan Crowe, and David Barton—
three of the greatest Americans I know. These men have dedicated their lives
to collecting and preserving our history so that future generations
can hold the real story of America in their hands.

Contents

Author's Note

I t's easy to look back at our history and picture it as a simple collection of events: a war, a constitution, an election, another war, and so on. But history isn't really about events—those are just labels we give to things. It's the people who really matter.

People can spend their time working for good or evil. They can be heroes or villains. They can choose to fight for love and courage and truth, or they can fight for their own egos and agendas.

Sometimes, even in retrospect, it's not that easy to figure out who a person really was. Steve Jobs, for example, features prominently in this book as a dreamer, but he was certainly not without his flaws. And, as we now know from accounts published after his death, Jobs was not always a good man. He certainly wasn't always a fair one. According to Walter Isaacson's book *Steve Jobs*, Jobs once said some pretty nasty things about me and even tried to get me fired from Fox News.

But when I look back at Steve Jobs's life, I see a man who tried his best and whose contributions will leave a lasting mark on the world. Perhaps, in the end, the lesson is that it's as important to say "I tried" as it is to say "I succeeded."

My admiration for Steve Jobs's contributions demonstrates one of the best things about America: We live in a country where agreeing with someone and admiring them don't have to be mutually exclusive. There are plenty of people who have done things I admire even though I don't agree with some of their actions or beliefs.

Henry Ford is a good example. He was a horrible anti-Semite, a man who blamed the Jews for almost every evil in the world. In fact, Ford is the only American mentioned in Hitler's *Mein Kampf*. But Henry Ford was also a genius when it came to perfecting the automobile assembly line—an innovation (originally conceived by Ransom Olds) that changed the world.

I don't have to agree with someone, or even like them, to be able to recognize their achievements. In fact, instituting some kind of likability litmus test leads us down a pretty dangerous path toward a modern version of McCarthyism. I don't like what you stand for so I use my power to try to take you down. It's something that is seriously being proposed by many on the Left, and even some on the Right—and it's got to stop.

What if instead we all agreed to no more blacklists. No more blind loyalty oaths. No more trying to take people down or get them fired simply because we disagree with them.

Steve Jobs talked a lot about his belief that the axis in America is no longer "liberal and conservative," but "constructive and destructive." I could not agree more. But I think where we disagree is in identifying *who* gets to decide which category a person falls into. Thomas Edison was not a good guy—but would you prefer he had been blacklisted and put out of business before he ever got started? Would you give up everything he created simply because you didn't like something about his personality or his political views?

I, for one, am glad Steve Jobs lived and created what he did. He changed our world for the better. I would never sacrifice that because he and I didn't agree on politics.

That same rule applies to many of the people we selected for this book. I'm sure there are plenty of "deceivers" who were actually very nice and generous people. The reverse is also true: I have no doubt that some of the "dreamers" we feature were selfish or malicious. The goal of this book is not to generically categorize someone's entire life; it's only to look at an often narrow slice of their accomplishments.

As with the previous book in this series (*Miracles and Massacres*), I attempted to adhere to a few guiding principles when deciding which people to include. I tried to select:

1. People whose names are mostly familiar but who are either misunderstood or who have a side to their lives that is not well known;

2. People with stories that have messages or lessons with clear relevance to today;

3. People who represent both sides of our past—the selfless and the selfish; the dreamers and the deceivers.

There is a great mix of people with stories that I think will really surprise you. From incredible deceptions perpetrated by sitting presidents, to the world-changing genius of people like Desi Arnaz, Alan Turing, Walt Disney, and, yes, Steve Jobs.

Finally, just as with *Miracles and Massacres*, these stories have been written in a style that puts you right next to the characters. It's my hope that you'll feel like you're reading a novel more than a history book because we learn best when we engage with stories, not when we try to memorize meaningless details.

Once you've finished each story, I urge you to read the section "About the Writing of This Book," as it will give you a good sense for the writing process and will explain what we took from the historical record and what we imagined or dramatized for the sake of crafting a compelling story.

Laos Deo,

Dallas, Texas
2014

Grover Cleveland: The Mysterious Case of the Disappearing President

Albany, New York
July 21, 1884

Governor Grover Cleveland stared in disbelief at the front page of the *Buffalo Telegraph*. Just ten days earlier he had received the Democratic Party's nomination for president, and given his reputation for unwavering honesty, he knew that he had a real chance to win. His Republican opponent, the notoriously corrupt James G. Blaine—a man who would soon become known as "Blaine, Blaine, James G. Blaine, the Continental liar from the state of Maine!"—was vulnerable. If Cleveland managed to parlay his sterling reputation into a victory in November, he would be the first Democrat elected since before the Civil War.

But now, as Cleveland stared in disgust at the newspaper sitting on his desk, victory looked a lot less likely. A TERRIBLE TALE, screamed the morning's headline. A DARK CHAPTER IN A PUBLIC MAN'S HISTORY.

The *Telegraph*'s article told the story of Maria Halpin, a widow in Cleveland's hometown of Buffalo, who had a child named Oscar Folsom Cleveland.

Cleveland, a bachelor, had never acknowledged that his former lover's child was his. After all, several of his drinking buddies had also shared Maria's bed—could he really be sure of his paternity? But those friends were all married, so Cleveland had agreed to give the child his last name and his financial support. When the boy was sent to an orphanage after Maria's excessive drinking and deteriorating emotional state led to her stay in a mental institution, Cleveland had dutifully paid the orphanage bill of five dollars a week.

Now, in the midst of Cleveland's presidential campaign, the nine-year-old child's very existence threatened to derail his White House hopes—unless he could find a way to turn this crisis into an opportunity.

As Cleveland read through the article, much of which was exaggerated and sensationalized, the governor began to formulate a strategy. The American people, he reasoned, would forgive a sexual indiscretion. In fact, if he was completely honest about something so embarrassing— something so many men lied about almost out of habit—voters might actually *reward* him. His candor would reinforce the trustworthiness that had been his calling card ever since he'd been elected to replace Buffalo's corrupt mayor in 1881 and New York's corrupt governor in 1882. Now, in a meteoric rise to national prominence, that same forthrightness would save his nomination for president of the United States.

"Write this down, and send it to all my friends in Buffalo," Cleveland ordered his press secretary and close confidant, Daniel Lamont. "I have a simple message for anyone who is asking anything about Maria Halpin." His voice now boomed with confidence and authority. "Whatever you do . . . tell the truth!"

Cleveland's strategy worked perfectly. By the narrowest of margins, and, in large part thanks to the trust inspired by his response to the Maria Halpin scandal, the governor of New York was elected president of the United States of America. Joseph Pulitzer, of the *New York World,* spoke for millions when he explained the four reasons he supported Grover Cleveland: "1. He is an honest man; 2. He is an honest man; 3. He is an honest man; 4. He is an honest man."

Nine Years Later
From Washington, D.C., to New York City
July 1, 1893

The president grimaced as he climbed into the presidential carriage for the trip down Pennsylvania Avenue to the Baltimore & Potomac train station. It took quite an effort for the six-foot, one-inch, three-hundred-pound chief executive to get from the ground to his seat. Even though Grover Cleveland was more than strong enough, the fifty-six-year-old didn't enjoy physical exertion. He'd once told Daniel Lamont, who was now serving as secretary of war, that even walking was an annoyance to be avoided whenever possible.

Lamont was at Cleveland's side for the ride to the train station, just as he had been for the better part of the last decade. The president thought of his friend, who was fourteen years younger, as the son he'd never had. Lamont even looked in some ways like a slightly thinner and balder version of Cleveland, right down to the bushy walrus mustache they both sported. Unfailingly loyal, Lamont and Cleveland shared an affinity for whiskey, cigars, hunting, and fishing.

Lamont was by Cleveland's side when he won the presidential election in 1884, and he was there when Cleveland lost the White House in 1888, despite having won the popular vote. Four years later, Lamont reprised his role as press secretary in Cleveland's bid to reclaim the presidency. They celebrated together in 1892 when Cleveland defeated Benjamin Harrison by a landslide.

In his second term Cleveland promoted his friend to secretary of war, but the president continued to rely on Lamont's judgment and counsel in all critical matters of state. First among those matters was the "money question."

The Silver Purchase Act of 1890 required the United States Treasury to purchase 4.5 million ounces of silver each month and to print large amounts of paper currency that could be redeemed for that silver. The consequence was inflation—wild, catastrophic, panic-inducing inflation. By Cleveland's inauguration in March, the United States was in the midst of the worst economic recession in its history: the aptly labeled Panic of 1893.

Cleveland and Lamont arrived at the train station and boarded a special car prepared for them by the railroad's owner. The president placed a supremely high value on discretion. Once aboard, his first priority was to order a cigar and a whiskey. His second order of business was to pull down the window shades. A private man even under ordinary circumstances, Cleveland knew the purpose of this trip was anything but ordinary. The press and public were on a "need to know" basis, and as far as he was concerned, there was nothing about this journey that any of them needed to know.

Cleveland had frequently received good press, especially as it related to his anticorruption efforts as mayor, governor, and president, yet he still despised reporters. As the train left the station, he recalled all the times journalists had poked their noses in where they didn't belong, beginning with their coverage of the Maria Halpin affair.

At times, Cleveland's rage at reporters turned to fits of anger. At other times, he found an outlet for his frustration by writing blistering letters to newspaper editors. To one publication, he wrote that "the falsehoods daily spread before the people in our newspapers are insults to the American love for decency and fair play of which we boast." To another, he blasted "keyhole correspondents" for using "the enormous power of the modern newspaper to perpetuate and disseminate a colossal impertinence."

The whiskey soon arrived, as did the cigar. With all the shades pulled down, Cleveland was able to relax for the first time since he'd hoisted himself into the presidential carriage. Only after he and Lamont were safely away from the Washington, D.C., area did Cleveland raise the shades to enjoy the views as the New York Express chugged northward.

The sights outside the president's window, however, were not always pleasing to his eye. Occasionally the train would pass by shantytowns filled with jobless vagabonds and homeless families making the most of what tin, cardboard, and spare lumber they could find to create shelter.

The train was moving fast, but he could still see the misery in the sunken eyes of the unfortunate inhabitants. Cleveland knew that unemployment was at an all-time high, that stocks were anemic, that banks, railroads, and factories were failing, that farm foreclosures were rampant, and that all the wrong rates were rising: interest rates, unemployment rates, and, if the papers were to be believed, suicide rates as well. Even so, Cleveland was not prepared for the wretched, impoverished conditions he saw from his window. The shantytowns looked like refugee camps in some third-world, war-ravaged country.

The tragic sights of suffering steeled the president's resolve to repeal the Silver Purchase Act. Just that morning, before surreptitiously leaving the capital, he had called for a special session of Congress to consider repealing the law he blamed for the country's woes. He was sure he could persuade them to eliminate the act. He was coming off a landslide election and the political momentum was squarely on his side. Only public disclosure of the purpose of the trip he was now on could stop him.

Cleveland arrived in Jersey City, New Jersey, and boarded a ferry for Manhattan. His destination was a luxurious yacht anchored in the East River, which would then sail him to his vacation home in Massachusetts, on Buzzards Bay, off Cape Cod. Before he could get there, however, he had to deal with a handful of reporters who had discovered that the president was no longer at the White House. They were curious to know why he had left Washington on the eve of debate over the Silver Purchase Act.

"I have nothing to say for publication, except that I am going to Buzzards Bay for a rest."

New York City
July 1, 1893
Early Evening

Among the reporters who had been on the ferry with Grover Cleveland was Elisha Jay Edwards, known to readers of his almost daily column by his one-word penname: Holland.

With a thick, light brown mustache that did little to obscure his handsome, angular face, Edwards was among the most diligent and respected journalists in the nation. A skilled researcher and writer, he had graduated from Yale Law School in 1873 and then stayed in New Haven to practice law. Those plans changed when he purchased an interest in New Haven's *Elm City Press*. Before long, his photographic memory, penchant for dogged investigations, and ability to write quickly, clearly, and elegantly made him the best reporter in that Connecticut city.

The early 1870s were the beginning of a drastic, two-decade media expansion. New printing technologies and a rise in literacy were the driving forces behind a threefold increase in newspaper sales. During that era, no publisher was as respected and feared as the *New York Sun's* Charles Dana. It was Dana who plucked the talented Edwards out of obscurity and brought him from New Haven to New York in 1879.

After ten years of twelve-hour days with Dana, Edwards took a job as the New York correspondent for the *Philadelphia Press*. It was there that "Holland" became one of the most read syndicated columnists in the country.

Six days a week, in newsrooms across the nation, reporters would begin their day by asking the same question: "What does Holland say today?"

As the evening sun set outside his window in the Schermerhorn Building on Manhattan's Lower East Side, Edwards wrote out the next day's column in longhand. It included a bit of gossip about Interior Secretary Hoke Smith, "the only member of the cabinet who has dared to assert himself in the presence of the president," and a little news about "a delegation of starving miners" who "may be sent to Washington from Colorado and Montana demanding from President Cleveland not bread but silver, which is the same to them." Finally, near the end of the column, was a note about how President Cleveland and his friend Elias Benedict were planning to spend much of July together at their vacation homes on Buzzards Bay. "Mr. Benedict says that Mr. Cleveland is as impatient for the sea bass fishing and as hungry for a day's sport trolling for bluefish as a schoolboy is for the first day of his vacation."

On Board the *Oneida*
East River, New York City
July 2, 1893
10:30 A.M.

As the *Oneida* pulled anchor on a warm, sunny morning and set sail northward, the president of the United States smiled and relaxed comfortably on her deck. He always felt his best when surrounded by old friends, and he had plenty of them now lounging beside him: his friend Elias Benedict, Lamont, and Joseph Bryant, who was his brother-in-law, family doctor, and frequent fishing companion. Over the years, Cleveland had traveled more than fifty thousand miles on the *Oneida*, often with some combination of these three men at his side and a fishing pole in his hand.

Cleveland's affinity for the boat was understandable, perhaps even unavoidable. With two masts and a glistening white 144-foot hull, she was a sleek, spectacularly gorgeous yacht. In 1885, the vessel—then named the *Utowana*—won the prestigious Lunberg Cup race. Soon after that, Elias Benedict purchased it and rechristened her *Oneida*.

The president chatted amiably with his friends about matters large and small while the *Oneida* glided past dozens of other boats in the East River. Their destination, Buzzards Bay, was no secret, and a typical trip would take about fifteen hours. But Cleveland and his friends were all too aware that this was no ordinary journey. The expected departures from their usual route, as well as what would happen on that route, were known only to a handful of people—including the four gentlemen currently lounging on the ship's deck, as well as a small number of passengers who had been hidden belowdecks, out of sight from the utterly unsuspecting public and press corps.

Shortly before noon, Cleveland watched as Joseph Bryant rose from his deck chair and walked toward the steps leading belowdecks. "If you hit a rock," Bryant called to the captain, "hit it good and hard, so that we'll all go to the bottom!"

Cleveland was not amused.

On Board the *Oneida*
July 2, 1893
12:05 P.M.

One of the small, tastefully decorated rooms belowdecks was a saloon. Grover Cleveland walked into it and stood in the middle of the room.

A socially active ladies' man back in his Buffalo days, Cleveland had been in hundreds of saloons over the course of his fifty-six years. But there were at least two unusual, even bizarre, aspects about the appearance of this particular one and the man who now stood in it.

The first was that the saloon had been stripped of all but one piece of furniture.

The second was that the three-hundred-pound president of the United States was standing nearly naked, wearing only his underwear and walrus mustache.

"I am ready for you," said the commander in chief. "Are you ready for me?"

New York City
July 3, 1893

Elisha Jay Edward was midway through the *New York Times* and all but done with his cup of tea when he noticed it.

No Sign of the Oneida
The President Has Not Yet Arrived at Gray Gables

The dispatch was buried in the middle of a tall column, below other short reports about a shooting at a boardinghouse and a political quarrel between an Irish-American organization and the mayor of Newark, New Jersey.

Buzzards Bay, Mass.—The weather is thick in Buzzards Bay, and there are no signs of the yacht Oneida, *having on board the*

Presidential party. Nothing has been heard of the party since they left New York.

The report's last paragraphs noted that the "usual run" from Manhattan to Buzzards Bay was "fifteen hours," and it stated that "inasmuch as the boat has not been reported at any of the ports, it is the opinion here that the yacht is at anchor down the bay awaiting the clearing of the fog, which will allow her to proceed."

Despite the breezy tone of the *Times* report, one fact was unavoidable: The president was missing.

New York City
July 4, 1893

E. J. Edwards's curiosity was further aroused when he arrived at the Schermerhorn Building on Independence Day and learned from the morning papers that President Cleveland was still unaccounted for. It had been three days since the *Oneida* slipped through the narrow channel between Manhattan and Queens, and no one on dry land had heard from the president since.

Dressed in a dark suit, necktie, high-collared shirt, and high-topped leather shoes, Edwards continued to skim the morning papers and noticed that the more sensational of them were speculating that Cleveland was somehow in trouble. There were rumors of a serious illness, although Edwards thought that to be unlikely, as it would be cause for a return to shore, not a reason to remain at sea.

Edwards knew that if Cleveland were gravely ill, it would spell doom for the repeal of the Silver Purchase Act. Foisted on Cleveland's ticket for political balance at the Democratic convention, Vice President Adlai Stevenson was a staunch silverite. If fence-sitting congressmen sensed that Stevenson would soon be assuming power, they wouldn't dare cross him and his pro-silver allies.

Edwards believed there was little sense in dwelling on such far-fetched possibilities. Newspapers could speculate as much as they wished about the president's seventy-two-hour absence, but Edwards thought Cleveland's disappearance didn't seem out of character. The president was famous for his desire for privacy, and he wasn't the kind of man who needed much of a reason for keeping his whereabouts a secret.

The possibility of a serious illness seemed especially unlikely to Edwards for one additional reason: On the ferry to New York, Cleveland had said that he was merely "going to Buzzards Bay for a rest." He had assured reporters there was nothing out of the ordinary about the trip. And, as everyone knew, Grover Cleveland was nothing if not honest.

New York City
Morning, July 7, 1893

Six days after Cleveland had set sail from Manhattan, E. J. Edwards was finally beginning to have doubts about the president's story. The morning papers reported two pieces of intriguing news.

The first concerned the president's reemergence. Yesterday morning, the eight reporters awaiting his arrival at Gray Gables on Buzzards Bay had learned that Cleveland, Lamont, and Bryant had reached land in the middle of the night and slipped into Gray Gables without informing a single member of the press. When reporters pressed Lamont for an explanation of the president's arrival—four days late and seemingly clandestinely choreographed—Lamont assured them the trip was "leisurely," the party had "found good fishing grounds," and that Cleveland's health was "excellent, excepting that he was suffering from a slight attack of rheumatism."

The second news item detailed the transcript of an interview with Dr. Bryant conducted the previous evening by an unidentified reporter for *United Press*.

> **United Press:** Doctor, a number of conflicting stories are told concerning the illness of the president. Some of them make the matter very serious. You would confer a great favor by making some sort of official statement.
> **Bryant:** The president is all right.

United Press: From what is he suffering?

Bryant: He is suffering from rheumatism, just as was reported this afternoon. Those reports were correct.

United Press: Then, Doctor, the report that he is suffering from a malignant or cancerous growth in the mouth and that an operation was necessary and had been performed to relieve it is not correct?

Bryant: He is suffering from the teeth; that is all.

United Press: Has an operation been performed?

Bryant: That is all.

Gray Gables, Massachusetts
July 7, 1893
7:15 P.M.

Bryant's failure to unequivocally deny that an operation had been performed led to a feeding frenzy in the press. In an effort to alleviate the growing suspicions, the doctor quickly assembled the reporters. "The president is absolutely free from cancer or malignant growth of any description," he told them. "No operation has been performed, except that a bad tooth was extracted." Bryant categorically denied that any interview with a United Press reporter had taken place the night before.

But it was too late. By midafternoon, the number of reporters staying at Walker's Hotel near Buzzards Bay had swelled from eight to fifty. Each of them was demanding answers to the question of what exactly the president of the United States had been doing for four unexplained days at sea.

As Secretary of War Lamont entered a large barn on the Gray Gables grounds, he felt an enormous sense of responsibility. Assembled there were the fifty reporters he had asked to gather for a 7:00 P.M. press conference that was intended to answer their questions once and for all.

Lamont had been willing to reprise his role as Cleveland's press secretary, not because he relished a return to the lion's den, but because he believed no one else was up to the task. If he could convince reporters that the president's health problems were nothing worse than rheumatism and a toothache, Cleveland would retain the public's confidence. More important, he would still be able to pressure Congress into repealing the Silver Purchase Act. On the other hand, if the reporters did not leave the barn satisfied that the rumors of cancer surgery were false, Cleveland's reputation, and his political capital, would be gone.

According to the *New York Times*, cancer was an "incurable" disease. If politicians in Washington believed Cleveland's life was in jeopardy, then his plans to revive the abominable economy would be as well. More banks would collapse; more farms would be foreclosed on; and millions more Americans would lose their jobs.

"I have a brief statement to make," Lamont began, doing his best to affect a confident and casual air. "There has been quite a stir over a trivial occurrence of rheumatism. I think the reactions to the president's minor aches and pains have been rather foolish, but I understand how unfounded rumors tend to take on a life of their own."

As reporters scribbled Lamont's words into their notebooks, the secretary of war continued. "It was nothing but dentistry that occasioned President Cleveland's journey on his friend Elias Benedict's yacht. The president had been too busy attending to affairs of state in Washington to see a dentist, and he used the occasion of his boat trip from New York to Buzzards Bay to have some dental work performed in a comfortable environment. President Cleveland understands the public's curiosity about his health, and he is grateful for their concerns about his well-being."

It was a hot and stuffy July evening, and sweat poured from the brows of the journalists packed into the barn. Lamont, on the other hand, looked as cool as a cucumber. There was no hesitation in his words or doubt in his tone. "President Cleveland's dentist performed admirably, as did the patient, who has spent a relaxing day playing checkers with the First Lady."

Having swatted away the "unfounded rumors," Lamont turned to the silverites who Cleveland blamed for the country's economic woes. "The only dishonorable behavior in the past week," he said coolly, with the slightest of smiles, "has come from quarters opposed to the president's attempts to revive the American economy. The opposition knows that the public stands firmly behind President Cleveland's monetary policies, and their attempt to portray the president as ill or injured is a sign of their desperation."

For the next half hour, Lamont fielded questions asking for details about the dental procedures performed and the identity of the dentist employed, but time and again, Lamont dismissed the questions as "trivial" and "unworthy of a response."

There was, in fact, only one question Lamont answered directly.

"Is it true," asked a correspondent from the *New York Tribune*, "that Vice President Stevenson left the World's Fair in Chicago yesterday and is travelling to Buzzards Bay?"

"No," Lamont answered emphatically. "Although, the Vice President did apparently make the mistake of believing some of the more sensational reports of the president's health in your newspapers. It's true he *did* leave Chicago yesterday, and *was* heading here out of concern for the president's health, but President Cleveland telegraphed him en route, reassured him of his general fitness, and requested Mr. Stevenson embark on a tour of the West Coast. There are important party leaders out there, and the administration desires that they know they have our respect and attention. For the next month, Vice President Stevenson will be visiting San Diego, San Francisco, Seattle, and cities in between."

When Lamont returned to the main residence at Gray Gables he telegraphed the secretary of state to reassure him of the information he had just shared with the press. "To Walter Q. Gresham, Secretary of State," Lamont wrote: "The president is laid up with rheumatism in his knee and foot, but will be out in a day or two. No occasion for any uneasiness. —D.S. Lamont."

As his last official act of the evening, Lamont instructed an assistant to send a copy of the telegram to the reporters staying at Walker's Hotel. He was unsure how much of his story in the barn they believed, but he figured it couldn't hurt to show them the same information was being sent to President Cleveland's own secretary of state. Even if reporters believed Cleveland would allow Dan Lamont to mislead a group of reporters, surely they wouldn't believe Cleveland would allow Lamont to lie to his own secretary of state.

New York City
July 8, 1893

As the morning sun streaked through his window in the Schermerhorn Building, E. J. Edwards leaned back in his desk chair, puffed on his pipe, and skimmed the *New York Tribune*.

> Mr. Cleveland Is Better
> Likely to Recover in a Few Days

The *New York Times* agreed:

"The assertion that President Cleveland is afflicted with any malady is all nonsense."

Most ardent in its defense of the president's good health was the *New York World*'s editorial page.

> *The persistent attempts to misrepresent and exaggerate President Cleveland's ailment are something more than scandalous at this time. If these reports were believed by the public, they might very easily, and probably would, precipitate a financial panic.*

In a lecturing tone, the *World* went on to call it "a pity if a president cannot have a 'touch of rhoumatix' and a toothache without giving rise to a swarm of rumors and false reports—some of them more malignant than his disease."

Edwards closed the paper and took a sip of his coffee. Like the rest of the country, he had been perplexed by the president's disappearance. After reading the United Press's interview with Dr. Bryant the morning before, he began to wonder whether there was some truth to the rumors about Cleveland's ill health. However, the press corps covering the president seemed to believe what Lamont had told them. Now, in light of the morning papers' consensus about the president's medical condition, Edwards suspected that little more would be heard regarding the rumors.

Greenwich, Connecticut
August 27, 1893

It had been nearly two months since E. J. Edwards had given much thought to President Cleveland's mysterious disappearance. In that time, he had taken a summer vacation and then returned to Greenwich, Connecticut, where he kept a home.

As Edwards rode down the sweltering streets he heard a voice calling, "Edwards! Edwards!" The reporter instructed his driver to stop the carriage and then he poked his head out the window. Outside, he saw his friend Leander Jones running toward him.

Jones was a local doctor, and although Edwards wasn't surprised that his friend would want to say hello and catch up, he was taken aback when, upon arriving at Edwards's carriage, Jones, half out of breath, asked "Can you have your driver pull to the side? I have incredible news to share!"

New York City
August 28, 1893
8:45 A.M.

In the late nineteenth century, the elegant brownstones of Harlem were among the most prestigious addresses on the continent. Inside their tony walls lived the leading men of New York City: doctors and lawyers, bank owners and industrialists, and a dentist named Ferdinand Hasbrouck, who happened to be among the nation's leading experts in anesthesia.

E. J. Edwards rang the doorbell of Ferdinand Hasbrouck's town house so early that the dentist was still in his nightshirt when he opened the door.

"I apologize if you were sleeping, Dr. Hasbrouck," the journalist said, extending his hand. "The name's E. J. Edwards."

The two shook hands as Edwards continued: "I write for the *Philadelphia Press,* and it's only because I'm on a deadline that I'm here so early. Would you mind taking a few moments to confirm a couple facts for an article I'm working on?"

Edwards was somewhat surprised when Hasbrouck invited him in, excused himself to change out of his nightclothes, and returned with a polite and pleasant demeanor. The reporter wasn't sure why Hasbrouck had received him, but he tried his best to hide how thrilled he was to be sitting in the parlor of a man who might have the answer to the biggest mystery in the history of the presidency: What had Grover Cleveland really been doing for four days on the *Oneida*?

"I happened to be returning home in Greenwich yesterday," said Edwards, "when a friend shared some details about your assistance with the president's surgery on the *Oneida* last month."

Edwards was doing his best to make his information seem unimportant—as if he were just nailing down some details for a story that everyone already knew about. The truth, of course, was exactly the opposite: Dr. Hasbrouck might be able to provide first-person confirmation for the biggest scoop by any reporter of E. J. Edwards's generation.

As Edwards told Hasbrouck what he'd heard the day before, the dentist's face grew ashen. His eyes widened with Edwards's every word, and after just a few minutes, he flung himself back in his chair and sank down into it.

Finally, after Edwards described what happened on the *Oneida* in exacting detail, Hasbrouck exclaimed, "Some of the physicians who were aboard the yacht must have told you that story! You could not have obtained it any other way!"

In fact, the first person from the ship to speak with E. J. Edwards was Ferdinand Hasbrouck. His time on the *Oneida* had caused him to miss an appointment to provide anesthesia for a July 3 surgery in Greenwich with a doctor named Carlos MacDonald. In an attempt to explain his absence and protect his reputation against charges of unreliability, Hasbrouck revealed to MacDonald exactly where he had been on the first three days of July and exactly what he had been doing. MacDonald then told enough friends and colleagues that rumors about Cleveland's health swirled around New York social circles well before the president ever reached Buzzards Bay.

Among those MacDonald told was a Connecticut doctor named Leander Jones.

New York City
August 28, 1893
6:45 P.M.

"I'm calling with the biggest scoop you've ever heard in your life!"

E. J. Edwards spoke quickly into the phone to a stenographer for the *Philadelphia Press*. "It's too big for me telegraph it to you, so I'm going to dictate everything I've written over the phone. Are you ready?"

The real question, Edwards believed, was whether the country was ready.

"Make seven headlines. The top one should say:

THE PRESIDENT A VERY SICK MAN

Then, below it:

AN OPERATION PERFORMED ON HIM ON MR. BENEDICT'S YACHT

PART OF THE JAW REMOVED

A DISEASE WHOSE SYMPTOMS GAVE INDICATIONS THAT IT MIGHT BE SARCOMA

Follow that with:

MR. CLEVELAND'S PRESENT CONDITION SUCH AS TO GIVE ENCOURAGEMENT

THE CASE NOT UNLIKE GRANT'S

Finally:

FOUR DAYS IN BED AFTER THE USE OF GAS AND KNIFE—
SEVERAL OF NEW YORK'S EXPERT PHYSICIANS CONCERNED "

Edwards's voice was full of excitement. For decades, he had tracked down every lead, cultivated countless sources, and had taken care to write one of the most reliably accurate and eloquent columns in the country. Now he was ready to inform the nation that their president had recently been diagnosed with cancer.

Cleveland, Edwards would report, had assembled a dream team of doctors on the *Oneida* to surgically remove his malignant tumor in an environment that would be free of leaks to the press. He had enlisted his friends—in particular his secretary of war—to cover it up with lies, all in the service of a president twice elected by the American people on the basis of his reputation for unwavering honesty.

Edwards continued dictating into the phone. "Mr. Cleveland, with Mr. Lamont, whose faithful attendance . . . approaches that of filial affection and has been a matter of much comment during the summer, left Washington quite suddenly upon the day when the call for the extraordinary session of Congress was issued.

"Arrangements were made in this city with celerity, and Mr. Cleveland was met when he arrived here by Dr. Bryant and another physician, and by Dr. Hasbrouck, all of whom boarded the yacht with him. The baggage of these physicians contained the instruments of surgery and the apparatus for anesthetic administration."

When Grover Cleveland had presented himself, per doctor's orders, in his underwear, Edwards reported, the saloon he stood in had been converted into an operating room. Its only piece of furniture was a reclining chair for him to sit on during the surgery. Oxygen and nitrous oxide were stored in tanks beside it. Before him was his friend Joseph Bryant, along with three other surgeons, plus the White House physician, and Dr. Ferdinand Hasbrouck, who would administer anesthesia and pull the teeth blocking the tumor.

"When the time came, the President of the United States submitted himself to the surgeon as calmly, as gently, and as willingly as though he were merely lying down for brief slumber," Edwards told the stenographer. "The operation did not require very long, but it entailed the cutting away of a considerable part of the upper jaw bone upon one side, the instrument boring through the bone and tissue as far as the orbital plate."

After the operation—which caused Cleveland's heart rate to fall and his temperature to surge—the president was left with a two-and-a-half-square-inch hole in his mouth where five teeth, a third of the roof of his mouth, and a considerable chunk of his upper jawbone had once been.

Faced with the most deceptive and audacious disappearing act in presidential history, Edwards took care not to exaggerate any aspect of the story. If anything, he felt he downplayed the peril the president was in. After all, only about 5 percent of patients who underwent surgery to remove a cancerous tumor survived for more than three years. In other words, the odds were only one in twenty that Grover Cleveland would serve the remainder of this presidential term.

Nevertheless, Edwards assured readers that, although the president was "perhaps a very sick man," his doctors expected him to recover. "Mr. Cleveland recovered from the shock even better than the physicians had dared to hope he would. He was kept in bed, so well treated that he slept much of the time, and after four days' absence, during which time the country was wondering where he was, it was deemed safe to permit him to land at Gray Gables."

Of course, Edwards did not need to exaggerate anything in his exposé. The truth was incredible enough.

It was so incredible, in fact, that a strange thing happened after it was reprinted in newspapers from coast to coast over the next few days: The public didn't believe it. The nation simply wasn't willing to take E. J. Edwards's word over their president's.

EPILOGUE

On the president's behalf, his allies in the press waged a vigorous onslaught on Edwards's veracity. The reporter was labeled a "panic-monger," "a disgrace to journalism," and a "calamity liar" whose reporting was "the very depth of despicable journalism." Not a single person with firsthand knowledge of the president's surgery went on record to confirm Edwards's story and vindicate the maligned journalist. Edwards could have boosted his own credibility by revealing Hasbrouck's name—or even the dentist's connection to the surgery—but to protect his confidential source, Edwards refused to do so.

Edwards endured attack after attack from Democratic-leaning newspapers like the *Philadelphia Times*. Its front-page story the day after the exposé was published was typical:

> *The only element of truth in the latest story of President Cleveland's illness which has been printed in Philadelphia is that he suffered from a toothache and that the teeth which pained him were removed on board E. C. Benedict's yacht.*
>
> *Mr. Edwards surrounded his report of that event with all the cruel and cold-blooded details, true and false, which his imagination could call up.*

The article added that Cleveland's tooth extraction was "one of the commonest, simplest operations known to dentistry" and that "there was no question of cancer or of sarcoma. Any comparison between Mr. Cleveland's toothache and the serious malady from which General Grant suffered and which caused his death was only another evidence of the exquisite heartlessness of the newspaper correspondent."

Without hesitation or exception, Cleveland, Lamont, and their allies tenaciously held on to their "toothache" story, and when the dust settled in the wake of Edwards's article, the American people believed that, from July 1 to July 5, 1893, President Cleveland had gone fishing, suffered from some rheumatism, and had a few teeth extracted.

On the back of Cleveland's popularity, and after one of the longest Senate filibusters in American history, Congress repealed the Silver

Purchase Act on October 30, 1893. The president's gambit to protect his political capital had worked—and the result was a radically new economic policy for the United States.

Thanks to Cleveland's deception, silver was out and gold was in, where it would remain until 1933, when the gold standard was abandoned by another former governor of New York, a Democratic president who shared with Cleveland a talent for covering up medical conditions: Franklin Delano Roosevelt.

Although he never regained all his energy or weight—or, unfortunately for the White House staff, control over his temper—the president served out every remaining day of his term in office. In a stroke of immense luck, Cleveland's cancer turned out to be unusually slow growing. When he died in 1908 (there is some debate about whether the cancer caused his death), not a single obituary mentioned his disappearance in July 1893 or the radical surgery his doctors performed in the saloon of the *Oneida*.

Not only did the president physically and politically survive the surgery—his tumor survived as well. Retained by one of his doctors as a souvenir, the clump of bone, tissue, and teeth today sits at the bottom of a glass jar on display in the New York Academy of Medicine's Mutter Museum. The caption beside it reads, "Tumor—Specimen Removed from the maxillary (upper) left jaw of President Grover Cleveland on July 1st, 1893."

In light of all the misreporting and obfuscation about the president's time on the *Oneida*, there is something fitting about the caption at the Mutter Museum: The date is wrong and the word *cancer* is not mentioned.

Perhaps the only thing that did not survive this bizarre episode of history intact was E. J. Edwards's once sterling reputation. Although he would continue to write his column and investigate with tenacity and success, his readers and peers were unwilling to place the trust in "Holland" they'd once had. Cleveland had salvaged his political strength and his economic agenda only by slandering and irreparably injuring a blameless reporter who dared to expose the truth.

It was not until 1917—nearly twenty-five years later—that one of the surviving doctors from the *Oneida* operation admitted publicly that Edwards's story "was substantially correct, even in most of the details." In a lengthy article in the *Saturday Evening Post,* Dr. William Keen, the most prestigious surgeon in the country, explained in intricate detail how he assisted Dr. Bryant and the other doctors who had operated on Grover Cleveland.

It had taken more than two decades, but in E. J. Edwards's seventieth year, his readers finally learned once and for all that he was an honest man—and that Grover Cleveland was not.

Cleveland was, of course, hardly the last president to lie to the American people or engage in a nonstop war against transparency. Nor was he the last to have his word held in high esteem by a compliant press corps. What has changed in modern times, however, is that the media—the so-called fourth estate made up of America's best and brightest journalists—are no longer trusted.

Sadly, that leaves the American people with no one to rely on: not the politicians; not the media.

Nature may abhor a vacuum, but political systems abhor a vacuum of trust even more. If we don't find someone to fill it—someone who can unify the country behind the truth—then that vacuum will be filled for us.

2

"I Did Not Kill Armstrong": The War of Wills in the Early Days of Radio

January 31, 1954
River House Apartments, 13th Floor
East 52nd Street, New York City

Numbers don't lie, Armstrong thought. That fact had always been a cold comfort, even through the worst of times.

In the quiet of his room he let his mind tick through the equations once again. The results were still the same: There was a high probability that his remains would be smashed beyond recognition by his impact with the sidewalk far below.

He'd done the math on his impending suicide because he was, above all else, an engineer. But there were still many variables to consider: the winter breezes gusting over the East River, updrafts and downdrafts flowing between the tall buildings, humidity, air density, and drag coefficients—even the courage with which he would take his fatal step from the ledge. To a layman, these concerns might seem minor compared to the most obvious unknown that he faced: *What kinder world, if any, might await him on the other side?*

His mind turned back to the matters at hand.

Armstrong knew that when it was all over—after the police and the coroner arrived—a quick identification of his body might ease the burden of his loved ones. So, in the likely event that his features would be destroyed by trauma, he had dressed himself in the usual careful fashion that his neighbors would immediately recognize.

He stood before the mirror, straightened his tie, and saw himself as he would soon be discovered: an evening overcoat, a wool scarf, gloves, and his favorite walking hat. All was as it should be.

On the corner of the desk lay his last words. The pages were placed under a paperweight to protect them from the winds that might sweep in upon his exit through the open window. He'd intended to leave only a brief goodbye, but once he'd begun, writing a lifetime of memories had passed before his eyes. Many things long denied had finally become clear to him, but in the end, none were more certain than this: Every one of his inventions, all of his achievements, and everything he'd once dreamed for the world would soon be buried and forgotten—right along with his name.

His signature was the last detail to consider. Most acquaintances addressed him only by his middle name of Howard, while old friends often called him *the Major* in recognition of his permanent army rank and his many contributions to his nation's victories in wartime. Whoever should first find this note might not know him at all. For clarity, then, he'd signed his name in full, as one might put a finish to a legal document.

> *God keep you; and the Lord have mercy on my soul.*
> *Edwin Howard Armstrong*

At the turn of the twentieth century, the national mind was alive and brimming with wondrous possibilities. Our heroes were the adventurers, the explorers, the visionaries, and the inventors. Even small children knew their names.

Their promises were breathtaking: One day soon winged vehicles would fill the skies and rockets would venture beyond Earth's atmosphere; automobiles would be as common as horse-drawn carts and buggies; synthetic materials and mechanized workers would revolutionize manufacturing and agriculture; great works of art and theater would be beamed to every living room in moving pictures, real as life; new medicines would eliminate dread diseases; new forms of abundant energy would bring security and prosperity to every hearth and home; and thinking machines would sit upon our desks to help us solve the profound mysteries still facing mankind.

It was not an era for timid bystanders. The means to pursue the next amazing breakthrough were available to every thinking man and woman. Their laboratories were attics, basements, and garages, and every citizen scientist with the will, the intellect, a blackboard, and hand tools could feel in their grasp the potential to change the world.

As that new century dawned, a great unexplored frontier awaited man's conquest: the still primitive, misunderstood medium that would one day be called *radio*. The wireless transmission of information across many miles through invisible airborne waves was the stuff of dreams, and its pursuit captured the ambitions of three very different men.

Lee de Forest, David Sarnoff, and Edwin Howard Armstrong all ran the same race on separate courses toward an unknown finish line.

Only one would ever cross it.

48 Years Earlier
Yonkers, New York
April 4, 1906

"Edwin! Edwin Armstrong, you come down from there this instant!"

He could barely hear his mother's voice over the noise of the wind singing through the wires all around him. He'd heard enough to know she was angry, though—she only brandished "Edwin Armstrong" when she was mad as a wet hornet.

The young man was sitting in a bosun's chair a hundred feet above the ground, suspended by four thin ropes alongside his latest and greatest antenna. He'd finished work on the tower almost an hour before, but he loved the feel of the air up there. If given a choice he would probably never come down.

"I'll be inside in a few minutes!" he shouted.

"Not in a few minutes, *now*. And I mean *right now*! And if you break your neck, Howard Armstrong, don't you dare come running to me!"

When his mom had turned and gone back inside in a huff, he made his way down to join the family for dinner. It was a generous meal at one of many regular gatherings with his parents and sisters and most of his uncles and aunts and cousins. As the food was passed around the table, his relatives quizzed him about his latest experiments, and then listened intently as if his words were the most important ever spoken.

Though his mom was still a little miffed at his earlier high-wire act, Howard could tell she'd forgiven him yet again. She believed in him, they all did, and there was never a doubt in his mind that within the comforting walls of this big, beautiful home, he was loved.

Howard never blamed his mother for being overly protective. She'd almost lost him when he was eight and came down with rheumatic fever. There were complications—he'd missed two years of school, and the disease had left him with a tremor and a tic in his face that still dogged him to this day, especially when he was nervous. That's why they'd moved from their beloved Manhattan to this spacious home in tranquil Yonkers. His parents wanted the best for their only son, and his entire family had been there to nurse him through his long recovery.

In addition to his fascination with great heights and his love of all things electrical, Howard had also learned to treasure solitude. In the quiet and safety of his attic laboratory, his mind was free to explore. Although he was humble to a fault, he also understood that he was gifted. When a family friend had seen his first crystal set—a cobbled-together little wonder that he'd created from scratch—the friend had declared him to be a true prodigy. Though he'd had to look up that word *prodigy* in the dictionary, something told Howard that what this visiting engineer had whispered to his dad might really be true.

Where others saw just a tangled box of components and wires, Howard couldn't help but visualize the myriad ways they might be connected. As he read through *The Boy's Book of Inventions* the concepts came alive before his eyes. He could see within the black-and-white circuits and schematics the interplay of flowing currents, the ebb and flow of resistance, impedance, reactance, capacitance, and induction. He could see in these forces the seeds of great discoveries—a world-changing treasure just waiting to be found.

Then there was radio—which was currently nothing more than a curiosity, a hobbyist's toy beyond the means of most laymen. An elaborate antenna, a pair of sensitive headphones, and an expensive receiver were required just to pull in a weak, scratchy signal from any distance at all. But in those waves of airborne electricity and magnetism, young Howard Armstrong saw an amazing untapped potential.

It was an idea that consumed him. To bring the wonders of radio—not just simple code, but voice, and someday even music—loud and clear into every American home. Just the thought of it made his heart race.

Howard's prized possession was a strange glass tube, placed in a position of honor on his attic workbench. He'd saved his pennies and sent away for it by mail, after reading all about it in the back pages of an inventors' magazine.

The thing was called an Audion—and while the flashy ad had promised miracles, in retrospect, Howard had to admit that the copy had been very short on actual facts. Even its inventor—a man named Lee de Forest—seemed to have very little concept of the Audion's practical use.

But Howard knew his savings hadn't gone to waste. Like Jack with his magic beans, he sensed a mystic potential in this odd glass tube and believed with all his heart that it was the pathway to an undiscovered realm—one that Edwin Howard Armstrong knew he was born to explore.

Six Years Later
October 1912

In the closing months of his twenty-second year, Armstrong still sat in that same chair in his attic lab, but many things had changed. He was now a student at Columbia, excelling in the engineering program under the tutelage of the great physicist Michael Pupin. Most of his boyhood dreams were in the process of being realized, but one had continued to elude him throughout his college years.

Tonight, however, he thought with a smile, that just might change.

Between classes Howard had continued his obsessive work with the Audion, commuting to Manhattan every day by motorcycle so that he could return to a long night of experimentation in his workshop at home. That evening he could feel in the air that all his hard work and sacrifice was about to pay off.

He stared hard at the circuit he'd just constructed—a design that had come to him in a flash of inspiration—and thought back to how he'd arrived at this point.

Current radio signals were far too weak to be heard without head-phones pressed against the ears—even at a moderate distance. Mere audio amplification wasn't enough—that only made the faint signals fade into the background noise. The answer had to be to somehow amplify the *signal* itself, not just the resulting sound.

The Audion produced only a modest improvement in the faint signals, but what if . . . *what if the output of the Audion were fed right back into its input again?* Electrons travel at the speed of light—he could feed the signal back a hundred times, a thousand times, even twenty thousand times, all in the blink of an eye, and the Audion would compound its tiny amplification with every single pass.

That electronic snowball effect was the very idea that Howard was about to put to the test.

Armstrong sat in the dim candlelight, making final adjustments. When all was ready he set the tuning capacitor all the way to the bottom of the band and turned a potentiometer that he'd labeled *regeneration* ever so slowly clockwise. Near the middle of the range he backed it off as a high-pitched squeal began to develop.

So far, so good. Now, with the delicate touch of a safecracker, he twisted the metal tuner knob gently up the scale.

Silence.

Again, and then again, another fraction of a turn.

Still nothing.

He sighed heavily and, for the first time in months, felt the nervous tic flaring up at the corner of his eye. He was dog-tired from another day of hard study and a night spent on this fruitless work. Maybe it was finally time to throw in the towel, focus on finishing his degree, and save this wandering experimentation for his idle retirement years.

In frustration, he tweaked the control hard, one last time.

A deafening tone pounded into his ears and he tore off the headphones in surprise. He could still hear it, though, loud and distorted, from where the 'phones dangled down at the end of the cord.

Stunned, his ears ringing, Armstrong reached out for the switch that would route the sound from the headphone jack into the tall amplifying horns he'd mounted beside his desk.

The windows rattled from the blast of clear, strong sound that suddenly filled the room. It wasn't just sound—*it was a signal.*

He stumbled his way down the stairs to the second story, pounding on every door he passed until he burst into his eldest sister's room.

"I've done it!" Armstrong yelled. "I've done it!"

"Done what?" she answered, her voice registering her sudden fright over what he might be talking about. "Howard, have you set the house on fire again?"

"Come with me now! You have to hear this!"

But she could already hear it, even from the floor below. As he ran up the stairs with his sister close behind, the Morse code continued booming into the attic, clear as a bell.

"Remember this night, sis," he said. "This is the night you'll tell your grandchildren about: the night that radio changed forever."

"It's so loud!" she shouted back, with her hands cupped over her ears. "Where's this guy transmitting from anyway, our kitchen?"

Armstrong held up his hand for silence, his eyes growing wide as he mentally translated the incoming dots and dashes.

"Honolulu," he whispered. "It's coming from Hawaii. Five thousand miles away."

Michael Pupin, Howard Armstrong's self-appointed mentor, often felt like a fretting mother hen. Armstrong could be strong-willed, even obstinate, and he often showed little regard for his own safety, either physically or legally. But Armstrong was also, hands down, the most

brilliant student he'd ever taught—maybe the most gifted and princi-
pled man he'd ever *met*. Given that Pupin had worked with the greatest
names of his day, that was saying a lot.

"Howard?"

Armstrong didn't answer. He was working away in his corner of the
lab at Columbia, in the basement below Philosophy Hall, up to the el-
bows in a new receiver he'd spent months perfecting.

"There's a little Christmas party tonight, Howard. Some of the students were asking if you'd come."

"Busy," Armstrong said.

"Howard, you told me you finished your patent applications, and I'd
like to review them now."

"On the table, over there."

As Pupin waded through the legalese he identified a problem almost
immediately.

"This is incomplete," he said.

"Then talk to the paper pushers," Armstrong replied. "I've spent too
much energy on that mumbo jumbo already."

"Too much energy? Howard, you're a year behind in completing this
filing. You have to protect yourself. This is important—"

"No," Armstrong said, "*this* is important, this work right here in front
of me."

"This application describes a patent for a radio receiving system."

"Yes—"

"But that's only a small part of it," Pupin continued. "You've shown
me that your regenerative system can actually *modulate* a signal, and
when you push it into oscillation, it becomes a transmitter as well. One
unit that can both send and receive, clear enough for voice and even
music."

"I haven't had time to perfect all that yet."

"Perfection be damned, it's the heart of the invention!" Pupin said.
"With this idea the guts of a radio transmitter can be shrunk from the
size of a closet down to a box I can carry in my hands."

"When it's ready, I'll announce it."

"You have a neighbor in Yonkers who's a patent attorney, and a very good one. He's of national renown. Why haven't you asked him for his help?"

"I don't trust lawyers."

"Howard, listen to me. That Audion tube in your circuit is the work of a dangerous man—"

"*Dangerous?*" Armstrong laughed. "Lee de Forest? I've heard the man speak at the Institute of Radio Engineers. He doesn't even know how his tube works."

"It doesn't matter if he knows how it works, it only matters what a judge and jury will believe." Pupin came closer, and sat by Armstrong's side. "I know for a fact that he pickpocketed the work of Reginald Fessenden, and then he tied him up in court for years. And de Forest won. Then he sued John Fleming, the man who invented the Fleming valve, the very basis of the Audion, and he won again. He shouldn't have won, but he did. De Forest seems to thrive on legal wrangling, and I've heard it said that you're the next name on his blacklist. You have too much to offer to waste your life in litigation. I don't want that to happen to you."

"It won't happen to me," Armstrong said. "Yes, my work incorporates the Audion. Does that mean de Forest invented regeneration? Could the caveman who first chipped out a stone wheel claim to be the father of the Model T Ford? It's absurd."

Absurd, yes, Pupin thought. But there were so few true geniuses to be found in the pages of history, and there has never been a shortage of opportunists and predators. Armstrong was a young man of great integrity, and such men can make the fatal mistake of assuming integrity in others.

He wanted to say more, but he knew that at some point the teacher must let the student venture forth from the safety of the nest.

"Don't work too hard tonight, Howard," he said.

"There's no such thing as working too hard," Armstrong replied, but by then his mentor had already left the room.

He surveyed his work one last time, then sat back and smiled.

Absolutely perfect.

Belmar, New Jersey
January 31, 1914

A very important man had contacted Armstrong for a demonstration of
his latest receiver. Armstrong had been preparing for their meeting for
weeks now.

He arrived early to set up, but when he pulled into the drive his appointment was already there, waiting for him.

To his surprise, Armstrong noted the man was around his own age,
maybe twenty-one or twenty-two, but he was dressed to the nines like a
Wall Street wheeler-dealer.

"I'm Edwin Armstrong," he said, as the two shook hands. "My
friends call me Howard."

"And I'm the chief technology inspector and contracts manager
for the Marconi Wireless Telegraph Company," the other young man
replied. "I don't have any friends, but my enemies call me Mr. David
Sarnoff."

They hit it off right away.

The conversation was easy, like a reunion of old acquaintances. They
talked of many things as Armstrong opened the trunk and the two of
them worked together to set up the equipment.

Sarnoff was a son of Jewish immigrants who'd come to America with
little more than the clothes on their backs and hopes of a better life.
A natural businessman, he'd been earning his keep since childhood,
and overcoming every hurdle of prejudice and poverty as he clawed his
way up the ladder. By the time he was fourteen he'd bought his own
newsstand and put his four siblings to work for him. Now, less than a
decade later, he held a position that would have been coveted by ambitious men twice his age.

Though their backgrounds and disciplines were very different, it
turned out their dreams of broadcast radio were the same. Both believed the radio receiver would one day be a treasured fixture in every
American living room. Sarnoff seemed to have a plan to actually make
that happen.

"Wait a minute, I've heard of you," Armstrong said, as he connected
the feed line and completed his final checks. "David Sarnoff, yeah.

When the *Titanic* went down, the newspapers said you stayed at the telegraph key for three straight days, getting messages out to the families. The reporters called you the wonder boy of radio."

"That's me."

Armstrong looked him over again. "Is all of that really true?"

"Well, it wasn't true back then," Sarnoff replied, with a conspiratorial wink, "but brother, it sure is now."

As Armstrong fired up the receiver, the two took turns tuning in far-flung stations and copying the incoming Morse code. They hit Ireland, Nova Scotia, Hawaii, and San Francisco—there seemed to be no limit to the range from which this amazing apparatus could receive.

"I've seen enough," Sarnoff said at last, laying his earphones on the table.

"Let me tell you how it works."

"I don't really care how it works."

"But—"

"Howard, relax. This receiver you've made, it's not just a break-through, like you said in your letter—it's the most remarkable radio receiving system in existence. It's a revolution."

"So, that means . . ."

"That means I'm going to recommend that Marconi license your invention. And that, my friend—assuming all your paperwork's in order—means you'll be making as much every month as most people make in a year."

"Say that again."

Sarnoff smiled. "Probably five hundred dollars per month, Howard, for this invention alone. And I've got a feeling this is only the beginning."

Twenty miles away, Lee de Forest paced the floor in his small studio.

In his youth, both Nikola Tesla and Guglielmo Marconi had turned down Lee de Forest's generous offer to lend them his genius. That blowhard Marconi hadn't even bothered to answer de Forest's formal letter of introduction.

At twenty-eight years old and on the verge of greatness, de Forest had been fired from his job by the dolts at the American Wireless

Telegraph Company. His crime? He'd refused to surrender all rights to his work and into the grasping hands of his greedy employer! He'd then bravely struck out on his own, only to see his dreams crushed again and again by unscrupulous partners and overzealous minions of the law.

Since the failure of his first company, he had ridden several more of them into the ground. Some of his new partners had been convicted for stock irregularities, and de Forest himself had only recently been narrowly acquitted on a trumped-up charge of fraud. The prosecutors had accused him of selling worthless pieces of junk—including his precious Audion!—and thereby fleecing hundreds of unsuspecting hobbyists by mail order.

Mistreated, disrespected, and misunderstood—such was the path of a genius in a backward world. Over the years he'd been twice married and divorced, and betrayed many times over by a series of businessmen who only wanted to use his brilliance for their ill-gotten gains. But at last he was free from all of them, and determined to make a fresh start.

Soon, he swore, he would show them. When *de Forest* was a household name, etched into history alongside those of Ohm, Volta, Faraday, Watt, Hertz, Joule, Henry, Galvani, and Ampère—then they would all be cursing the day they'd dared to disrespect him. This would be marked as the moment in history when Lee de Forest began his Phoenix rise into legend.

With the last of his dwindling savings, de Forest had begun to broadcast little short-range programs of music and news in the city. It was a humble rebirth, but a foundation he could build on. He had made a firm resolution that he wouldn't be stolen from again. More than that, he would take back what was his from all those who sought to rob him of his rightful legacy.

Several months earlier, there'd been rumors floating around that some local upstart had used his Audion in a receiver of extraordinary design. Now that wop bastard Marconi had licensed the design, no doubt to rub salt in de Forest's wounds, and he was soon to begin cranking out receivers like link sausages.

There was more. This young thief, fourteen years his junior, this

Edwin Howard Armstrong, actually had the unmitigated gall to patent the stolen goods under his own name. When the true inventor, de Forest himself, had tried twice to submit his own registration for his new Ultra-Audion receiver, he was flatly turned down in favor of the younger man's fraudulent precedent.

This could not stand.

Lee de Forest vowed he would win back his greatest invention, secure all rights to its use, and destroy this charlatan, Howard Armstrong—even if it took the rest of his natural life.

1917

Howard Armstrong stood outside the courtroom, waiting. He could feel the twitching in his neck and at the corner of his eye, and he wished hard that for once he could just make it stop.

When Lee de Forest had filed this patent suit against him in 1915, the lawyers all assured Armstrong that the case would never get to trial. When it did get to trial, they told him it would all be over soon. Now, almost two years later, his bank account was almost empty and still the case showed no sign of resolution.

"Try to relax, Howard," his attorney said. "You've got a big afternoon ahead on the stand."

"How can I relax? Yesterday I had to listen to de Forest blather on for four straight hours. Any thinking man could tell that he doesn't understand even the most basic principles of radio. He couldn't even explain oscillation! And the judge sat there nodding his head through it all, as though what he was hearing made perfect logical sense!"

"The judge isn't an expert."

"Then where are the experts to testify on my behalf? Three days ago, the Institute of Radio Engineers awarded their first ever Medal of Honor to me for the development of the regenerative receiver—the very invention in conflict here. That's how important this discovery is. *My discovery.* And those men and women at the institute, above all others in the world, they know who rightfully deserved it—"

"Nevertheless," his attorney interrupted, "de Forest claims he discov-

ered regeneration two years before you did. He just didn't get around
to patenting it."

"Balderdash! So the fox catches a rabbit, and then waits two years
to eat it? De Forest files patents like Carter makes pills. Any fool could
see that if he knew how to create what I created he never would have
waited."

"And they'll bring up the fact that you didn't answer the allegations
in the suit immediately."

"My father had just drowned that very month, and I had to take
up the support of my family. I couldn't be bothered with this claptrap
then, and I haven't the time or the money or the patience to be bothered with it now! I must get back to my work—"

"Howard, please, just lower your voice and calm down. You don't
want to look nervous, or angry, or insulted to be here. We'll present your
case as we've laid it out. You'll answer the questions simply and honestly,
and trust me, we can wrap this thing up in another week or so."

But a month passed, and another, and it still wasn't over. Then one
morning, the world turned upside down.

Woodrow Wilson had been reelected president on a solemn promise
to keep the United States away from the bloody battlefields spreading
across the world. But on April 2, 1917, the president had gone before
Congress to request a declaration of war on Germany. Four days later,
both the Senate and the House had voted to commit U.S. troops to join
in the conflict.

The Great War, they called it. The war to end them all.

Though no one had asked him, Lee de Forest had immediately gone
on record to say that he wouldn't be supporting the effort. Why should
he risk his own life, he'd asked, to defend the characterless, incohe-
sive goulash that was the American people? He would gladly sell the
military anything they needed from his inventory, however, just like any
other paying customer, at the current retail price.

For his part, Armstrong enlisted immediately into the Army Signal
Corps. At the same time, he turned over the patents to all his inventions, free of charge, for the wartime benefit of the U.S. government.

All domestic transmitters were immediately commandeered, and
production of new units flew into high gear. Though the technology

was still primitive, it was clear that wireless communications would play a vital role for the Allied and Associated Powers.

Naturally, all trivial matters such as patent lawsuits were suspended by fiat until further notice. At least that burden was lifted from Armstrong's shoulders, if only temporarily.

As a captain in the Signal Corps, his first base of operations was the radio labs in Paris. Advanced German aeroplanes were terrorizing the skies over Europe, and the tactical use of their own young radio technology was a major factor to be overcome. Howard Armstrong was charged with helping the United States to level this key playing field.

First on the agenda was the improvement of wireless radio links between Allied airborne scouts and fighter aircraft and their commanders on the ground.

"Don't go so easy!" Howard Armstrong shouted forward to the pilot. "Fly her like you'd take her into battle!"

"You'd never catch me flying this hunk of junk into a fight!" the pilot shouted back. He put the open-cockpit Sopwith Scout into a hard bank and swooped into a descending turn. The wings flexed and the canvas-covered wooden fuselage creaked and complained, but the craft seemed to be holding together for the moment.

This outdated model had a nickname among the aviators at the Paris base—they called it the Spinning Jenny. But, death trap or not, it was the only two-seater available for Armstrong's tests, so the rickety old plane would have to do.

He put on his headphones and set about tuning and adjusting the transceiver in his lap. It was almost impossible to hear anything at all. The wind, vibration, and engine noise were compounded by a whine of ignition static fouling the receiver. Signals from other planes and ground stations crowded in and jammed one another. When he transmitted, the base seemed to hear only a small portion of what was sent.

On top of these problems, the radio was heavy and complicated, with multiple interacting controls. It would be a headache to tune this properly on a workbench indoors, much less in the jump seat of an aircraft in the midst of a bombing raid. There were so many delicate parts inside that breakdowns would be a daily occurrence.

"Okay, take her down!" Armstrong shouted. "I've seen what I need to!"

Back at the lab he left the notes with his new assistant, Sergeant Harry Houck, and then went out for a walk to think through his current stack of challenges.

The Germans used innovative, high-frequency methods in their communications—"short waves" that were far outside the reach of older receivers. Intelligence services first needed to intercept those transmissions before they'd have any hope of decoding them. Bombing raids were a growing danger, and if radio could be used to detect the faint ignition noise from incoming planes it might be possible to get an early warning. Wireless location-finding also had to be improved so enemy ships and even troop movements could better be detected. As Armstrong had just seen firsthand, portable receivers required a complete redesign if two-way radio was ever going to be put to effective use in the war.

Many lives depended on quick solutions to these problems. Despite the relentless pace, Armstrong's nerves hadn't bothered him once. This was exactly the sort of pressure he loved. For the first time in years there was a blessed refuge of calm and quiet in his mind. With no lawyers, writs, subpoenas, or injunctions to drain his spirit away, he was finally able to once again devote himself to pure invention.

In the midst of that thought Armstrong stopped walking, right in the middle of the street. A schematic circuit diagram was revealing itself before his eyes, like the dawning image on a photographic plate in a cloudy darkroom tray. It was the solution—not only to one of the challenges he faced, but to possibly *every* one of them.

He turned and began to run back toward the lab, suddenly frightened this image might fade and decades of progress in radio might be lost in trying to summon it forth again.

"Harry, I've found it!" Armstrong shouted as he burst into the workroom and set about erasing the long blackboard by his bench. They'd spent the previous week writing out their long-term research plans there, but his assistant knew better than to object.

"What have you found?" Houck asked, but Armstrong was already deep inside his own mind, drawing whatever it was that had possessed him.

When Houck began to understand what he was seeing, he joined his leader at the board, and for hours the two men worked without a word until the diagram was finally complete.

Inventors don't always see the potential of a stroke of genius in the moment it arrives. But as they stood back and took in what they'd just brought into the world, both men knew they'd made history, and had changed the science of radio forever.

Armstrong had set out to provide a leap forward in the clarity of radio signals, to improve long-distance reception and dampen interference, to make receivers simple to tune by an untrained operator, and to open the door to wireless direction-finding breakthroughs that could change the course of the war. He'd solved it all in a single stroke

It would be called the superheterodyne.

1924

The Great War had been over for years, but David Sarnoff knew his corporate battles would probably never end.

Marconi had been absorbed into the new Radio Corporation of America, and though he was still only in his mid-twenties, Sarnoff found himself second in command at RCA. He'd dreamed of broadcast entertainment and a radio receiver in every American home. Now, with RCA booming and its fledgling National Broadcasting Company poised to take off nationwide, those dreams were fast becoming reality. That success had brought competitors crawling out of the woodwork on every side.

Howard Armstrong's superheterodyne had made practical the mass production of receivers that were simple enough for average people to use. Through some brilliant business hocus-pocus, Sarnoff had both confounded his competitors and leveraged his friendship with Armstrong to create a slim window of opportunity for RCA to be first to market. The admen had named the company's flagship set the Radiola, and the copy was right on target.

You will agree with Marconi
When you hear the sensational new
Radiola Super-Heterodyne
acclaimed by inventor of radio as "a great advance"

But there was trouble in paradise.

Armstrong's prototypes had worked like a charm, but after the R&D labs at General Electric and Westinghouse had put their thumbprint on the design, the result was noisy, quirky, and so heavy it was just barely portable.

Having created massive consumer demand, and with his nervous stockholders and dealerships awaiting a payoff on their investments, Sarnoff had just canceled millions of dollars in manufacturing orders for a product he considered too flawed to produce.

He was known as a man with all the answers, but for once David Sarnoff had no idea what to do next.

"Why not call Armstrong?" his secretary asked.

This bright young woman, Marion MacInnes, had already pulled Sarnoff's fat from the fire on more than one occasion. She was sitting at her desk, looking dreamily at a photograph of Howard Armstrong— the very picture that had gotten him banned from the corporate premises. The photo showed the still-boyish inventor balanced on the peak of the 450-foot antenna atop the RCA building at 30 Rockefeller Center. When the papers ran the shot, the insurance guys went apoplectic and probably would have had Armstrong arrested if Sarnoff hadn't intervened.

Armstrong—now that wasn't such a bad idea.

"Get him up here," Sarnoff said, "and alert security to let him through. But so help me, Marion, if he climbs that tower again, genius or not, he's going to spend the night in jail."

The two men met on the roof of the building, far from the prying eyes of the fretting RCA executives. As Armstrong pored over the production schematics for the Radiola, he and Sarnoff had a few quiet minutes to reminisce.

"I never got a chance to apologize to you," Armstrong said.

"For what?"

"For selling the rights to the superheterodyne to Westinghouse. I didn't want to leave you out, but I couldn't wait. I needed the money for the lawyers."

"I was pretty hot about that for a while," Sarnoff admitted, "but all's forgiven. Let's just say that deals were made, and I made sure I came out on top. Now I've got Westinghouse and GE right where I want them. AT&T is even trying to stick their nose into this business, but we're holding them off as well." He would have gone on, but as he watched Armstrong for a few moments more, he realized that his old friend really had no capacity for the nuance of this sort of war. "You're still fighting de Forest, then, on regeneration? How long has that been going on?"

"Almost ten years now. I won against him in '21, and then he appealed and now I'm set to win again. When that verdict comes down I'm going to run up a flag with my patent number on it, big enough that he can see it from his house on the Hudson."

"Why not just drop it? Settle, and move on?"

"He's sworn he'll never pay damages to me until he's lost in the highest court in the land."

"Then waive damages and take your win. Make de Forest buy a license if he wants to use your work. That'll burn him up."

"There are some things a man can't compromise on. It's not only the money I'm owed. You've heard what he says about me to any hack reporter who'll listen. He calls me a thief."

"You're in good company. You should hear some of the mud he slings about Marconi, though being an eyewitness, I can confirm that some of the more lurid tales of his appetite for the ladies are absolutely true."

"Well, that's certainly more than I ever wanted to know about Marconi's love life."

"Seriously though, Howard, as a friend, you should think hard about cutting your losses with this de Forest business. Put it behind you."

"I can't give it up, David. It's my reputation at stake."

"Ten years," Sarnoff sighed. "It's a crime, that's what it is." He could see a change come over Armstrong as he spoke of the case—the constant pressure must have been tearing him down, bit by bit. "Well, let's hope old Lee does as bad a job before the Supreme Court as he does at reporting the news. Remember the night when he called the 1916 presidential election? *'Breaking news! Charles Evans Hughes beats Woodrow Wilson!'* He splashed that scoop all over the tri-state area, and then he stuck by it for almost a week."

Armstrong smiled, but there was no joy in it. Sarnoff thought it probably best to change the subject.

"Speaking of money," Sarnoff continued, "I'm sitting on orders for one hundred thousand radio sets, and I don't have a single one to deliver. Do you think you can help me with that?"

Howard Armstrong put the drawings aside.

"I'll tell you what. If I can do it, I want a signed letter on your stationery, giving me permanent permission to climb that antenna tower behind us any damned time I want."

"I'll do better than that," Sarnoff said. "I've got a lovely young woman downstairs, right outside my office, who's got a crush on you to beat the band. You give me the Radiola, and I'll introduce you to her."

This time Armstrong's smile was genuine. He held out his hand, and they shook on it.

"And there's one other thing I want you to start thinking about," Sarnoff said. "I was listening to our stations the other night, during that big rain, and the static was awful. From March until October we have to print a damned weather report right next to the program listings in the paper so people can see if the storms will wipe out their reception. You find me a way to eliminate that noise, clean up our signal regardless of the weather, and we'll own this industry for the next fifty years."

"I'll give it some thought."

"And Howard, listen to me," Sarnoff said. His tone was serious. "It's a bitter world we're operating in. There are empires at stake, and that's much bigger than you and me. That's bigger than friendship. This suit with de Forest? You must know he's got AT&T behind him now. You can't win alone anymore. The age of the independent inventor is over and done. You've strayed in the past and I understand why. But if you stick with me, you'll own the future."

"I won't believe that, David. I think the world of you, but I'll never be a company man. You've got big ideas, I know, but I've got a few of my own."

Sarnoff nodded. "I've heard that assistant of yours call you 'the Major.' That's from the war, right?"

"That's right."

"Well, around here they call me 'the General.' I'm going to be running this place before you know it, and RCA is only the beginning. And Howard?"

"Yeah?"

Sarnoff put a hand on his old friend's shoulder.

"You mustn't ever forget that a general outranks a major."

1934

The ten years that followed ushered in a world of change.

There were times of happiness greater than Howard Armstrong had ever known. He'd found his one true love in Sarnoff's assistant, Marion MacInnes, and after a blissful courtship they'd been married. Together with Harry Houck, Armstrong had solved the mass production problems and David Sarnoff had sold his hundred thousand receivers, and then many hundreds of thousands more.

With eighteen thousand shares of company stock as his reward, Armstrong had become the largest single shareholder in RCA. But the Depression took its toll. Stock that had been worth $572 per share in 1929 had plummeted to just $12.25 by 1933.

As an industry, radio was coming into its own. They were already calling it the "Golden Age of Broadcasting." Even as unemployment soared, people who struggled to buy food and pay the rent never missed a payment on their radio sets. It was a gathering place for the troubled nation. The airwaves were filled with popular music, news, and sporting events, as well as comedy and drama from the greatest stars of the day. Even the president regularly went on the air to reassure his fellow Americans that happy days would soon be here again.

It certainly didn't seem that way to Howard Armstrong.

By then *de Forest vs. Armstrong* had been heard by a dozen courts, with wins, losses and stalemates claimed by both litigants. After all this, the Supreme Court of the United States had just issued its decision on the matter.

Through what could only be explained as a complete misunderstanding of the technical foundation of the case, the court had ruled against Edwin Howard Armstrong.

Finally, after almost twenty years, the verdict of history was now etched in stone: Lee de Forest had won. Armstrong was a thief.

May 29, 1934

Howard Armstrong stood in the wings awaiting his introduction at an annual meeting of the Institute of Radio Engineers.

He'd been invited to give that night's keynote speech long before the Supreme Court's decision had come down. It was a standing-room-only crowd, and by now most everyone in the audience knew of the ruling.

Though Armstrong dreaded yet another round of public humiliation, he had never broken a commitment to his peers. He was sure, however, that his planned presentation on frequency modulation would now be inappropriate to deliver. He would keep his notes in his pocket. There was only one thing he needed to say.

As he took to the stage the crowd was mostly silent.

"My friends," Armstrong began, "and my colleagues. As you may be aware, my long fight with Mr. de Forest has finally come to a close. It has been the longest such case thus far in American history, and it was brought to determine who is the rightful inventor of regeneration. The verdict of the high court has now been rendered, and it was not the outcome that I'd hoped to see."

He could feel a twitching begin in his neck, and he held a grip on the podium to try to keep it down.

"In 1917, this organization saw fit to award to me its Medal of Honor for the discovery of that very principle. I will never forget that night. To me it seems like only yesterday, and yet it was so long ago."

Emotion rose into his throat and took hold there. Only a few more words needed to be spoken, and he prayed he could deliver them.

"With the Supreme Court's decision, I no longer have a right to the honor that you so graciously bestowed upon me." He took the small engraved plaque from his coat pocket and placed it on the table beside him. "I only wish—"

A single shout of "No!" arose from the back of the auditorium.

Another man yelled out, "It's yours, Howard, and we all know it!"

"My friends," Armstrong began again, but his voice failed him. He felt the first tears begin trailing down his face.

Others in the audience started to join in the vocal protest. Applause began slowly and then spread throughout the room until the roar of it was ringing in his ears. The engineers were coming to their feet in an ovation that seemed as if it would never end. They were cheering and chanting his name, and then one of them ran up onto the stage and put Howard Armstrong's treasured award right back into his hands.

When he got home from the meeting he told Marion all about it, and the two stayed up most of the night talking about the future. She'd been by his side through virtually every trial and tribulation, lending him her strength, and he loved her more every single day.

By morning, for the first time in years, the road ahead seemed bright.

Ever since David Sarnoff had asked him to tackle the static problem, Armstrong had been quietly at work. The challenge had been monumental, but now the prototype was nearly done—and wide-band frequency modulation would be an invention all his own that no man alive could ever dispute. Outside his wife and Harry Houck, only Sarnoff, now the president of RCA, had been privy to the progress so far. Finally, it was ready to be announced.

Armstrong wrote in his journal that morning:

An era as new and distinct in the radio art as that of regeneration is now upon us. After ten years of eclipse, my star is rising again.

A few sleepless days and nights later, a team of company engineers assembled in Armstrong's temporary lab at RCA headquarters.

Howard turned on the latest model of the Radiola and then tuned in a signal until the sound was as clear as he could make it. There was music playing, a classical piece, exhibiting the thin, tinny audio of a typical program of the day.

"There are two transmitters upstairs," Armstrong said. "One is broadcasting with yesterday's technology, and that's what you're hearing now. Watch, and listen."

Armstrong flipped a switch near him and a spark generator began spitting bright white arcs of electricity across its gap. The radio signal was immediately overwhelmed by interference and the program disappeared into the hiss.

With a sweeping gesture, Howard Armstrong then switched the output to the new FM receiver right beside him.

The same orchestra music filled the room, but the difference was breathtaking. For minutes they all listened in utter fascination—for the first time, a broadcast signal carried the full audio spectrum discernible to the human ear. And despite the static generator that was still going strong, the reception was so pure and clear that one could hear the whisper-quiet sound of the violinist turning his pages of music.

When the demonstration was over, David Sarnoff dismissed his team of engineers to the next room and took Armstrong aside.

"Well, you've done it again, Howard," he said. "This FM business, it's going to change everything one day."

"One day?" Armstrong replied. "It's changed everything already, starting *today*."

"Let's sit down over here," Sarnoff said. When they arrived at the table, Armstrong saw what looked like a corporate contract was already waiting for them. "This is an agreement between you and RCA. Among other things it entitles you to a significant share of the profits that might come from your work here."

Armstrong began to read. His enthusiasm began to leave him, though, before he'd even gotten halfway through.

"This transfers all my patents for FM over to your company."

"That's right. You and I will always know who invented it, but to the rest of the world, FM will belong to RCA. And that's not all."

"What else?"

"I'm not going to announce these results," Sarnoff said, "and neither will you. Nothing you showed us here today will be made public."

"What do you mean? You said this was another revolution—"

"And it is, but we're not ready for it yet. We've only just gotten AM into widespread acceptance. I've got millions of radio sets out there in the market, and tens of millions more on the production line. That gear would all be obsolete, not to mention the stations and broadcasters who'd all have to replace their equipment overnight. Once people hear your new system, they'd never want to listen to AM radio again."

"But that's wonderful—"

"No, Howard, it's not wonderful. It's a threat to the fortunes of a thousand men that you don't want to cross. More than that, they would never allow you to cross them, and neither will I. You're right about one thing, this is the future, and you should be proud of what you've done. But the future has to wait."

Armstrong was getting angry.

"I won't do it. What if I don't sign? Then what are you going to do?"

"You don't want to find that out, Howard. Don't you read the business section? I don't get ulcers, brother, I give them."

"You're going to threaten me now? Don't make me laugh! The patents are mine—"

"Did de Forest teach you nothing at all? Do you really imagine you can walk out on this deal with any hope of beating me at my own game?"

"I'm not walking out," Armstrong said. "This is my laboratory—"

"No, it isn't, Howard, not if you turn this down. And I take it your answer is no."

"That's right."

"Okay," Sarnoff said. "You've got until the end of the day to pack up and clear out. You can go back to that basement at the university because I need my space here for another team. While you've been playing around with radio, we've been working on something much bigger."

Sarnoff paused to let the tension build.

"Television."

•   •   •

Over the next few years Howard Armstrong poured every ounce of time and energy into the uphill battle of promoting the benefits of FM radio.

The costs were astronomical. He created a production chain to make and sell receivers to a growing number of enthusiasts along the East Coast. He sold franchises and licensed other entrepreneurs to manufacture his name-brand sets. At the same time, he built a 40-kilowatt FM radio station, W2XMN, to transmit his high-fidelity broadcasts for a hundred miles in all directions. He also inked a deal with the Yankee Network to help them found the first FM radio conglomerate. Before long more than 200,000 listeners were tuning in to FM every day.

It was grueling work and the budget was always down to the bone, but he and Marion were happier than they'd ever been. Their destiny was in their own hands.

One afternoon, Armstrong returned to his small office to find David Sarnoff sitting in his chair.

"I like what you've done with the place," Sarnoff said.

"What are you doing here, David?"

"I've got one last offer for you," Sarnoff said, sliding a document across the desk.

At first glance it looked like the same offer that Armstrong had turned down long ago, with one notable change: Rather than a permanent share of all future profits from his FM patents, the figure was now a flat fee: one million dollars.

"Why on earth would I accept this?" Armstrong asked.

"Because it's the only way you're ever going to win."

"Are you kidding me? I'm on my way to half a million listeners. I have new stations on the drawing board from here to Chicago. Before long we'll be as big as NBC."

"If you don't believe any other thing I say today, Howard, believe this: That will never, ever happen."

"A million dollars? Just my facilities here are worth more than that, not to mention future earnings on FM. I wouldn't sign my rights away for a hundred times what you've offered."

"Last chance," Sarnoff said, but there was no reply. He shook his head and stood, and then he took his time to fold and pocket the rejected contract. "Very well, then. Get a long last look at this friendly face, Howard. Because the next time we meet, I'm afraid you're going to see another side of it."

In the back of his limousine on the way back to New York, David Sarnoff picked up the handset of the car's intercom.

"Make a note on my schedule," he said. "When I walk into my office I want a conference call waiting with Frank McNinch in Washington, D.C. . . . Yes . . . The office of the director at the Federal Communications Commission."

The lawsuits began almost immediately. Some were filed against Howard Armstrong, and others Armstrong was forced to file himself.

The months tied up in court once again turned into years.

RCA was openly using FM technology for its television arm, while blatantly ignoring Armstrong's patents. Rumors flew that Sarnoff was encouraging other corporations to disregard Armstrong's patents as well. It became a sort of unspoken coalition, with a single unarmed man on one side and ten Goliaths on the other.

Everywhere Armstrong turned a new wall rose in his path, but still he pressed on. At one point the opposing lawyers kept him coming back to the witness stand for over a year, asking him questions of no consequence to the case just to stall for time and wear him down. Then, one day, it was finally David Sarnoff's turn to testify. Much of this time was a blur to Howard, but he would never forget what Sarnoff was about to say.

"Mr. Armstrong has asserted," the opposing attorney said, "that you once offered to pay him for the rights to develop FM technology, which he now claims to be his own original work. He's put the figure in question at one million dollars. Is this true?"

"It is not," Sarnoff said.

"You never offered to pay Mr. Armstrong, on behalf of RCA, for the use of his work?"

"At some point, I may have offered him something. We were old friends, you see, and he always seemed to be having legal troubles—"

Armstrong's lawyer objected to this, and as usual, was overruled.

"In any case," Sarnoff continued, "if I offered him anything it would have been nowhere near the figure you mentioned. It would have been a gesture, nothing more."

"Mr. Sarnoff," his attorney began, "I'll close with a simple question for you. Who developed FM?"

David Sarnoff leaned forward to make sure the court could hear every word that he said.

"The FM system that is in question here today was developed, beginning to end, by RCA. It is the sole invention of our corporate engineers."

1941

On December 7, 1941, the United States was again thrown into war.

As before, despite his own ongoing battles, Howard Armstrong immediately offered his services, and turned over every patent he held for the use of his country in the war effort.

Lee de Forest, now sixty-eight years old, and always game for publicity, announced his development of a self-guided bomb to be used against enemy forces in the air campaign. At the demonstration, the bomb veered off course and nearly fell among the generals who'd gathered to witness its power. All in attendance left feeling lucky to have escaped with their lives.

While David Sarnoff had been denied a navy commission back in 1917, this time was different. For the duration of the war he left the safety of the boardroom for an active role in support of the Allies. In the end, he directed the development of a communication system that helped make possible the invasion of Normandy.

When the war was finally over, it was back to business as usual.

Unbelievably, Howard Armstrong was still hanging on—refusing to back down. But Sarnoff had an ace in the hole that he'd hoped he'd never have to play.

Sarnoff made another phone call to Washington, and within a month of American Telephone & Telegraph joining his lobby, the ruling he'd requested came down from the FCC:

The FM broadcast frequencies were to be permanently moved, far up the spectrum from where they'd always been. In that one stroke, every unit in existence that was designed for FM transmission and reception was rendered obsolete.

River House Apartments, 13th Floor
East 52nd Street, New York City
January 31, 1954

Edwin Howard Armstrong had held on for nearly nine years more. Royalties had dwindled, debts were piling up, his health was failing, his savings were gone, and his hard-fought patents were about to expire. Just over two months earlier, on Thanksgiving night, he had finally taken all he could stand.

"They'll never let me alone!" he'd shouted. "They'll keep after me until I'm broke or dead, and nobody cares which it is!"

"I do, Howard," Marion pleaded. In all these years together she'd thought she'd seen him at his worst, but this was different. "We can still get through this—"

"But I can't! Why won't you see that? I've wasted my life and yours! Everything I've ever done means nothing!" In the midst of his rage he'd grabbed a fireplace poker and swung it again and again at the walls, the family photographs, and the many awards that were carefully arranged on the mantelpiece.

When he'd looked at his wife again he was horrified by what he saw. In his blind anger he'd struck her. Marion's arm was bleeding. For the first time since he'd met her he'd put fear into those beautiful eyes.

The metal bar in his hand dropped to the floor and he fell to his knees in front of her, but she had already left him and run for the door.

That was the last time he'd seen her, and the very last time he ever would.

And so it ends, Armstrong whispered.

It had been quite a chore to remove the air-conditioning unit from the bedroom window, but at last it came free and the way was clear.

The night was cold, but he was well dressed for it. All that lay before him was that final step.

He had always loved the feeling he got from standing way up high. That night, at that moment, the feeling was no different. His regrets were all behind him.

And with that thought, Edwin Howard Armstrong took a last deep breath, and then walked off into the air.

EPILOGUE

Armstrong's body lay hidden until the next morning, crumpled and still on a third-floor landing. The maintenance man who discovered the body knew immediately who he'd found.

The suicide made the front page of every paper in town.

Lee de Forest got the news and quietly made a number of calls in pursuit of the gory details. He then issued a statement regarding the death of his long-standing enemy: *"Armstrong is dead, and I am alive, and hope to live on for many years. What a contrast!"*

De Forest spent those remaining years constructing what he hoped would be an everlasting place for himself in history. He lobbied for a Nobel Prize and, also unsuccessfully, tried to convince his fourth wife to pen a glowing biography to be titled *I Married a Genius.* Among the source material was a sampling of future predictions he had made along the way:

> *While theoretically and technically television may be feasible, commercially and financially it is an impossibility.*
>
> *I do not foresee "spaceships" to the Moon or Mars. Mortals must live and die on Earth or within its atmosphere!*
>
> *The transistor will more and more supplement, but never supplant, the Audion.*

As a PR stunt, his publicist once sent a letter made out to "The Father of Radio, Hollywood, California." Upon its successful delivery to him, de Forest was to use it as proof to the newsmen of his unchallenged legacy.

The letter was soon returned by the Postal Service, marked *Addressee Unknown.*

Though money isn't everything, history records that when he passed away in 1961, Lee de Forest had less than $1,300 to his name.

When David Sarnoff was told of Armstrong's suicide, he was quiet for a time, and then, as though he stood accused by the messenger, he said, "I did not kill Armstrong." The company was closed on the afternoon of the funeral, and Sarnoff himself led a large group of mourners down the street to attend the service.

Marion Armstrong did not suffer her husband's death in silence. Not long after he'd been laid to rest, she took up his many legal battles against some of the most powerful corporations in America.

Using funds from a settlement with RCA, Marion stood up to the giants one by one. Motorola, Philco, Admiral, Emerson, Sylvania, Packard Bell, and many others, by intent or oversight, had profited from the work of Howard Armstrong—and she believed that it was long past time for them to pay for it. But, for Marion, as with her late husband, it was never about the money.

In his ruling against Emerson Radio & Phonograph, Judge Edmund Palmieri found the corporation's arguments on the up-for-grabs origins of FM to be "speculative, inconclusive, and unconvincing," and declared that "Major Armstrong was truly a pioneer in the field in theory and in fact." At last, FM belonged to Armstrong.

The decision was so definitive that Emerson's lawyers saw no hope in an appeal. Upon learning of this result, several other companies who'd banked on similar cases suddenly proposed generous out-of-court settlements. The last holdout, Motorola, lost their final appeal in October 1967. More than half a century since the legal challenges began, and thirteen years after his death, Edwin Howard Armstrong had finally won.

Long after he was gone, Armstrong was honored by the International Telecommunication Union. There, among his peers, his name is forever enshrined alongside those of André-Marie Ampère, Alexander Graham Bell, Michael Faraday, and Guglielmo Marconi.

Edwin Howard Armstrong's discoveries formed the basis of communications technology for many decades to come. In fact, his FM broadcast system was later used by another pioneer who bore the Armstrong name, though the two were related only in spirit.

In 1968, in a moment that would have delighted one of the twentieth century's greatest unsung inventors, Neil Armstrong spoke to the world via FM radio from his station on the surface of the moon—the very place that Lee de Forest believed mankind would never visit.

3

Woodrow Wilson:
A Masterful Stroke of Deception

PROLOGUE

Berlin, Germany
May 17, 1933

The somber-faced man with the Charlie Chaplin mustache and stubbornly straight black hair looked confidently upon the members of the Reichstag. He had waited for this moment ever since his release from prison years earlier. Now, as chancellor of the German republic, his power was absolute and his real mission just beginning.

He had spent years railing against the Treaty of Versailles that had ended the Great War. But repudiating the "Treaty of Peace"—the brainchild of the French, British, and Americans under Woodrow Wilson— had only gained traction in recent years. The Great Depression had hit Germans hard and, as a result, citizens were restive, angry, and vengeful.

These were qualities that a man like Adolf Hitler could appreciate.

"All the problems which are causing such unrest today lie in the deficiencies of the 'Treaty of Peace,' which did not succeed in solving in a clear and reasonable way the questions of the most decisive importance for the future," Herr Hitler charged. He decried the "absurd" terms of the treaty, including the harsh reparations imposed on Germany that would lead to the "economic extermination of a nation of sixty-five million."

"These terms," he declared to his approving audience, "will become a classic example in the history of the nations of how seriously international welfare can be damaged by hasty and unconsidered action."

The worst part of Hitler's latest diatribe was that it contained an element of truth. Even his fiercest opponents now recognized that the treaty's harsh terms had played right into the Nazi Party's hands. Ironically, those very same terms had once been opposed by one of the treaty's prime architects: Woodrow Wilson. But, in the end, Wilson was too infirm and confused to be of any real use. At a critical moment in world history, the leader of the free world's power was increasingly and secretly transferred to someone who was wholly out of their league when it came to international affairs.

This, in many ways, is the story of how the Second World War really began.

Princeton, New Jersey
Spring 1906

"Father!"

"How was the doctor, Father?"

The girls rushed to greet Woodrow Wilson and his wife, Ellen, at the front door. Wilson, a thin, bespectacled man of forty-nine, was the president of Princeton University and a growing celebrity not only within academia, but liberal progressive circles.

"All is well," he told them, scooping them into his open arms.

Beside him, he saw Ellen's smile freeze across her face.

Poor woman, Wilson thought. *She's not much of an actor*. He knew the children could see that she was a portrait of nerves and terror. She had no talent for deception or guile, even when it was in the family's best interest. He'd always felt women lacked a certain intellectual brain matter or, as he once put it while teaching at Bryn Mawr, his female pupils exhibited "a painful absenteeism of mind." This, of course, was another reason why the progressive Wilson had long held his view that women would be useless in positions of leadership. He remembered the whimsical delight he took when he once visited a so-called "Women's Rights" conference in Baltimore that resulted in him telling Ellen about "the chilled, scandalized feelings that always overcome me when I see and hear women speak in public." Women's lives must supplement men's lives, he believed.

Despite the assurances to his children, the truth was that all was *not* well. Just the other morning, while preparing for Princeton's graduation festivities, he'd awakened to find that he couldn't see out of his left eye. He figured a visit to the doctor would resolve the problem quickly, but instead the doctor had grilled him about his entire life history.

Despite the doctor's being a German immigrant, Wilson put up with the questions. The doctor was, after all, a far higher quality of immigrant than those Wilson typically encountered. Most immigrants, he noted, had "neither skill nor energy nor any initiative of quick intelligence." It was as though Europe was "disburdening themselves of the more sordid and hapless elements of their population."

He told the doctor that he'd had episodes like this before—once, years ago, he'd lost sensation in his left arm for months. But the situation had rectified itself, through rest and sheer force of will, and he knew this problem with his vision would do the same. He also mentioned the other symptoms he'd had on and off in the past: Vision problems when trying to play golf, occasional weakness and numbness, and plenty of headaches. It was all nothing, he insisted. Nothing that couldn't be easily treated. Besides, didn't the physician know that he had important things to do?

Rather than give him a clean bill of health, as Wilson anticipated, the doctor declared that Wilson had arteriosclerosis—the same disease that had killed his father. Pressure was building on his brain, causing more frequent and severe incidents. The doctor had insisted that Wilson immediately curtail his activities and lead a quiet, sedentary life.

All the way home, Ellen fretted that her husband was dying by inches. But Woodrow Wilson wasn't quite ready for such dire predictions. He'd already decided to get a second opinion. Then a third. Perhaps even a fourth.

Whatever it took to keep his plans on track.

Prospect, New Jersey
March 17, 1910

As usual, Ellen was a flawless dinner hostess. Colonel George Harvey, the editor of *Harper's,* and his wife were having a great evening in the tastefully appointed family dining room. The Princeton president held forth from a carved wooden chair as the candlelight reflected from the chandelier above them.

"Wonderful dinner, Mrs. Wilson," said the grateful Harvey, whose eyes revealed a man of sophistication and savvy.

Wilson placed his napkin onto the white lace tablecloth. "Shall we, Colonel?"

Leaving the women to gossip, Wilson showed Harvey to his library.

"I want you to suppose something, Mr. Wilson," Harvey began as soon as they were seated. "If I can handle the matter so that the nomination for governor shall be tendered to you on a silver platter, without you having had to obtain it, and without any requirement or suggestion or any pledge whatsoever, what do you think would be your attitude?"

"Well, the suggestion is flattering," Wilson replied, feigning modesty.

"I already have Senator Smith on board," Harvey added, referring to the New Jersey power broker and former United States senator James Smith Jr.

It was clear to Wilson that the case for him to run for governor was a powerful one. The Democratic Party had suffered major losses in the last election. They needed a fresh face, someone who, as laughable as the concept was, given his pedigree, could run as a reformer against the political machine.

Of course, the tempting proposition was not without drawbacks—and Wilson mused about them aloud. Though he'd given a number of speeches, he was largely unknown outside academic and media circles. Surely there were more prominent men who might take up the banner. Would voters really believe that an academic was qualified to serve as governor?

As Wilson played the Hamlet role to perfection, agonizing one way and then the other, Harvey made sure to present a trump card.

"And of course," he added, "if you were governor, we'd push hard to make you the party's nominee for president in 1912."

The presidency—now *that* was appealing. Wilson had dreamed about it since he was a little boy. And why wouldn't he have a shot at the nomination? Without him, the Democrats were sure to lose anyway. It would take an improbable implosion by the Republicans, the nation's majority party, to give the Democrats any chance at all.

His mind raced as he thought about the possible outcomes of his campaign for governor. The Republican candidate was knee-deep in scandals that would contrast sharply with Wilson's exemplary personal character. Wilson would run as a reformer, an agent of hope and change. But, for now, he would have to play the reluctant supplicant, grateful for the consideration of the party bosses.

When Harper finally finished his pitch, Wilson did his best to appear unmoved. It was always best to look like the reluctant politician even if you were nothing of the kind. "I should regard it as my duty to give the matter very serious consideration," he said.

In truth, Wilson knew he would give it more than just serious consideration. He'd entertained dreams—visions even—of being a great statesman for quite some time. He felt he was destined for high office, though he would gladly defer to others should someone ever come forward with ideas as brilliant and forward-thinking as his own. But he knew that few people could ever match his sterling reputation or unimpeachable integrity. If Colonel Harvey and his crew were a means to that end, he'd humor them . . . at least until he took office.

The White House
Washington, D.C.
March 3, 1913

Cary Grayson, with his bushy dark eyebrows, large nose, and five-
foot, seven-inch frame, was a distinctive figure in the White House.
As he stood at attention, President William Howard Taft escorted the
next president of the United States through the Executive Mansion.
Grayson had met Taft while assigned to the presidential yacht, the
Mayflower, as the ship's physician. And it was Taft who, after taking a
liking to the young doctor, had transferred him to the White House last
December.

Grayson liked Taft as well. He found him to be a gregarious sort, always eager to chat, even if he had proven to be a rather poor president.
But his humiliating loss in 1912—trailing Wilson and former president
Teddy Roosevelt, who'd run as a third-party candidate—didn't seem to
affect his mood. Indeed, he seemed to Grayson to be downright jovial
as he showed President-elect Wilson around.

Grayson had voted for Wilson and looked forward to the new era
of progressive, activist leadership he promised. Just before leaving the
governor's office, in fact, Wilson had pushed the New Jersey legislature
to approve the Sixteenth Amendment and impose a federal income tax.
Wilson, Grayson figured, was a man of action.

"Mr. Wilson, here is an excellent fellow that I hope you will get to
know," Taft said cheerfully, pointing to Grayson and grinning beneath
his thick mustache. "I regret to say he is a Virginian and a Democrat,
but that's a matter that can't be helped."

It wasn't clear if Taft had intended to gently tweak Wilson, who
shared both attributes with the doctor. Regardless, Wilson let out a
small laugh—which was a lot for a serious man from academia like
him—and extended a hand to Grayson.

"Pleased to meet you, Mr. President-elect," Grayson said.

The White House
Washington, D.C.
March 1, 1914

President Wilson had quickly drawn Cary Grayson into his confidence.

Almost a year earlier Grayson had impressed the president with his skill and discretion after Wilson's sister had tumbled down a marble staircase at the inauguration luncheon. As the young doctor stitched her cut, President Wilson was soon on hand admiring his work. "I am astonished that you were able to act so promptly," the president told Grayson. "Do you always have such equipment on hand in case of medical emergencies?"

Now, as Wilson's personal physician, Grayson understood why the president had been so curious about his preparation: Wilson's health wasn't exactly robust—he seemed to constantly suffer from stomach ailments, exhaustion, and headaches.

Grayson had recommended the president take long walks and horseback rides, and Wilson asked Grayson to accompany him on many of those trips. He did so gladly. They even attended church together when Ellen was away, with the president praising Grayson for making an excellent imitation of a Presbyterian.

Over the past year, Wilson had confided in Grayson about his wife's declining health. The occasional fainting spells and general weakness that had plagued her for months was not a topic the president discussed easily.

"It's her nerves," Wilson told Grayson as they stood at Ellen's bedside. "She's had too much strain."

The Washington social scene could make anyone queasy, Grayson knew, especially a hardworking and devoted woman like Ellen Wilson—someone whom most of the White House workers had grown quite fond of.

"Yes," Grayson said, in agreement while giving her a brief exam. "There's nothing organically wrong with her."

Rest and time away from Washington. That was what her husband felt Ellen needed. And that, in turn, was exactly what the doctor prescribed.

The White House
Washington, D.C.
August 2, 1914

When it was just the two of them alone in the room, Ellen Wilson lifted her head and turned to Grayson. He could see in her eyes she had something important to say.

As her condition worsened, she could no longer move her arm. She could barely retain any food or water, and she was having some sort of kidney trouble, which he again attributed to a nervous breakdown.

Grayson and the president had been working to keep any distressing news from her, such as the war that had been declared a few days earlier across Europe. They also shielded Ellen from the toll that world tensions were taking on the president. Though he was in reasonably good health, Wilson's complaints of various ailments prevailed.

Despite their best efforts, Ellen's health continued to deteriorate. Others recommended bringing in outside experts, but Wilson and Grayson always refused, convinced that it was nothing but nerves. They both adored Ellen. They did not want to think the worst, and so they didn't. But the First Lady herself was under no such delusions.

"Doctor, I realize that I am going," the First Lady whispered. Her eyes were wet.

Grayson shook his head. "No, Mrs. Wilson," he replied, startled.

"You know him and he is devoted to you," she continued. "Take good care of Woodrow."

Grayson nodded and vowed to do just that.

The White House
Washington, D.C.
August 12, 1914

Grayson took out his pen and paper and began to write.

Earlier that morning, he had found Woodrow Wilson in tears. The president had been despondent ever since his return from Ellen's burial service in Georgia, and his condition showed no improvement today.

Wilson confided in Grayson that he no longer took any joy in the presidency. Not without Ellen around. He wanted to escape. At night, he would lose himself in his detective novels. He couldn't bear to be alone.

Grayson had urged the president to rest. There was no use, Grayson argued, in exacerbating his own maladies, or the greater calamity they might bring on to his own health. Reluctantly, the president had agreed.

It was "a heartbreaking scene," Grayson now wrote as he reflected back on the day. "President Wilson is a great man with his heart torn out."

He knew the letter's recipient would understand. Edith Bolling Galt was, after all, a widow herself.

The White House
Washington, D.C.
March 18, 1915

Edith Galt arrived that afternoon wearing a long black dress imported from Paris and with a severe preoccupation about her shoes. Her walk to 1600 Pennsylvania Avenue had been a muddy one and her shoes were now unrecognizable.

The forty-two-year-old Galt, who readily informed friends that she was a direct descendant of Pocahontas, entered the old, elegant mansion and cast a glance at Ike Hoover, the chief usher. Hoover stared back at her with a look he might've given to someone suspected of stealing the candlesticks.

Galt had arrived at the White House that afternoon at the request of the president's cousin, Helen. The poor girl had been in a state of deep depression since the death of the First Lady. Edith's friend, Cary Grayson, had implored her to come and visit Helen for months. Over time, Edith and Helen had formed a friendship—so much so that they had spent that afternoon walking the muddy streets of Washington. Now, at Helen's insistence, she had come inside the White House for a cup of tea.

Though she did not think herself a political sort, Edith marveled at being in the same building where Jefferson had dined, where Lincoln had planned for war, where the Roosevelt children once roamed. As she turned the corner of the old house, Edith struggled not to gasp: there, walking down the long hallway toward them, were her old friend Cary Grayson and a tall man with graying hair. Both were dressed in golf clothes that seemed to have been made by a blind tailor.

"Mr. President, this is Edith Galt," Grayson said.

Wilson's eyes twinkled. "Mrs. Galt," he said. "How do you do?"

She smiled. "Good afternoon, Mr. President."

As she apologized for the state of her shoes, her curious violet eyes looked down to note that the president's boots were just as muddy. They both laughed at their unseemly attire.

Edith knew immediately that she had captured the president's attention, though it was hardly a surprise—she was quite accustomed to attracting the interests of men. They seemed to like her boldness.

Eyeing Grayson, who watched the meeting with great interest, Edith never for a moment considered that he and Helen might have engineered this seemingly chance encounter.

The White House
Washington, D.C.
March 21, 1915

As the motion picture finished—the first ever to be screened at the White House—President Wilson declared it a triumph. D. W. Griffith's *The Birth of a Nation* was "like writing history with lightning," the president gushed. "And my only regret is that it is all so terribly true."

The film, which depicted the Civil War era, had caused riots in major cities like Boston and Philadelphia for its praise of the Ku Klux Klan and its depiction of domineering and deceitful former slaves taking advantage of white southerners during Reconstruction. The president, whose own administration had worked to resegregate portions of the civil service and the U.S. military, found little in the film to quibble with. In fact, Wilson knew that news of the film's White House screening would only help the Klan's efforts to use the film to boost recruitment—and he was just fine with that.

Washington, D.C.
March 25, 1915

Edith tore open the package that had arrived at her townhome directly from the White House.

In the weeks since they'd met, President Wilson had invited her over to dinner and welcomed her to frequent private discussions in his Oval Office study, where they'd held forth on issues great and small. They bonded over their mutual status as widowed spouses and their southern heritage. They reminisced about the poverty of plantation owners and farmers after the Civil War and about their bewilderment over the loyalty that Negroes still seemed to show their old masters. They discussed the state of Europe and Wilson's fears of American involvement in the Great War.

Now the president had taken the next step in a hurried courtship. Opening the package, she pulled out a note, signed "From your sincere and grateful friend." Then she glanced over the accompanying book, one that had been the subject of a recent conversation. British author Philip Gilbert Hamerton was one of Wilson's favorites, as was this particular book: *Round My House: Notes of Rural Life in France in Peace and War*. The book advanced a theme that he'd spoken about often in their private discussions: that the nations of the world weren't so different. They just needed to understand each other better.

That he would share so many insights with a woman who was basically a stranger demonstrated to Edith just how much Wilson longed for a replacement for his recently departed Ellen. Edith found him to be such a desperately lonely man that it made her sad.

But she liked him, too. He was kind and attentive, and she could also see he was brilliant. Edith was sure he had great things ahead for his presidency, as long as someone was there to help keep his spirits up.

The White House
Washington, D.C.
May 4, 1915

After the dinner guests dispersed, Wilson escorted Edith onto the South Portico. In the two months since they'd met, he'd been sending her letters like a lovestruck teenager. "I need you as a boy needs his sweetheart and a strong man his helpmate and heart's comrade," he had written. But even she was shocked by his latest declaration.

Under the moonlight of a clear night sky, the president of the United States had fallen to one knee and proposed marriage.

Edith tried to conceal a gasp. Marriage was so impractical: She was sixteen years his junior; he was still mourning his wife; and the White House staff eyed her like a soldier would an enemy walking into his camp. "It's too soon to be asking such a question," she replied. "What would people say?"

"I don't care," Wilson said. "I need you."

"If I must give you an answer tonight," she replied, "then my answer must be no."

Wilson offered a wide grin. "You don't have to answer me tonight."

Washington, D.C.
September 24, 1915

Edith and Colonel House sat across from each other, a teapot stationed in the middle of the table. "May I pour you another cup, sir?" she asked him softly.

House nodded. "Thank you, madam."

She knew why they were meeting. Colonel Edward House was Woodrow Wilson's confidant, longtime advisor, and close friend. And she was the usurper that he intended to tame. This meeting, Edith knew, was to be House's chance to put her in her place—at least, that's what he believed. Ellen had a different plan in mind for their discussion.

For some time after Wilson's unexpected proposal, Edith had gone back and forth about what to do. She knew that Ellen was considered something akin to a saint since her passing. The White House servants sneered when Edith entered the mansion or deigned to sit in a chair where St. Ellen had once rested. She had feared, too, the reaction of the press—not to mention the snobbish society ladies whose whispers filled the city. Then there was the reaction of the president's children: What must they think of their father replacing their beloved mother so soon?

Edith prided herself on being a woman of considerable means, and cherished independence. She didn't need a husband.

Still, she mused, Wilson was a loving, gentle man. A visionary. And how many women would turn down a chance to be the First Lady of the United States?

After days of indecisiveness, Edith's mind was finally made up by something her lawyer said. Confiding her dilemma in him, the lawyer told her that it was her destiny to hold in the palm of her hand the weal or woe of a country.

That was all she needed to hear.

The rest of Wilson's team was not as certain of Edith's potential as her lawyer had been. Edith suspected they were conniving to delay the wedding, or even to break up the couple altogether. She also knew that Colonel House would be the linchpin of any of these plans. Which is exactly why she had decided to meet with him.

"You know, the president speaks of you with great affection," Edith told House, as wisps of warm mist rose from their teacups. "He admires your ability to place problems in perspective."

She watched as House beamed with delight. "That's wonderful to hear, Mrs. Galt."

House told her that he believed Wilson had the potential to be a great peacemaker in the war. He said that the president's proposal to end the conflict could be "the greatest event in human history excepting the birth of Christ."

Edith nodded sagely as the old, puffed-up fool prattled on. She'd taken an almost instant dislike to him, and she resented Wilson's naïve declarations of House's wisdom and prudence. She suspected that House did not approve of her, or of their upcoming wedding, but she was also confident that he would leave their meeting believing that he had Edith's support and approval. House was a necessary evil, at least for now.

After tea, she drove him around the city in her electric car and then deposited him at the White House, where she was certain he would provide a favorable report to the president and not object to their plans for a December wedding.

United States Capitol
Washington, D.C.
March 5, 1917

"I, Woodrow Wilson, do solemnly swear that I will faithfully execute the office of President of the United States and will, to the best of my ability, preserve, protect, and defend the Constitution of the United States."

Chief Justice Edward Douglas White paused. "So help you God?"

Wilson paused to regain the steam in his voice, then responded, "So help me God."

Edith was at her husband's side when he, in a long frock coat and silk top hat, removed his hand from the Bible, the same he'd used as New Jersey governor, and bent down to kiss it.

She was the first First Lady in American history to stand beside a president at the public swearing-in ceremony, and also the first to ride with a new president in the inaugural parade—a sign to most Wilsonians of Edith's utter devotion to her husband.

The day had started overcast and misty, Edith noted, but then the sun had broken through—an encouraging sign, she hoped, that the country would also see sunshine rather than the dark cloud of war. Indeed, Woodrow Wilson had won reelection under the slogan "He kept us out of war."

Wilson's narrow defeat of Republican Charles Evans Hughes had been a little too close for comfort. But now it was all over, and Edith's tireless support during the campaign had won her praise from nearly all corners.

Now standing at the apex of power, she could scarcely believe she had ever let something as trivial as finding out about her future husband's long affair with Mary Peck stand in the way of her destiny to become First Lady. She was confident she'd cured him of his serial infidelities, just as she'd cured the press of their irrational distaste for her. She particularly enjoyed the favorable coverage she was now receiving from many Washington journalists, whom she'd worked assiduously to charm since becoming First Lady while accompanying her husband on nearly all of his official trips. Noting her influence, the *Louisville Courier-Journal* wrote that "[o]mnipotence might be her middle name."

She could live with that.

United States Congress
Washington, D.C.
April 6, 1917

The discovery of a German plot to encourage Mexico to go to war with the United States left the president with no other choice. Addressing both sessions of Congress, Wilson announced that a state of war now existed between America and Germany.

When he signed the war declaration, Edith handed him the same gold pen he had given her as a gift.

"Use this," she said.

Washington, D.C.
July 14, 1917

Edith looked on with disgust. From the window, she could see the crowds of women swarming Lafayette Park across from the White House and making their way to the front gates. The National Woman's Party was commemorating Bastille Day by demanding the right to vote. They carried outrageous banners with the French Revolution slogan, "Liberty. Equality. Fraternity." But to make such a vulgar display with the country at war? It made her sick.

Privately, she and the president had long bemoaned the suffragist movement, finding it to be a deplorable embarrassment. "Universal suffrage," Wilson had once declared, "is at the foundation of every evil in this country." During his reelection campaign, Wilson had differed sharply with Republican Charles Evans Hughes, who supported a constitutional amendment granting women the right to vote.

The group continued their display on her front lawn, until finally they were arrested for unlawful assembly. The president had counseled leniency toward the women—but Edith, thinking him too benevolent and forgiving, was adamant that they all be arrested.

United States Congress
Washington, D.C.
January 8, 1918

Wilson had a mission. With an overriding belief in his own abilities, he thought it might not even be too much to say that it was a mission from God. The Great War was proving to be one of the bloodiest conflicts in history. So much senseless violence. So much that might have been prevented had nations simply reasoned together.

Encouraged by a plea for peace from Pope Benedict XV the previous September, President Wilson had assembled a brain trust to help craft a plan. The participants were pulled from top Ivy League universities and met in New York, under the direction of Colonel House, to devise a plan that would end all future wars.

Now, addressing both chambers of Congress, Wilson declared his Fourteen Points for peace. The last, and most important, of these called for the formation of an association of nations guaranteeing "the principle of justice to all peoples and nationalities, and the right to live on equal terms of liberty and safety with one another, whether they be strong or weak."

Wilson's League of Nations proposal, as he first envisioned it, would ban "unethical" behavior, such as espionage or dishonesty, by member states. These rules would be enforced by a global governing body that could punish offenders by cutting off trade and imposing blockades.

An international tribune would administer justice, just like a court might do in the United States.

Wilson put forth this plan before the war ended, hoping to terminate hostilities without a surrender on either side. It was an effort to create "peace without victory." Other Allies did not seem so keen to surrender their sovereignty to an international body, but Wilson knew that he could persuade them.

The speech received triumphal reviews from the only voices that really mattered to him: Edith and the *New York Times*. "No public utterance you've ever made was greeted with such acclaim," his wife said later that night. The *Times* soon agreed, declaring that the Fourteen Points rivaled the Emancipation Proclamation in their importance.

Republicans, however, begged to differ. They did not like the idea of an international body usurping America's sovereign rights. The president worried about building enough support, but Edith assured him that opposition would soon be wiped away by popular acclaim.

Wilson realized his wife was right yet again.

Aboard the USS *George Washington*
North Atlantic Ocean
March 4, 1919

The president was gray. He had a temperature and the chills. His head throbbed. The voyage to Europe for peace negotiations had only just begun, and Grayson already feared for the president's ability to handle what might be weeks of tedious debate and negotiation. He urged the president to rest, but Wilson dismissed his advice.

Since the armistice in the Great War had been declared the previous November, the president had worked nonstop in pursuit of his League of Nations dream.

His most vociferous opponent, Senator Henry Cabot Lodge, had been expressing grave misgivings about any plan that might subjugate U.S. sovereignty or range of action to an international body. He did not want America bound to what he called "the intrigues of Europe." He also wanted the United States to be able to deploy forces wherever it wished, whenever it wished, without the consent of an international body.

"I have my own diagnosis for my ailment," Wilson told Grayson with only half of a smile, "I suffer from a retention of gases generated by the Republican Senators—and that's enough to poison any man."

Paris, France
April 14, 1919

Grayson had attended to his patient day and night for weeks now. Ten days earlier, the president had been seized with coughing fits, severe diarrhea, and shortness of breath. Grayson had at first suspected food poisoning, but he changed his diagnosis to severe influenza after Wilson's temperature reached an alarming 103 degrees. In the days that followed the president looked like a walking dead man.

Despite his patient's dire condition, Grayson put on his game face for reporters and other delegates, issuing a constant stream of hopeful and optimistic updates. Only in private did his confident smile fade. In a letter to a friend Grayson confided: "From your side of the water you cannot realize on what thin ice European civilization has been skating. I just wish you could spend a day with me behind the scenes here. Some day perhaps I may be able to tell the world what a close call we had."

Paris, France
April 28, 1919

"It's House," Wilson muttered. "He's got the servants acting as spies. They're monitoring everything we say."

Grayson assured his patient that this wasn't true. In recent days, the president had seemed to rally from the worst of his illness, only to plunge into even deeper distress. His face twitched and his hands shook so much at times that he could not even shave himself.

Now he was spewing seemingly paranoid or incoherent ideas, like this accusation of spying against Colonel House, his friend and most loyal advisor.

Grayson knew that this was only the latest incidence of Wilson's bizarre behavior. Recently, after a luncheon on the peace process, the president had noted the arrangement of chairs in the room. "This isn't in order," he'd said. He then urged Grayson to help him put red chairs in one section for the Americans, green in another for the British, and the remainder of chairs in place for the French.

To Grayson's growing astonishment, the president had also reversed himself abruptly on a multitude of important decisions. In earlier discussions, Wilson had proven reluctant to support the severe punishment that the British and French were advocating against Germany, such as cutting up some German territories, disarming the nation completely, and imposing huge reparations. Then he completely reversed himself. Before he became ill, Wilson had adamantly opposed a proposal to put German's former kaiser on trial. After he returned to negotiations, he put forth a resolution to do just that.

Leaving the sick room, Grayson found himself confronted by curious reporters. He again told them the same thing he'd been saying for weeks. "It's influenza. I'm afraid the president has suffered a relapse." He blamed Wilson's toiling away in poorly ventilated rooms and unfavorable weather for the most recent bout.

Returning to his room, Grayson fretted. What if the press learned that he'd sent for two medical experts from America to rush to the president's side? What if someone with authority suggested what Grayson already knew to be a very real possibility: that the president wasn't suffering from the effects of influenza, but from a stroke?

Washington, D.C.
September 3, 1919

As he boarded the train at Union Station, Cary Grayson tried to conceal his distress—but it was largely a futile effort. Only he and Edith knew the true state the president was in: He was peaked; his face was pale; and he twitched involuntarily. Over and over Grayson had tried to persuade Wilson to see the disastrous consequences that could result from this impending trip, but, as always, he refused to listen.

Grayson agreed with the president's vision for the League of Nations and believed it would be an historic effort to end all wars. He was less sure, however, about Wilson's refusal to consider any compromises to the proposal. Grayson believed that such rigidity bordered on insanity. Moreover, it was politically impractical. Anyone who read the papers knew that the League, at least the way Wilson insisted on it being constructed, was a nonstarter with both Congress and the American people.

Never lacking confidence in his own ability to persuade, Wilson was convinced that this three-week train trip would turn the tide of public opinion in favor of the League—thus forcing buckling senators to vote in its favor. He had scheduled dozens of speeches in places from Ohio to Indiana to Montana to Colorado to California and back in an effort to round up support.

But Grayson thought the trip was far too onerous for the oft-ailing president. He'd noticed that flashes of rage came more quickly to Wilson now. The president was frustrated that everyone was treating him like he was a different person. Even if they didn't say it to Wilson directly, Grayson knew that his friends and advisors all thought the president was missing a step.

Now, as the train began to make its way out of the capital, Grayson wondered if Wilson might ever make it back home to Washington.

Indiana State Fair
Indianapolis, Indiana
September 4, 1919

Wilson stood on a platform at the state fairgrounds and held forth before thousands of curious people. He saw in their eyes the profound effect he was having on them as he thundered against opponents of the League. Citing Article XI, one of his favorites in the Covenant of the League of Nations, Wilson declared "that every matter which is likely to affect the peace of the world is everybody's business, and that it shall be the friendly right of any nation to call attention in the League to anything that is likely to affect the peace of the world or the good understanding between nations.

"Under the Covenant of the League of Nations, we can mind other peoples' business and anything that affects the peace of the world, whether we are parties to it or not, can by our delegates be brought to the attention of mankind!"

The crowd roared—and Wilson smiled, knowing that victory was now only a matter of time.

On Board the Presidential Train in Montana
September 6, 1919

With each day of travel, Cary Grayson saw that Wilson's condition only seemed to worsen.

The president was muddled in his speeches: He said Baghdad was in Persia, rather than Iraq; he confused the dates of treaties he was citing; and he claimed to have descended from American revolutionaries, when, in truth, none of his ancestors had lived in the colonies during the Revolutionary War. Most of these occurrences could be laughed off, the inevitable result of too many speeches, but Grayson knew Wilson was a man of precision. His faltering was, Grayson feared, a sign of greater trouble.

Wilson could barely eat, so Grayson prepared a daily diet of liquids and soft foods for him. Now severe throat pain was making it hard for the president to even swallow. Grayson, having watched the steady progression of symptoms, now had a new diagnosis in mind. With Edith listening anxiously by his side, he told the president that he had developed a throat infection, an alarming sign that his overall health was beginning to fail.

Pueblo, Colorado
September 25, 1919

As her husband delivered his fortieth speech in half as many days, Edith looked on with growing concern. He was not sleeping. His breathing was labored. He would sometimes appear to be choking. He would lose his train of thought during speeches, and he'd often repeat himself. He was more rigid than she'd ever seen him. Even with her.

Just before his speech, Edith asked Wilson to stop and take a respite. "No," he told her. "I have caught the imagination of the people. They are eager to hear what the League stands for. I should fail in my duty if I disappointed them."

It was true that thousands were turning out to see him. What wasn't quite as clear was whether any of them actually opposed the League to begin with. Sure, there were occasional signs of dissenters—"Shall American boys police the world?" men would call out to him—but they didn't seem to Edith to be likely converts to her husband's cause. Which made her start to wonder: What was the point of this trip? Preaching to the choir would not change anything.

Speaking outside a large hall, underneath splendid red, white, and blue bunting, Wilson greeted the crowd. "Mr. Chairman and fellow countrymen, it is with a great deal of genuine pleasure that I find myself in Pueblo, and I feel it a compliment that I should be permitted to be the first speaker in this beautiful hall. One of the advantages of this hall, as I look about, is that you are not too far away from me, because there is nothing so reassuring to men who are trying to express the public sentiment as getting into real personal contact with their fellow citizens."

Wilson, his voice gathering steam, then accused opponents of the League of being disloyal to their country. "I have perceived more and more that men have been busy creating an absolutely false impression of what the treaty of peace and the covenant of the League of Nations contain and mean.

"I find, moreover, that there is an organized propaganda against the League of Nations and against the treaty proceeding from exactly the same sources that the organized propaganda proceeded from which threatened this country here and there with disloyalty."

He went on for an hour, until his head throbbed and his voice was hoarse. He defended the League and attacked his opponents. He said his efforts were essential to a just and lasting worldwide peace. And then he brought the audience, and some journalists as well, to tears as he closed his speech by citing the sacrifices of the American dead. "There seems to me to stand between us and the rejection or qualification of this treaty the serried ranks of those boys in khaki, not only those boys who came home, but those dear ghosts that still deploy upon the fields of France."

As Wilson basked in the thunderous applause, Edith cried as well. Not because of her husband's words, but because she knew he would not make it much longer.

Edith Wilson beckoned the maid into her compartment. It was very late at night, so the First Lady said little as the maid brushed her hair and then offered a massage. With her husband sleeping in the next room—at last, he was getting some rest!—the women made a special effort to keep quiet.

Before long, they heard a knock on the door. It was the president.

"When you are finished," he called out, "will you come in here?"

A pause, and then: "I'm very sick."

Quickly summoning Dr. Grayson, Edith listened in horror as her husband now admitted what they'd all known for so long. He had tried to sleep, but the pain was unbearable. He couldn't breathe. He was nauseous. She could see the muscles on his face twitching. He had difficulty moving his left side.

She saw a worried look crossing Grayson's face and her heart began to race. She wondered if her husband would even survive the night.

On Board the Presidential Train to Kansas
September 26, 1919
5 A.M.

Cary Grayson came to the same conclusion as the First Lady: The western tour was over. The reporters would be told the president had an illness attributed to exhaustion. A telegram would be sent to Wilson's daughters informing them of his early return, but assuring them there was nothing to worry about. All other stops were canceled. The conductor would send messages down their route to clear the tracks for the train's speedy return to Washington.

Everyone agreed to the plan, except for the president, who, despite having managed to dress himself, still looked piteously ill.

"No," Wilson told them. "No. I must keep on."

Grayson could not relent to his friend's whims. Not this time. "Any other course than returning to Washington," he warned Wilson, "might bring disastrous, even fatal, consequences."

But Wilson would not relent. Grayson and Edith looked at each other with exasperated expressions. The First Lady knew what she had to do.

Edith went into the bathroom and retrieved a small mirror. With tears in her eyes, she brought it to her husband. "Look at yourself."

Wilson took the mirror and, for the first time, saw the reality. He swallowed hard and choked back tears. "I don't want to be a quitter."

"You have done your part, sir," Grayson said. "You cannot continue. Not any longer."

Wilson sighed and looked at the man who, other than Edith, was his closest confidant. "If you feel that way about it," he submitted at last, "I will surrender."

The tears fell freely down his cheeks. Wilson had pledged to give all he had for passage of the League. Now, Grayson knew, that's exactly what he had done.

The White House
Washington, D.C.
October 2, 1919

Just as she had done each night since their hasty return home, Edith awakened every hour or so to check on her husband. At around 8 A.M., she found him on the side of the bed, trying to reach for a glass of water.

He had been unsettled ever since their return. Some days, his head ached so fiercely that he could do nothing except pace around the bedroom. Much to his discontent, Grayson had put him on bed rest. The *New York Times* reported that the president had experienced a nervous breakdown, caused by the strain of trying to gain passage of the Treaty of Versailles. Most people, including foreign visitors, had been barred from seeing him. Even Vice President Thomas R. Marshall was turned away.

Edith handed the glass of water to her husband and noticed his left arm hanging loosely by his side.

"I have no feeling in my hand," he told her. "Will you rub it? But first, would you help me to the bathroom?"

She took his hands and helped him from the bed. He gripped her tightly, wincing with every step.

Once they made it inside, Wilson propped himself up on the sink. "Woodrow, I'm going to leave you for just a moment," Edith gasped. "I'm going to call Grayson."

The president nodded.

After making the call she hung up the phone, only to hear a loud crash from the bathroom. Running back inside, she found the president lying on the floor.

He was not moving.

Cabinet Room
The White House
Washington, D.C.
October 6, 1919

"The president's mind is very active. He is very engaged," Grayson told
the assembled cabinet members. "And he's very much annoyed that
this meeting has been called. By whose authority? For what purpose?"

Of course, Grayson already knew the answers. It was the talk of
all the newspapers. He understood that the cabinet was considering whether to put the vice president forward as temporary leader of
the government, or perhaps to convene a temporary government-
by-cabinet in Wilson's absence.

Grayson was not happy about being called away from his patient to
attend to such matters. Addressing the entire Wilson cabinet, he made
it clear, as if there were any doubt, that the president and Mrs. Wilson
resented the decision by Secretary of State Robert Lansing to convene
an emergency meeting without the president's knowledge or consent.

"The president's condition is encouraging," Grayson told them,
adding that Wilson was still on bed rest and that only urgent matters
should be presented to him.

Grayson had been a reluctant participant in this ruse. Immediately
after his friend's collapse, he had quietly suggested to Mrs. Wilson that
the president consider resigning for the good of the country. Edith
would not hear of it, and looked at him as if his very utterance was an
act of cruelty and betrayal.

"Woodrow Wilson is the most brilliant president we have ever had,"
she told him. "We can't deny the country his leadership. Not at a time
like this."

It was easy to succumb to such arguments because he agreed with
them. Cary Grayson loved Woodrow Wilson. Wilson was his friend, his
confidant, and the closest thing to a father he'd ever had. He did not
want for him to resign. He truly believed the president could recover.
How could he turn his back on him now?

And yet he watched with some unease as Mrs. Wilson reviewed and
approved documents for her husband. It was Edith who managed his

workflow, who decided which requests to answer and which to ignore. She was doing that, Grayson believed, out of loving devotion to a great man.

Sensing the awkwardness of the moment, Secretary of War Newton D. Baker spoke up. "We had only gathered today as a mark of affection for the president," he maintained, as others in the room looked on skeptically. "Please convey our sympathy to the president and give him our assurance that everything is going along all right."

The White House
Washington, D.C.
October 6, 1919

"If the Congress should ask questions concerning the employment of our naval forces in the Adriatic and Mediterranean, please refer the questions to me at once, informing the Congress you have done so by my direction and that the replies will be forthcoming in due course, unless the Executive should find that it was not compatible with the public interest to convey to the Congress at the time the particular information desired."

Woodrow Wilson's note to the secretary of the navy was precipitated by senators asking him for information on the reported landing of U.S. troops on the Dalmatian coast.

Now, as Edith reread the order, she couldn't help but feel a surge of power. The note was not signed by the nation's commander in chief. He was sleeping and far too ill to comprehend the issues anyway.

She had written every word.

The White House
Washington, D.C.
October 12, 1919

Under Cary Grayson's supervision, the White House released its thir-
tieth bulletin on the president's health, again labeling his illness as
"nervous exhaustion."

Grayson saw the skepticism in the eyes of the reporters he met with,
and he certainly read it in their words. Many of them believed that the
White House, preoccupied with the president's condition, was unable to address a slew of domestic issues, foremost of which was the
apparent lack of preparedness in welcoming troops home from the
Great War.

Many soldiers were ravaged with disease and injury. Some were
shell-shocked by the horrors of battle. With no plan in place to help returning veterans transition back into the domestic workforce, and with
soldiers finding that immigrants had filled their jobs, riots and unrest
had begun to spread. Unemployment and inflation were rising, and the
administration seemed unable to handle any of it.

"The secrecy, and even the deception, practiced by court physicians
in the case of a monarch similarly afflicted have no place in the proce-
dure of an orderly republic," the *San Francisco Bulletin* wrote. "We are a
grown-up people and if told everything will be better prepared to face
the worst if there is really no hope of improvement."

That was bad, but what irked Grayson more was a quote in the *New
York Times* from Republican senator George Moses of New Hampshire.
Moses declared the president a very sick man who'd suffered from
some sort of cerebral lesion. "[He] will not be any material force or factor in anything," the senator stated.

"Senator Moses," Grayson now told the press, taking the allegations
head-on, "must have information that I do not possess."

The State Department
Washington, D.C.
November 8, 1919

Secretary of State Lansing pleaded with the First Lady to allow her husband to offer him guidance on various important international matters.

First, he explained, there was the question as to whether the United States should recognize the new government of Costa Rica, which had a constitutional structure of the kind that Wilson had championed. In response Lansing received a note on White House letterhead and written in Mrs. Wilson's hand:

> *The President says it is impossible for him to take up such matters until he is stronger and can study them. So if an answer must be made—the Sec. of State can say he (the Sec.) cannot act without the President's consent and that the P. directs the matter be held in abeyance until he can act.*

Next, Lansing had asked for guidance on how to handle the friction between the United States and Great Britain over England's arbitrary seizure of German tankers. Again, Mrs. Wilson had replied that the president "does not know enough about this matter" to act.

Now a new political crisis in Syria demanded American attention. And again, the United States president was unable to offer his chief diplomat any guidance at all.

But the worst consequence of Wilson's illness was, Lansing believed, the resolution of the Great War. Had Wilson been able to have a stronger voice in negotiations at Versailles, Germany's punishment might not have been so onerous, which played into the hands of radical groups, like the growing Nazi Party. Instead, the Allies had carried out an act of revenge that many now feared would open the door to an even worse armed conflict in the years ahead.

The White House
Washington, D.C.
November 19, 1919

Edith glanced at the draft statement that Democratic senator Gilbert
Hitchcock of Nebraska planned to read aloud to his colleagues who
were still wavering over the matter of the League. She took a pen and
scratched out the sentence that stated that if the treaty failed as it was
written, as almost everyone expected it would, then "the door will
probably be open for a possible compromise."

Woodrow had never been open to compromise on the League.

And neither was she.

The White House
Washington, D.C.
December 5, 1919

Leaving her sleeping husband in bed, Edith Wilson left the room and
waited for the senators to arrive. Like everyone else in Washington,
they had been hearing rumors about the president's health for months.
Some of the rumors were more outlandish than others: that he'd had a
massive stroke, or a heart attack, or that he'd gone mad.

The senators' expedition to the White House came about due to the
ongoing border skirmishes between Mexico and the United States ever
since the end of the Great War.

The latest episode, which involved the kidnapping of an American
consul, led to Congress passing a resolution that broke off diplomatic
relations with the Mexican government. Senators were stunned to find
out later that Secretary of State Lansing hadn't spoken directly with the
president in months.

Amid the outcry over this admission from Lansing, a Senate subcommittee was quickly assembled to determine whether Wilson was
still fit for office. Republican senator Albert Fall of New Mexico and
Democrat Gilbert Hitchcock of Nebraska were suggested as congressional emissaries to the White House in the hopes of forestalling any

further action. Nobody expected the president to agree to see them. Until suddenly, through Edith Wilson, he did.

Edith nodded to the two men as they were escorted into a dark, windowless room on the mansion's first floor. She watched their eyes turn to the president, who had not been seen in public—or by any outsiders at all, for that matter—in months.

Wilson, dressed in a sturdy brown sweater, greeted Senator Fall with a firm handshake.

"We are all praying for you, Mr. President," Fall told him.

"Which way?" he asked with a wry smile.

Still suspicious, the senator cast a glance in the First Lady's direction, as she took dictation.

"You seem very much engaged, madam," Fall said.

"I thought it wise to record this interview so there may be no misunderstanding or misstatement made," she replied.

The senators spoke with the president for a few minutes longer. Wilson raised various points that seemed to indicate he was up to date on the situation in Mexico. Then the senators were quickly shown out of the room.

Edith breathed a sigh of relief. In preparation for the senators' visit, she had consulted with Robert W. Woolley, the Democratic Party's head of publicity, to determine how to give the impression of a vigorous and engaged Wilson. With Woolley's counsel, and her husband's active assistance, she had carefully constructed the scene.

The dark, windowless room was chosen so that it would be more difficult to see Wilson's pallor. The president's useless left arm was hidden under his bulky sweater and a blanket. The chair for Senator Fall was deliberately placed to Wilson's right, so that Fall could not see the paralyzed left side of the president's face. Edith had spent hours coaching her husband on the details of the Mexican crisis so that he could at least mutter a few intelligible points. For the most part, the president had spent the past months unable to focus on anything. For weeks he hadn't even been able to speak.

Her elaborate staging, it seemed, had worked. The *New York Times* reported that the meeting "silenced for good the many wild and often unfriendly rumors of presidential disability."

The White House
Washington, D.C.
January 12, 1920

Woodrow Wilson had come down with another bout of influenza. Although Grayson had successfully kept this news from reporters and
cabinet members, the latest setback troubled him greatly.

"I am not well," Wilson said to Grayson, stating the obvious. He was
in a gloomy state. The League of Nations had failed to pass and Wilson
took the news hard. "It would have been better if I had died last fall."

"We are doing all we can to relieve your affliction," Grayson replied.
But, for the first time, the doctor had real doubts about whether that
was true.

"I fear I have no choice but to resign," the president said quietly.

Considering the steel will of his patient, the notion stunned Grayson. That Wilson himself was musing about stepping down only underscored the severity of his latest affliction. But Grayson reluctantly
agreed with him. How much more could one man take?

Together, the two men discussed taking a wheelchair to the Capitol
so that Wilson could announce his decision to the Congress in person.
But as soon as Edith caught wind of the idea, all talk of resignation
ended. The country *needed* them in the White House, she reasoned.
Quitting now was out of the question.

Besides, Edith was hard at work with her ailing husband on another
urgent matter: exacting revenge upon the senators who had hindered
the ratification of the League of Nations Treaty.

Her list had already reached a total of fifty-four names.

The White House
Washington, D.C.
March 1, 1921

Woodrow Wilson was in tears. Addressing his cabinet for the last time
as president—Republican Warren G. Harding, who'd beaten Ohio
governor James Cox in the general election, would take the oath of

office in three days—he apologized for not being able to control his emotions.

Though many people seemed to think Wilson had changed dramatically since his stroke—he was more paranoid, more accusatory, more unstable—Wilson didn't see any of it. He still felt the same, though he'd had to abandon his musings about a third term.

Regardless, he was outraged whenever anyone suggested he had any physical or mental shortcomings. Sure, he had relied on a cane to enter the Cabinet Room, but he thought that was of no real consequence. The cane, Wilson joked, had become his "third leg."

Before adjourning, the president posed for photos with the cabinet. In one of them, he was holding his cane. But in a second photo, the cane appeared to have been erased.

23 Years Later
Hollywood, California
1944

Edith watched an early cut of the film about her late husband's life. It was a fair rendering, she concluded. Hollywood had done a great man justice.

Of course, she hadn't left the outcome of this project up to chance: The film was based on her own memoir, and biographer Ray Stannard Baker, an advocate of her version of events, was on the set, carefully looking over every word of the script. Along with a cooperative Hollywood scriptwriter, Edith and Baker had made sure the record was straight about her husband's illness in October 1919.

Now, as she watched the scene in which Dr. Grayson informs her that the president is fully capable of continuing on with his duties and that resignation was never considered, she marveled at the masterpiece they'd created.

It was the final step in preserving her husband's memory.

EPILOGUE

46 Years Later
Upperville, Virginia
March 27, 1990

The two men stood together as they released their late father's papers to the press. James Gordon Grayson and Cary Travers Grayson Jr. knew they were contributing to history, even if they were exposing a story that their own father had worked so hard to keep concealed.

For the first time in history, the public was able to see the extent of Wilson's incapacitation as a result of a massive stroke. They saw Grayson's private assessment that Wilson should have announced his malady to the public, as well as a separate physician's statement that the president's condition was irreversible.

In response to the news, Arthur S. Link, one of the most prominent historians of Woodrow Wilson, felt compelled to amend his original conclusion that the rumor of Edith Wilson as president was "more the realm of legend than scholarship." His new view was starkly different:

"Edith emerges as the master of the cover-up."

Inspired in part by emerging revelations of Woodrow Wilson's deception about his long and crippling illness, the Twenty-Fifth Amendment to the U.S. Constitution was adopted by the United States Congress. The amendment established procedures for presidential succession in the event of a presidential disability. Section 4 allows the cabinet to overrule actions like those taken by Edith Wilson and Cary Grayson:

> *Whenever the Vice President and a majority of either the principal officers of the executive departments or of such other body as Congress may by law provide, transmit to the President pro tempore of the Senate and the Speaker of the House of Representatives their written declaration that the President is unable to discharge the powers and duties of his office, the Vice President shall immediately assume the powers and duties of the office as Acting President.*

4

Streets of Gold:
Charles Ponzi and the American Scheme

Boston, Massachusetts
July 23, 1920

William H. McMasters was one of Boston's top public relations experts. He'd handled political campaigns for everyone from Calvin Coolidge to former Boston mayors John F. "Honey Fitz" Fitzgerald and James M. Curley. It was this reputation that led the treasurer of the Hanover Trust Company to secure McMasters's services for one of their top new shareholders: an overnight financial sensation named Charles Ponzi.

At fifty-six years old, McMasters had wavy graying hair, a small nose, and prominent lips. A lawyer and Spanish-American War veteran with political aspirations of his own, he was never averse to having a multimillionaire for a client—especially a guy who seemed to be throwing money around with abandon. Whether it was friends, staff, family, or charities, practically everyone Ponzi came across got money. McMasters liked that.

"Mr. McMasters!" Ponzi greeted him. "I've heard so much about you!"

The well-dressed lawyer smiled as the exuberant diminutive Italian approached him.

"I am in need of a PR agent," Ponzi said. "And I have been assured you are the best in the business."

Oozing charm and confidence, Ponzi shared with McMasters his plans for building a larger financial empire. He told him that he was bringing in hundreds of thousands a month and giving his shareholders a 50 percent rate of return in just ninety days.

McMasters was shocked by the numbers. "A fifty percent return? In ninety days? How is that possible?"

"It's very possible, I assure you," Ponzi replied. "Just ask my investors."

"But how do you do it?" McMasters pressed.

"Well, I can tell you only so much," Ponzi said. "Otherwise I might give away trade secrets that would put me out of business."

Ponzi was self-assured, McMasters saw that right away. But he also saw something else, something that filled the seasoned lawyer with doubts. After all, a person who spins the truth for a living can always see when someone else is doing the same.

19 Years Earlier
University of Rome
April 12, 1901

"I am studying hard," Carlo wrote his mother. He regaled her with stories about his grueling class schedule, the good marks he was making at university, and the laudatory comments of his professors. "I hope you will be proud."

Of course Carlo knew that she was already proud. Imelde Ponzi had big dreams for her only child, who had ventured from the northern Italian countryside into the city. She had told Carlo again and again, especially after his father died, that he was the family's future. Only he, with his brilliance, tenacity, and many capabilities, could bring them the wealth and recognition they deserved. He would build "castles in the air," she often said, whatever that meant.

Perhaps that was why Carlo was drawn to his circle of friends at school. These were young people of sophistication and wealth. They wore the finest clothes, drove the finest vehicles, partied at all hours, and had seemingly unlimited funds. They lived *la dolce vita*.

Satisfied with his letter to his mother, Carlo had a few more drinks, scrounged together some money for gambling, and stumbled out into the night.

Parma, Italy
May 4, 1902

One year later, Carlo was sitting in his uncle's house in Parma. Since his father's death, his uncle had seemed to think it was his duty to offer counsel and guidance.

"College is over," his uncle said. "I think it is time you found a job.

"Maybe you could apply to be a clerk. Or maybe you could join the postal service like your father. It doesn't pay much, but you could earn an honest living and contribute to the family."

The young man winced. Carlo Pietro Giovanni Guglielmo Tebaldo Ponzi was not meant for a life of middle-class drudgery. Working at a monotonous job for meager wages? That was humiliating. And what a disappointment it would be to his mother. They were a rather ordinary middle-class family, but they had million-dollar designs. Carlo's mother was a descendant of Italian dons—and Carlo believed it was time to return the family to wealth and prominence.

Imelde had been heartbroken when her only son had dropped out of the University of Rome. She was astonished when she learned of his poor marks. She couldn't believe he had lied to her for so long.

Carlo hadn't set out to deceive her. He never expected to flunk out of university. His rich friends had seemed to coast through their studies and stay in school. He couldn't figure out why that same strategy hadn't worked for him.

"I appreciate the suggestion," Carlo said. "But I need to do something bigger. Something that would make Mama proud. I want to show her that her faith in me was not misplaced."

"Well, then, what about America?" his uncle asked. Stories about uneducated, poor Italian boys leaving for America to get rich were everywhere.

"America?" Carlo asked, his face brightening.

"In America, the streets are paved with gold," his uncle said. "All you have to do is reach down and pick it up."

Boston, Massachusetts
November 17, 1903

Twenty-one-year-old Carlo Ponzi arrived in the United States amid choppy seas and an icy wind that whipped up the rain and ocean mist. He walked onto the docks and wiped the saltwater from his thick, expressive eyebrows. He barely spoke a word of English and had just $2.51 left in his pocket. The rest, his entire life savings, he had gambled away during the voyage. Ponzi bore no ill will toward the Sicilian who'd cheated him out of his money. To the contrary, he was impressed by the man's skill.

But his current sorry state was of no consequence to him. At five feet four, Carlo may have been short of both height and money, but he had million-dollar dreams. America would be the place where great things would happen for him. He could feel it. This was his destiny.

As he exited the ship, he was wearing his best suit. He'd learned from his former classmates in Rome that one always had to look the part. With a smile on his lips and a twinkle in his eye, he was sure he looked as if he had just walked out of one of Boston's finest homes.

Carlo dutifully submitted himself for inspection to the officer at the U.S. entry point. Like every other immigrant arriving in America, he vowed that he had never been in jail or the poorhouse, and that he had no communicable diseases. It was all rather demeaning for someone of his merit, but what could he do?

"What's your occupation?" the officer asked.

"Student," Carlo replied.

Walking through the inspection gates, he felt an unpleasant texture beneath his finely polished Italian shoes. As he looked down, he made a surprising discovery: The streets of America were not paved with gold.

They were in fact caked in mud.

Banco Zarossi
Montreal, Canada
April 4, 1908

Luigi Zarossi chomped on a cigar and eyed the young men carefully as he listened to them outline their plans for the bank.

In a matter of months, Charles, with his steady smile, confident gaze, and infectious optimism, had won his boss's trust. Zarossi had promoted him from assistant teller to manager of the bank in record time. *A bank manager*—his mother couldn't help but be impressed with that!

Charles's English, if not his finances, had improved enormously over the last few years. He had drifted from one job to another, working in all sorts of odd places, including as a dishwasher at a restaurant, where he'd slept on the floor to save money. But he knew none of those jobs were going to help him achieve his dreams. It wasn't as though he was starving—he wasn't. He knew he could lead a perfectly comfortable lower-middle-class existence like any number of his fellow immigrants. Find an Italian woman. Raise some Italian kids. But that wasn't for him.

In his frustration, he sometimes turned to dice or card games to try to make some extra money, but, for whatever reason, luck rarely took his side. That was why, after hearing about an Italian immigrant who had started a successful banking business in Canada, he'd decided to head north.

And so he was starting over again. He was now in a new country, with a brand-new name to match: Charles Bianchi. "Charles" was more acceptable than "Carlo" and "Bianchi" was Italian for "White." White like a piece of paper. A blank page. A clean slate.

Under the direction of the jovial Luigi Zarossi, Banco Zarossi catered to Italian immigrants, luring them in with promises of competitive interest rates and fair dealing—not to mention speaking their native language. Banco Zarossi became one of the fastest-growing financial institutions in Canada, but Charles knew it was also a troubled one. Zarossi had been dipping into customers' deposits to pay for some bad investments. His boss was a nice man, Charles thought, but a stupid one.

It was during his time at the bank that Charles ran into Antonio Salviati, a friend from the old country. Salviati was still the same slick guy he'd known at the University of Rome, complete with the small scar on his cheek from a knife fight. It was Salviati who had helped Charles come up with the plan they were now presenting to Zarossi.

"Mr. Zarossi, what if you could offer customers a ten percent interest rate on their accounts?" Salviati asked.

"Ten percent?"

Charles smiled and said, "They would be beating down our doors!"

"I agree with you—but, Charles, you understand banking enough to know that such an interest rate is impossible. We'd never be able to turn a profit."

Charles exchanged a look with Antonio. "Mr. Zarossi," he said, "haven't a good number of the bank's customers given you money to wire back to their relatives in Italy?"

Zarossi nodded.

"Well, take the money, but don't actually send it," Salviati advised. "Use it to pay off your debts instead."

Zarossi's eyebrows rose. "But what will happen when the customers realize their money never reached their relatives?

"That's why we should pay a ten percent interest rate," Charles said. "To bring in big depositors." He explained that by the time anyone was wise to the scheme, the bank would have more than enough money to wire to customers' families in Italy.

Charles smiled. "Everyone will win. The customers will get ten percent interest. You will be able to pay off your debts. And more and more money will flood into the bank's coffers."

Ponzi's confidence was infectious. "Yes," Zarossi said, puffing on his cigar. "Maybe this plan could work."

Montreal, Canada
May 1, 1908

Alone in his room at the boardinghouse, Charles threw his clothes into suitcases. His train was leaving in thirty minutes. He hoped it would free him from both Montreal and from his latest mess.

He quickly looked around the room for anything he might have forgotten. Suddenly he heard a knock on his door. Then another.

"Who is it?" he asked. Opening the door, he saw two somber-looking men. Although they were dressed in plain clothes, they had the aura of law enforcement. His heart raced. Why had he lingered in Montreal? He should've been gone by now. He thought he would have had more time.

"Are you Charles Bianchi?" one of the men inquired. His tone did not suggest a friendly call.

"No," Charles replied. The Bianchi name hadn't brought him new luck after all, so he tried another. "My name is Clement."

"I'm Detective McCall," the man said. "I know who you are."

"Okay, okay," Ponzi replied, with a sigh. "I'm guilty."

Nobody had said a word two days earlier when Charles had walked into the main office of Canadian Warehousing. And why should they? After all, the company was a customer of Banco Zarossi, and Charles had visited them often.

Entering the director's empty office, he had opened a desk drawer and written himself a check for $423.58. He thought the precise number was an especially nice touch, making it seem more credible. At the bottom he signed the director's name. Then he put the check into his suit pocket and walked out the door.

Charles didn't want to take money from one of his customers, but what choice did he have? The scam at the bank had collapsed in just a couple of months, far sooner than any of them had expected. Customers received quick word from relatives that their money hadn't arrived—and that was it. Within days, Salviati had disappeared and Zarossi had fled to Mexico City with all the cash he could find.

But Ponzi had decided to remain—at least long enough to spruce himself up before returning to the United States. He walked from store to store, buying two new suits, an overcoat, a pocket watch with a chain, shirts, ties, and suspenders. He looked the part of a successful businessman.

Now those very clothes were being inventoried by Detective McCall, who also found what was left of the forged check Ponzi had cashed— a little over two hundred dollars.

"Carlo Ponzi," also known as "Charles Ponzi," aka "Charles Bianchi," aka "Charles Clement," was under arrest.

That night, Charles wrote to his mother in Italy from the St.-Vincent-de-Paul Penitentiary:

> *Dearest Mother, your son has at last stumbled on excellent fortune in this country. I have taken a position as special assistant to the warden in this institution, who can well use my fluency in language in conversing with some of the inmates. It is a three-year contract, darling mother, and during that time I shall not have to worry where my next meal or warm bed is to come from. . . .*

When he finished writing he shifted fitfully on his mattress, which was made from a sack of corncobs and husks. For Ponzi, the despair of being locked in a cell was nothing compared to the empty feeling of being dead broke. As he clawed at his makeshift pillow, he resolved never to let it happen again.

Three Years Later
Moers Junction, New York
June 7, 1911

"On your feet, wops!"

The U.S. border inspector walked through the crowded coach train and scrutinized the six men before him. They were obviously Italians. Five of them were big and burly and looked clueless. The sixth, however, was a short guy who appeared confident and composed.

Back in Canada, Charles Ponzi had told the five big Italians to board the train quietly and sit with him. He had ushered them on board as a favor to his old friend, Antonio Salviati, who was still managing to evade the authorities in Canada while undertaking a new scheme: smuggling Italian immigrants into the United States.

When Ponzi handed his ticket to the conductor, the five men were to follow suit. They were not to say a word or cause any trouble.

Intelligence, however, was not their strong suit. The moment an officer began to question them they started jabbering away in Italian. The jig was up moments later when their paperwork didn't check out.

The officer looked directly at Ponzi. "You've brought these men into the United States in violation of the immigrations laws," he charged.

"I did no such thing," Ponzi protested. "We were all merely on the same train."

"None of you have a permit to enter the country," the officer said. As an Italian citizen, Ponzi needed a visa since he had never bothered to obtain citizenship when he'd first arrived in America eight years earlier.

"We were interviewed by the inspector on the Canadian side of the border. If we were inadmissible for any reason, it was his duty to inform us!"

"We don't need you to tell us the law, Mr. Ponzi."

Charles lowered his head and closed his eyes. His run of bad luck had apparently not yet ended. He was on his way to another prison, and this time for one of the most serious of offenses: attempting to smuggle aliens into the United States.

Atlanta Federal Prison
Atlanta, Georgia
January 1912

Charles Morse was a filthy-rich Wall Street mogul—exactly the kind of man Charles Ponzi had always wanted to be. Now Morse was Ponzi's fellow inmate. The authorities had closed in on Morse over his involvement in a speculation scheme and the alleged misappropriation of bank funds—not unlike Ponzi's own crimes back in Canada. As Morse described what he'd done, Ponzi hung on his every word.

Morse had been known as the "King of Ice" in New York due to his ice delivery business. He'd also had a successful shipping company, which had made him a player with some of the biggest names around— not just in the city, but in the entire country. Even now, Morse bragged to Ponzi that his lawyers were pushing President William Howard Taft to show him leniency because of the mysterious illness he was suffering from.

Ponzi had noticed that Morse's curious malady always seemed to be most acute right before he was to be seen by the prison doctor. Then, moments later, he seemed to be fine again. Ponzi knew something was up, but he never said a word. He just watched.

The illness intensified the entreaties of Morse's wealthy friends for Taft to pardon him on humanitarian grounds. When news spread through the prison that Taft had finally granted the release, Morse quickly started planning a European vacation.

Over their periodic chess games, Morse told Ponzi many times that his sentence was one of the most brutal ever imposed on a citizen of the United States. "There is no one on Wall Street who is not doing daily what I did," he said.

Ponzi listened to his idol's words carefully, especially now that the great man was departing. "Always have a goal, Charlie, a goal that keeps getting bigger.

"It's all a matter of keeping your sights high. There are millionaires outside who make mistakes every day, but their sights are high and when things go wrong the money is there to cover their losses." *Their wealthy friends seem to be there as well,* Ponzi thought.

Charles later found out that Morse's illness had been just another one of his schemes. He had been eating soap shavings to put toxins temporarily in his body. In America, Ponzi was starting to realize, if you had money and power, you could get away with almost anything.

Six Years Later
Boston, Massachusetts
February 4, 1918

Charles Ponzi looked at the wooden pews of St. Anthony's Church and saw them filled only with Gneccos, his future in-laws. He couldn't afford to bring his mother or any other relatives to America for his wedding. It was the day's only disappointment.

Up until this moment, he'd endured a long string of disappointments since his release from prison. He had first kicked around the South for a while, finding temporary jobs in Alabama. Then he'd decided to return to Italy to see his mother and fight for his country during the Great War. He had convinced himself that fighting with honor for his homeland would fulfill the great destiny that had eluded him.

It was not an idle dream—Ponzi had, in fact, even gone so far as to board a steamship in New York Harbor. But as the ship weighed anchor, Ponzi learned via telegraph from the Italian government that he would have to bear the cost of his transit to Italy and back himself. Ponzi believed that to be unacceptable. He was returning home to fight for his country—it seemed to him that paying for his voyage was the least they could do.

Leaving his luggage on the ship, Ponzi walked out to the deck and jumped overboard.

It only took a few minutes to swim the short distance back to the pier. *Maybe,* he thought, *America is still my destiny after all.*

And now, as he stood at the altar awaiting his bride, he felt that destiny more strongly than ever.

Thirty-five-year-old Charles had wooed the much younger Rose Gnecco for months. Even with his meager salary as a clerk at the J. R. Poole Company, Charles had showered the woman with flowers, gifts, and nights out at the theater. He'd finally saved up enough cash to afford a modest ring.

During their courtship, Charles had always been vague about his past. He told Rose he was involved in various "investigations." He hinted that he'd worked for the Italian government.

"We will build a great empire," he told her. "We have a great destiny before us."

Rose smiled politely. "I don't care about any of those things. I just want to be with you. I want to raise a family."

Now, with the sun peeking through the church's stained glass windows, Charles and Rose were married. He truly loved her, and he felt honored beyond words to have found such a beautiful woman. It was another new beginning for him. Another fresh start. And, this time, his life really was going to take a turn for the better. Big things were about to happen. He could feel it.

Boston, Massachusetts
January 4, 1919

"We don't need to be rich to be happy," Rose told him. "It's okay, Charles."

Ponzi had quit his job and taken over his father-in-law's grocery business, determined to turn things around. The company had owed $11,000 to creditors when he'd joined. Charles had pled with the creditors' lawyers to loan him $6,000, and he'd promised to repay the money and the business's debts within a year. He had a plan. He could do it.

The lawyers didn't believe him.

As it turned out, they were right to be skeptical—and now, with the bankruptcy papers officially filed that morning, Ponzi was once again without a job. But this time was different. This time he had a wife to support.

Brooding over his most recent financial troubles, he sat at the kitchen table, examining his stamps. He loved collecting them because it allowed him to think without distraction. Rose marveled at his patience and how they seemed to be an endless source of fascination for him. As he sat at the kitchen table, poring over the colorful pieces of paper from around the world, he vowed that this failure would be the last. He'd seen scams and frauds and bankruptcies. He'd seen Boston, Canada, and the inside of two prisons. Now, he pledged, he would finally see the one thing he'd been missing all along: success.

He was going to be his own boss now.

Boston, Massachusetts
Summer 1919

Walking through the front door of the Hanover Trust Company, Charles Ponzi was confident he would receive the funds he needed to make his new company a success.

Seated across a desk from the bank's president, he outlined his business plan, then cut to the chase: "I'm going to need two thousand dollars," he said, assuring him that all of it would easily be repaid on time.

The *Traders' Guide* that Ponzi had devised was an enterprise of pure genius. He would charge other businesses around the country to advertise in the magazine, which would also promote his own import-export business for free.

Ponzi had outsized ambitions for the publication, planning to release it in multiple editions and languages, including English, French, German, Italian, Portuguese, and Spanish. To get things going, he would mail a hundred thousand free copies to companies he found in business directories. Advertisers, he assured the bank's president, would line up to buy ads in a publication with such a massive, business-oriented circulation.

Anticipating his success, Ponzi had already rented a large office and hired two stenographers. All he needed now was money for more staff, along with printers, translators, salesmen, and, of course, postage. He had tried to find investors throughout that spring and summer, but had come up with nothing. *What can you do?* he asked himself. *Some people lack imagination.* This meeting with the bank was his last resort.

"It is a very interesting idea, Mr. Ponzi. We would be happy to consider the loan, assuming the collateral you desire to pledge against it is sufficient."

Ponzi was prepared for the question. "Sir, I have an account in good standing with this institution. I believe that should suffice."

"I'm sorry, Mr. Ponzi," the banker replied. "I was hoping you had something else in mind. I cannot approve the loan and I cannot even send the proposal forward to the loan committee."

Charles was stunned. "I don't understand."

"While it is our policy to accommodate our depositors whenever we can," he said, "your account is more of a bother to us than a benefit." Its balance, the president pointed out, usually hovered around zero.

Ponzi stormed out of the bank. The *Traders' Guide* was going to be his ticket to a fortune. Why couldn't anybody else see its promise?

Later that summer Charles sorted through the letters on his desk and came across one postmarked from Spain. Unaware that Ponzi was no longer working on the magazine, its writer had seen a notice for the *Traders' Guide* and asked for a free copy.

A lesser man might have viewed the letter as a cruel mockery, but Ponzi saw it as a turning point.

He scrutinized the envelope and the strange, yellow piece of paper, the size of a half dollar, that was attached to the upper right corner. It wasn't a traditional postage stamp. He knew those well. What was it?

A smile spread across his face at the realization of what he'd just discovered. It was the spark of genius he'd always known was within him. Finally, after all of the false starts and all of the years of struggle and bad luck and misunderstandings with the law, the destiny his mother longed for him to fulfill was finally within reach.

Actually, it was more than within reach; it was currently residing in the palm of his hand.

Boston, Massachusetts
December 9, 1919

Even as he struggled to explain his new business venture, Ponzi could see that Joseph Daniels had no interest in the 1906 conference in Rome, or foreign exchange rates, or reply coupons. To Daniels, who was standing on the other side of Ponzi's desk with a frustrated scowl on his face, the equation was simple: Ponzi owed him money for the furniture he'd rented; Ponzi was unable to pay it; so now Daniels was there to repossess the furniture.

But the Rome conference *was* important, Ponzi insisted. It was the linchpin of his new idea, called the "Securities Exchange Company," and the key to his fortune. And so he tried again to explain it.

Back in 1906, nations participating in the Rome conference had agreed to allow International Reply Coupons—just like the one attached to the letter he'd received from Spain—to be placed on envelopes sent abroad in place of postage stamps. Those coupons could be redeemed in any participating nation for a stamp of the equivalent price.

It was pretty straightforward, but there was a loophole in the law: Because foreign exchange rates changed all the time, one could buy a coupon in Italy or Spain or Portugal for an amount that could end up being much less than what it was worth in the United States. And yet the coupon could still be redeemed in America for the full price.

Daniels still looked confused. How could he not see what this meant? Didn't he understand the potential? Buying a single coupon here or there was of no consequence, but if Ponzi got an army of employees to buy thousands, no *tens of thousands,* of these coupons abroad and then redeem them here in America at a higher price, the potential profits were enormous! Maybe, he told Daniels, even double or quadruple the original investment.

This was a can't-miss idea, and it was all perfectly legal. "Joseph, this is just common sense. I can guarantee my investors a fifty percent return on investment within ninety days—that is how confident I am that this will work. We are simply taking advantage of inefficiencies in the system!"

In truth, Ponzi had invented the "fifty percent in ninety days" pitch because it sounded impressive. He had absolutely no idea how much he could really make, but he also knew the actual numbers were irrelevant—he just had to sell the dream. *We are all gamblers,* Ponzi thought. *We all crave easy money.*

To Daniels, the idea sounded too good to be true, but he was intrigued enough by Ponzi's enthusiasm to invest $200 and to let him keep the furniture for a little longer.

Boston, Massachusetts
December 21, 1919

Ponzi was about to lose the potential investor. Ettore Giberti, a grocer
and fellow Italian immigrant in his thirties, had come to the office to
hear more about the new enterprise that Ponzi had been talking up all
over the neighborhood.

As Ponzi explained the idea behind the company—the coupons, the
Rome treaty, the currency rates, the 50 percent profits—Giberti grew
increasingly alarmed. Far from being entranced by the idea of easy
money, Giberti was skeptical. "I think I will pass."

Ponzi could not lose on his very first investor pitch after Daniels.
That would be an unwelcome precedent. So he made Giberti an offer:
"Why don't you become the first sales agent for the Securities Exchange Company?" He explained that Giberti wouldn't have to part
with any money and instead would receive a referral fee of 10 percent
of any money he brought in.

Free money, the grocer thought. What could be wrong with that?
"All right," Giberti said. "That sounds much better. I am in."

Now that Giberti was on board, Ponzi offered him a tutorial on
salesmanship and psychology. "The most important rule is to never
crowd a prospect," Ponzi advised. "Any attempt to force something on
an investor would create suspicion rather than confidence."

He also convinced Giberti to put up a nominal amount—maybe $5
or $10—just so he could tell the people he was soliciting that he was
also an investor.

Two weeks later, Giberti handed Ponzi $1,770 from a total of eigh-
teen different investors.

Now, as he spread the cash out over his desk to count it, Ponzi
had to make a decision. He could try to actually buy the coupons and
redeem them for cash, as promised. It was very likely to work, but it
would take a lot of work and coordination with people overseas. Or, he
could improve upon the idea he'd first been a part of at Banco Zarossi:
use the cash from later investors to pay off the earlier ones. Everyone
got their money, and there would be no hard work necessary.

In the end, there was no decision at all. Where Zarossi had failed, Ponzi knew he would succeed.

Boston, Massachusetts
February 1920

The first forty-five days were up, and now Ponzi was ready to pay his investors their money back, along with the promised 50 percent interest. Sure, he'd told investors ninety days at first, but he knew that paying them the promised interest in half the time would generate far more enthusiasm.

"How can you afford to do this?" some investors asked.

"My man in Europe, Lionello Sarti, returned earlier this month," Ponzi explained. "He works on a transatlantic liner that makes stops in various ports, so he collects reply coupons by the thousands and brings them back to the States.

"Mr. Sarti tells me coupons are available even in the small post offices across Europe!" Ponzi continued. "Our returns have been enormous already!"

Word of Ponzi's success began to spread. A young married couple had learned of the company from a friend who was an early investor. Now they wanted to talk to the man himself.

As Ponzi met with them, he noticed that the wife seemed especially skeptical of the strategy. He saw the dubious look in her eyes as she listened to him answer her husband's questions. She wasn't sold. So Ponzi went to work on her directly.

He showed her sample International Reply Coupons, told her all about Mr. Sarti and his missions to Europe. The investments were safe, he assured them. "Should you take ill or want your investment returned, you need only say the word. It is your money."

By the time he was finished, the wife took $15 from her purse and handed it to Ponzi. Her husband proceeded to turn over $400 more—the remainder of their bank account—and agreed to work for Ponzi as a sales agent.

When returns were due, Ponzi often told customers that he would gladly pay off their investments, but that if they wanted to *reinvest* their money—well, then the returns would be even greater.

Most agreed to do just that. And, soon, almost everyone was telling their friends about the financial wizard who had invented a plan that would make them all a fortune.

Even his wife's uncle, John Dondero, invested in the reply coupons, handing Ponzi a check that amounted to his life savings, $2,000. It was the biggest sum Ponzi had ever received from a single investor.

"An excellent investment," Ponzi replied. "I'm honored by your trust. I will be sending Mr. Sarti on another trip to Europe imminently."

Dondero did not worry that he had never met Mr. Sarti—though he might have if he'd known that no one else had ever met Sarti, either.

Boston, Massachusetts
March 1920

Charles Ponzi walked into the police station looking like the embodiment of wealth and success. One hundred and ten investors had come into his office over the past month alone, investing a total of around $25,000. It was more money than Ponzi had ever seen at one time—more than he would make in a decade doing the kind of "honest work" his uncle had envisioned for him.

A man always wants more, Charles thought. *More money. More possessions. More power. The more he buys, the more he wants to buy. It's human nature.*

He had begun to pay off his debts, including the $200 he owed to furniture dealer Joseph Daniels. He'd even bought more furniture from Daniels to show his appreciation for his previous trust.

Now, basking in his success, Ponzi had come to the police station to buy an insurance policy. Getting the attention of a police captain, he inquired, "Does anyone collect funds here for the widows and orphans of policemen?"

"We have the Boston Police Relief Association," the captain answered.

"Wonderful," Ponzi replied. He placed $250 in crisp bills on the counter. "I can think of no more worthy cause. Please make sure they receive my donation."

Boston, Massachusetts
April 19, 1920

Ten thousand dollars were flowing into the offices of Charles Ponzi each week.

Word of the Ponzi profit machine was now the talk of ordinary folks throughout the city. He couldn't go to a fruit vendor without hearing their excitement about investing in International Reply Coupons and the sky-high profits that would follow.

Of course, there were still questions. People weren't always fools. Some asked how he was buying all these reply coupons in Europe. Ponzi told them what he could, but explained that he could not divulge any corporate secrets. He *could,* however, tell them that he had built an elaborate network of agents throughout the Continent, people buying up coupons by tens of thousands, for redemption back in the States.

"How are you trading in the coupons for money?" others asked. It was a good question—*too good,* in fact. Ponzi told them that such information was a trade secret for competitive reasons. If he explained his methods of redemption then anyone could do it and he would no longer have a business. Besides, all of his initial investors were receiving the interest they had been promised and many were reinvesting with him. Who could argue with success?

Charles was charming everyone into investing—butchers, bricklayers, priests, local police officers, even their wives. It was almost too easy. People wanted to see for themselves how, as Ponzi told Rose one night, "a little dollar could start on a journey across the ocean and return home in six weeks, married and with a couple of kids."

Everything was going incredibly well, but Ponzi could not shake the feeling that he hadn't thought of everything yet. With each new investment, his stomach twisted further in knots. He was sure he was getting an ulcer. What if his investors all wanted to cash out at once? What if someone figured out that there was no Lionello Sarti or that there were no coupons being redeemed? What if the authorities shut him down?

Ponzi's growing angst turned out to be prescient. This became clear later that day when he received a letter from the U.S. Post Office, the contents of which he disclosed to no one.

Boston, Massachusetts
May 24, 1920

Charles Ponzi was the millionaire he'd always wanted to be. He and Rose had chosen a massive mansion in Lexington, Massachusetts, complete with a grand portico, a carriage house, air-conditioning, and a heated swimming pool. He had the finest clothes and he showered his wife with gifts, flowers, and jewels. He bought a new car—a cream-colored Hudson coupe—and he planned to hire a butler and a cook. He sent his mother money to come to America—first-class, of course.

But none of those trappings of wealth underscored his success as much as what he was doing today.

Walking into the Hanover Trust bank—the same bank that had re-fused to lend him money and had derided his account as a nuisance—Ponzi now deposited a small fortune of $60,000. Pretty soon, he thought, he'd buy up shares of the bank to gain a controlling interest. Maybe he'd even be named the bank's president. Revenge was sweet.

But this was about more than just revenge; it was about his destiny. Ponzi saw himself in the same vein as Italy's greatest hero, Christopher Columbus. The explorer had thought he was on his way to Asia and had discovered America instead. Nobody cared that he'd had no idea America existed when he started his journey, or that he had come across it by accident. He was famous anyway. Yes, Ponzi thought, he and Columbus were similar in many ways.

Ponzi's anxiety over his growing fraud lessened as he walked into the lobby of Hanover Trust. Using his profits to buy shares in other com-panies meant that he could use those company's success to help pay off his investors. It was perfect. He wasn't finished yet. Far from it.

Boston, Massachusetts
June 17, 1920

Ponzi jumped up and down like a child as he spotted the small, frail woman dressed in black who was exiting the ocean liner with the other first-class passengers. It was the first time he'd seen his mother in seventeen years.

Dressed in a dark blue suit with a carnation in his lapel, he approached his mom and wrapped her in a warm embrace. Imelde scrutinized her son carefully. She didn't seem surprised by his success—this was, after all, what she'd always expected from him.

As he took his mother to meet his wife, Charles laughed. "My hat!" he exclaimed to Rose. "She's worried about the price of my hat!"

He couldn't wait to show her his mansion.

Boston, Massachusetts
July 3, 1920

"Mr. Ponzi, I'm a reporter from the *Boston Post*." The voice on the other end of the telephone line was deep and serious. "I understand a chap named Joseph Daniels is suing you for one million dollars." The sum was all but unheard-of and had caught everyone's attention.

Ponzi had received the news only days earlier. Daniels, the furniture dealer, had decided that his loan of $200 had kept Ponzi's company afloat. Now he wanted a piece of the massive profits that had followed.

The lawsuit infuriated Ponzi. The company had been his idea alone! Daniels had wanted no part of it. He'd be damned if that furniture salesman would get a single cent.

"This is merely a nuisance suit," Ponzi told the reporter. "I think Mr. Daniels thinks he can get rich by suing people, rather than by working hard and investing."

Ponzi was eager to get the reporter off the phone, and off his trail. But then an idea struck him. One of his best—and that was really saying something.

"Tell me, can you come down to our offices?" Ponzi asked. "I'd like to show you what we're doing here."

Lexington, Massachusetts
July 24, 1920

It promised to be another glorious summer day. While Ponzi enjoyed breakfast with his wife and mother in the mansion's dining room, the maid brought in the *Boston Post*.

The front-page headline caused Ponzi to spit out his juice.

DOUBLES THE MONEY WITHIN THREE MONTHS
50 PERCENT INTEREST PAID IN 45 DAYS BY PONZI—HAS THOUSANDS OF INVESTORS.

As he eagerly turned the pages, absorbing every word of the article, he smiled with delight. He had been wooing the newspaper's reporters for weeks, and, of course, he had received an important assist from his public relations advisor, William McMasters—but still, he had never expected something this big. The story read:

> *The proposition has been in operation for nine or ten months, roiling up great wealth for the man behind it and rolling up much money for the thousands of men and women who are tumbling over themselves to entrust him with their money on no other security than his personal note, and the authorities have not been able to discover a single illegal thing about it.*

The article pegged Ponzi's net worth at $8.5 million and reported how his investors—"rich, poor, prominent, and unknown"—had seen their money "doubled, trebled, quadrupled."

Ponzi concluded that the story couldn't have been better if he had written it himself. He watched with pride as his mother glanced at the headline, the story, the pictures. He had finally proven himself to her. And to the world.

• • •

The next morning Ponzi arrived at his office to find an enormous crowd of people waiting for him. They had been lining up since 6 A.M., eager to invest their savings in Ponzi's can't-miss strategy.

The *Post*'s story had been picked up by newspapers across the country. Charles Ponzi was now more than just rich—he was famous.

"There's Ponzi!" someone shouted as the "wizard" arrived in a blue limousine. The sighting led to cheers as dozens of people rushed forward to see the genius in the flesh.

"Ponzi! Ponzi! Ponzi!"

As Ponzi walked through the crowd with his gold-tipped cane, he presented himself as the people's financial hero and savior.

"I want to see the man who can make a million in six months!" someone shouted, their voice rising over the din.

"That's me!" Ponzi replied, to laughter. "I'm the man! I'm doing it!"

As he entered his office, he received a phone call from Rose. She told him that reporters and others were standing in front of their house, all hoping to catch a glimpse of him. Someone from the Fox movie company had called to tell her they were going to send a camera over to put Ponzi in the newsreels!

Ponzi took a deep breath and smiled. Everything he'd worked for was now his. That day alone, his offices collected more than $3 million in new investments. It all came from people who were tripping over themselves to give their money to a man they knew solely through a newspaper article.

Boston, Massachusetts
July 26, 1920

What the newspaper gods have given, they now were quickly taking away.

Ponzi was riding in the backseat of his car when the *Boston Post*'s morning edition gave him another surprise. This one was far less pleasant. Top financiers, the paper noted, were now questioning what they called the "Ponzi scheme."

The article included a devastating quote from Clarence W. Barron, one of the country's most acclaimed financial experts. "No man of wide financial or investment experience would look twice at a proposition to take his money upon a simple promise to pay it back at interest of 200 percent annually."

Barron had checked with the U.S. Post Office and learned that an average of just $8 worth of International Reply Coupons had been redeemed per day over the last several months. If Ponzi was making his money by redeeming these coupons on a wide scale, Barron was wondering why the Post Office had no record of it.

Ponzi was infuriated by the accusations and considered filing a lawsuit against Barron for libel. But first he had to attend an important meeting, one that might well spell the end of everything anyway.

To settle all doubts about the company's legitimacy, McMasters had suggested that Ponzi sit down with the state district attorney and federal investigators and offer to put himself through an audit.

McMasters knew there was something funny about Ponzi's numbers and suspected the Ponzi would never agree to official scrutiny. But, to McMaster's surprise, a suddenly jovial Ponzi was all too happy to oblige.

Now, sitting across the table from the DA and other officials, Ponzi came right to the point. He said he welcomed an examination of his operation. He had broken no laws.

Pressed for how his company could possibly be providing such returns to investors, Ponzi shook his head. "That I cannot tell you," he replied. "I cannot give away my secrets to my competitors."

As his client spoke, smoothly and confidently, calmly answering question after question, McMasters became even more skeptical. Several times Ponzi had seemed to contradict himself. McMasters wondered if he was the only one who had noticed.

"Mr. Ponzi, if you can do these things that you claim, you will be the greatest Italian who ever came to America," one of the officials told him.

Ponzi smiled. "Don't forget Columbus!"

Everyone laughed.

"The real question facing you," Ponzi observed, "is whether or not I have the money to meet my outstanding notes. Isn't that right?"

The district attorney conceded that was so.

"Well, then, may I make one request?" he asked.

"What is it?"

"Instead of having multiple auditors from multiple state and federal agencies auditing my company's books, could the various officials settle on just one?"

The next day Ponzi closed his offices as the public audit got under way. But that didn't stop people from lining up outside. McMasters watched as a few of the investors asked for their money back—and Ponzi happily obliged. But most of them, McMasters observed, seemed inclined to wait out the audit. They still believed in the wizard who could make them a fortune.

"I've given back more than two million," Ponzi told McMasters. "But people still trust me! There are thousands out there who know I keep my promises, who are hanging on to millions of dollars of notes!"

McMasters was not among them. At Ponzi's office, he had begun to examine receipts and accounting slips. Then he went house to house and shop to shop, interviewing various investors. They showed him ticket stubs that indicated how much Ponzi owed them. And then he started to add up the sums.

As he met with hopeful citizens who had given everything they had to this man, a disturbing realization haunted McMasters: Charles Ponzi was hopelessly insolvent.

Boston, Massachusetts
August 2, 1920

The lines outside Ponzi's office circled the block. McMasters had witnessed this scene before, although under vastly different circumstances. Instead of joyful crowds eager to hand over their hard-earned money, people now looked terrified and angry. Some were in tears. A few had even fainted.

All of them seemed to have read the *Post*'s front-page article that morning, a story written by William McMasters himself, who was now a *former* employee of Charles Ponzi. Although he'd been paid $5,000 to write the piece, he had done it primarily to clear his conscience and tell the people of Boston the God's honest truth.

The headline said it all:

DECLARES PONZI IS NOW HOPELESSLY INSOLVENT
PUBLICITY EXPERT EMPLOYED BY "WIZARD" SAYS HE HAS NOT SUFFICIENT FUNDS TO MEET HIS NOTES

Ponzi responded to the story immediately. Showing up at his office, he denied the allegations and offered to pay off the investors who were circling the block. He also said he would sue the *Post* for $5 million.

"The issue now at stake is an issue between a man who wants to do all he can for the people and men who want to take as much money as they can from the people without giving adequate return!" Ponzi declared.

His former client's manufactured fury did not faze McMasters. He'd been around Ponzi long enough to know it was all a bluff—the last, desperate act of a failing showman.

Boston, Massachusetts
August 3, 1920

Ponzi greeted the reporters who were now watching his every step with his customary grin. "Well, they didn't break me yesterday," he said. "And they won't break me today." He told them that he was going to sue McMasters for $2,000.

"How are your newspapers selling?" Ponzi yelled out. "I ought to have a commission!"

Reporters marveled at his unflappable calm, but Ponzi knew what they didn't: One always had to look the part. Besides, as he'd learned years ago from Charles Morse in that Atlanta prison, a rich man could escape serious consequences.

Still, he felt the pressure. The ulcer was still there. Although many people were sticking by him, the run on his company from worried investors had now reached $400,000. Despite his public protestations, Charles Ponzi knew that he would soon be out of money.

Lexington, Massachusetts
August 8, 1920

Ponzi was still wearing his bathrobe and had not left the mansion all day. Rose was pacing back and forth in tears. She had never wanted this life in the first place. Her worst fears did not involve losing the house or the money, but losing her husband. She didn't want him to go to jail. She still believed in him.

She shared that sentiment with the reporter who came to visit them that Sunday. "I would much rather that he was a bricklayer working eight hours each day," she told him.

As his wife fretted, Ponzi told the reporter his life story—from his idyllic youth in Italy, to his journey to America, and then on to Canada, where he was involved in "confidential investigations." From there, Ponzi said, he was "sent south" to Atlanta and Alabama before making his way back to Boston.

As the reporter took notes, he couldn't help but notice that Ponzi had glossed over several years of his life.

Later that day, Ponzi received a telephone call from the reporter.

"Mr. Ponzi, a telegram has just come into our office from a reporter in Montreal. It seems that a man named Charles Ponzi, aka Bianchi, was once arrested for forgery there."

The reporter paused, then asked, "Are you that man?"

Ponzi scoffed. "Ridiculous!" A strong denial, he knew from experience, could buy him some much-needed time. The public audit of his books would be completed any day now. Maybe by some miracle the auditor would believe his claims of solvency and he could figure out how to make all of this work.

The *Post* reporter persisted. "But weren't you in Canada around that time?"

"What difference does it make?" Ponzi asked.

"This man worked at Banco Zarossi," the reporter said. "Did you work at that bank?"

"I might have," Ponzi said, hanging up the phone.

Reporters surrounded him now, everywhere he went. They hung on his every word. Many regular citizens did, too—convinced that he was a David standing up to the Goliath of the moneyed elites and corrupt authorities. People were still coming to his office with money to invest, including a group of immigrants who had pooled together $100,000.

"After I am proved on the level," Ponzi vowed, "I will demand that the authorities be investigated."

Boston, Massachusetts
August 12, 1920

Officials at the local jail thought Charles Ponzi was a marvel. He was still confident and smiling, even though he was under arrest and most of the city of Boston, indeed most of the country, now knew he was a con man.

On the day of his arrest, Ponzi told reporters, "I am not going to flee, but will stay here and face the music. I am going to prove that I'm on the level now." Other wealthy men had made similar claims and gotten away with their crimes. Perhaps, Ponzi thought, he could do the same.

Dressed in a dark, chalk-striped suit and polished shoes, Ponzi had his driver take him to the authorities, where he turned himself in.

"I have done nothing wrong," he assured them.

"But you agreed to accept the auditors' figures?" they asked him.

"Yes," he replied. "I have agreed."

New mug shots were taken at the Boston jail, and Ponzi was formally charged with scheming to use the mail to defraud investors, but he was a portrait of resolve. "The man's nerve is iron," a jailer later told reporters.

Ponzi would not admit defeat. Never. "No man is ever licked," he said, "unless he wants to be. And I don't intend to stay licked. Not as long as there is a flickering spark of life left in me."

The last few days had been especially unkind to him. First came the allegations in the *Boston Post* that Ponzi had been imprisoned in Canada for forging checks. The story included his mug shot, dispelling any lingering doubts about his malfeasance, even among the most loyal Ponzi acolytes. The revelations about his prison record horrified Ponzi, but not for the obvious reasons. He was more worried about Rose's reaction to finding out he'd lied to her for so many years.

That evening, Rose came to visit him in jail. His heart pounding, his shoulders slumped, Ponzi came clean.

"I'm sorry for lying to you," he said, sobbing. "For hiding my past."

"I've known all these years, Charles," she replied.

Charles lifted his head. "Known what exactly?"

"Your mother sent me a note years ago, right after we became engaged. She wanted me to know about all of your past crimes. She asked that I keep it to myself."

Ponzi, broken and defeated, could not muster his trademark smile.

"I married you anyway," Rose whispered. "Because I loved you."

His wife's revelation did not ease the final blow that Ponzi suffered when the government's auditor, Edwin Pride, concluded that Ponzi was $3 million in debt. By day's end that number would be revised to upward of $7 million. Overall, Ponzi's investors had lost, by some estimates, $20 million ($246 million in 2014 dollars).

Half a dozen banks that held now-worthless notes from Ponzi were on the verge of collapse. Thousands of ordinary citizens faced financial hardship or ruin, although a few hard-core believers still held on to their notes, hoping that the wizard could pull some last miracle out of his hat.

Ponzi was sentenced to five years in federal prison.

A complete audit of the company later turned up $61 of postal coupons, along with a letter from the U.S. Post Office that was dated April 19, 1920:

Dear Mr. Ponzi,

Post office inspectors have reported their interview with you concerning a proposed speculation in International Reply Coupons issued by foreign governments. They are not intended as a medium of speculation, and the department cannot sanction their use for that purpose.

The letter had made clear months ago something that would've made the whole scheme instantly collapse if it had ever been made public: International reply coupons could not be redeemed for cash.

Twenty-eight Years Later
Rio de Janeiro, Brazil
November 17, 1948

"Mr. Ponzi, how would you like people to remember you?" the reporter asked.

Ponzi raised his once-bushy eyebrows, now mostly wisps of white. Sixty-six years old, nearly blind, and partly paralyzed from a stroke, the white-haired and shriveled Charles Ponzi flashed his sly, ingratiating smile one last time.

He thought carefully about the reporter's query, as well as the thousands—no, tens of thousands, even *millions* of people back in America who hung on his every word.

"Without malice aforethought," Ponzi replied, "I gave them the best show that was ever staged in their territory since the landing of the Pilgrims!"

He'd finally become the legend he had always wanted to be—if not in the exact manner that he'd intended.

January 14, 1949

"Everything all right, Señor Ponzi?"

Ponzi's friend, a nearly blind Brazilian who shared his wardroom at the free government hospital, surely already knew the answer to that question.

Charles Ponzi was penniless and ravaged by the effects of a stroke. He was awaiting another operation on his eye, which he hoped would improve his vision. After being deported from America as an "undesirable alien" (he had never obtained U.S. citizenship) and divorced from Rose, he'd endured a string of failed business ventures.

During World War II, Ponzi had been in Brazil, and then Argentina, where he bought a boardinghouse populated by prostitutes, along with a hot dog stand. He had hoped it would be the start of a national chain. Instead, it had gone bankrupt.

Now he was utterly alone. He occasionally sent letters to Rose, who was still living in Boston. They always went unanswered.

"Yes, yes," he replied to his roommate. "Everything is fine." It was always going to be fine. And then he closed his eyes for the last time, his final dream undoubtedly brightened by a street paved with gold.

EPILOGUE

Boston, Massachusetts
1962

By the time William McMasters finished his 206-page manuscript he was eighty-eight years old. He had believed his role in exposing his former employer's massive fraud had been lost to history. Now, thanks to this book, the record would be corrected forever.

McMasters, never one to keep his opinions to himself, was sure to include a final prediction in his book.

"I do not anticipate that another Charles Ponzi will ever appear in the financial world."

Just two years earlier, a twenty-four-year-old law school dropout had pooled together $5,000 to start his own investment company.

His name was Bernie Madoff.

5

He Loved Lucy: The Tragic Genius of Desi Arnaz, the Inventor of the Rerun

PROLOGUE

Desilu Studios
Hollywood, California
July 12, 1962

It was the first day of production. *The Lucy Show*—which was Lucille Ball's first effort since the end of her hit show, *I Love Lucy*—remained a "Desilu" production, co-owned by Lucy and her ex-husband, Desi Arnaz, as part of a divorce settlement. The duo could have sold the company and split the proceeds, but that didn't seem like a good business move. "Instead of divorce lawyers profiting from our mistakes," Lucy said, "we decided that we'd profit from them."

Though it might have seemed a little awkward to spectators, Desi, the show's producer, walked onto his ex-wife's set to say hello to the cast. He gave Lucy a kiss on the cheek and a gift: a small four-leaf clover made out of antique emerald jade.

"Lucy, dear," he said, "I wish you all the luck in the whole everloving world. You really deserve it, kid."

Lucy smiled. "Oh, Desi. How thoughtful." They embraced. Then Lucy walked back in front of the cameras to rehearse the show.

Desi moved to a nearby catwalk that was used for lighting. Leaning against the railing, he watched his ex-wife for a moment. Then he broke down.

Wiping his tears away with a handkerchief, Desi looked up to see Lucy's costar, the actress Vivian Vance. Vance had played Lucy and Desi's wacky neighbor Ethel Mertz in their first series, and was now reprising her role as one of Lucy's closest friends in real life. "Veev"—as Desi called her—was crying, too.

"Oh, Desi," she said, as she stood beside him. "It just isn't the same, is it?"

Desi shook his head. Their seemingly storybook marriage was over. His drinking and gambling was taking its toll. In fact, the empire Desi Arnaz had meticulously built since those impossible beginnings at a boardinghouse in Florida was slowly crumbling all around him.

Twenty-nine Years Earlier
Vista Allegre
Santiago, Cuba
August 12, 1933

"Get your mother out of the house right away! They're coming for you!"

The young boy with the bronze skin, expressive face, and thick black hair was confused. His uncle Eduardo, screaming at him from the other end of the telephone, sounded panicked.

"Who? Who's coming for us?" sixteen-year-old Desiderio Arnaz asked.

"Machado has fled the country," his uncle answered. The Cuban president had been under siege for some time as a result of the island's hard economic times. Now a full-scale revolt had been mounted, led by a collection of anarchists, students, Bolsheviks, and other malcontents. A general strike had been called across the nation. Once the Cuban generals turned against the president, the government fell.

"All *Machadistas* are being arrested or killed," an unnerved Eduardo insisted. "Their houses are being burned." Desi's father, as mayor of Cuba's second-largest city, was undoubtedly on the list of targets, as was his family.

"For God's sake, don't waste any more time!" his uncle snapped. "Get out of there!"

As Desi hung up the phone, he remembered back to the celebration for his father, Desiderio II, only months earlier. He was a beloved and respected politician. It was inconceivable that people could turn on him so quickly.

Desi heard what sounded like rumbling outside. From the window, he could make out a vast mob carrying guns, pitchforks, and torches. They seemed to be heading directly toward the Arnaz home. Desi thought there must've been at least five hundred of them.

Desi's mother ran into the room. "*Dios mio!* What is happening?!"

Only one thought made its way through Desi's frazzled head. *Run!*

Desi helped his mother with her coat, ran around the house gathering whatever cash he could find, and then grabbed his father's pearl-handled revolver from the nightstand drawer.

Across the privileged neighborhoods of Santiago, thugs on horseback were slaughtering cows and setting buildings on fire.

Desi's mother grabbed their pet Chihuahua while he took one last look at his beloved family home.

And then they ran.

Desi was in the backseat of the family car the next day as they drove past their home en route to a relative's place in Havana where they would be safe. The beautiful old house was in ruins, with parts of the rubble still smoldering. All the windows had been broken. Shards of glass dotting the yard reflected the sun like cruel flashes of light. In the garden, the family's piano was smashed into pieces. One of their cars was upside down on the sidewalk. His bicycle was twisted like a pretzel. Looters were still going in and out of the house, looking for more to take.

The scene was particularly shocking to Desi's mother, who was still reeling from the knowledge that her parents had almost been killed earlier that day by a bomb planted in front of their home. A well-

known Cuban beauty and an heiress to the Bacardi rum fortune, she
was now homeless. And hopeless.

"Mi casa!" she said between sobs, her face pressed up against the car
window. *"Mi casa!"*

Her brother Tony was driving and he looked on with great concern.
"I know you are not in the mood now to believe what I'm going to say,"
he began, "but take my word for it, you will recover. You will go on. You
will again have the things you had and perhaps even more. But you will
have to be strong."

He then turned to the terrified teenage boy sitting in the backseat.
No one had heard from Desi's father in days. They all feared for him,
but refused to consider that he might be dead. "Especially you, Desi,"
Tony said. "You're a young boy. You have your whole life ahead of you."

At sixteen, the handsome, carefree Desi had owned his own mo-
torcar and speedboat and lived in three different homes. Now all that
he had left were the clothes on his back. Desi nodded his head, then
closed his eyes and vowed that he would still make the life for himself
he dreamed of.

U.S. Immigration and Naturalization Service
Key West, Florida
May 1934

As the border patrol guard inspected his visa and gestured him forward, Desi's eyes focused on the familiar face waiting for him on the
other side of the gate.

The man was laughing and held his arms open wide as his eldest
son approached. Desi's father had been arrested and jailed with other
members of the former government when the revolution began. After
six months in prison, he was released and allowed to flee in exile to
Florida, where he now awaited Desi's arrival.

"Bienvenido a las Estados Unidos de Norte America," he said, embracing
Desi tightly.

Desi smiled and breathed his first sigh of relief in many months. He was happy to be out of Cuba—even though his mother and many other family members still remained there.

His father looked at him sternly. "Now," he said, "those are the last words I will speak to you in Spanish. You must learn English."

"I got A's in English at school," Desi reminded him, reverting back to his native language.

"Then try to say something."

"Okay," Desi said. But nothing came out. English was a lot easier to study than to actually use.

The two men boarded a bus bound for Miami, where Desi's father had found them a place to stay. "I am very sorry I couldn't have you join me here sooner, Desiderio. I didn't have any money to support us both. I don't have much now."

Desi was struck by his once proud father admitting such a thing.

"It's okay, Dad," Desi said. "We'll start all over again."

Miami, Florida
February 15, 1935

Desiderio Sr. was visibly ashamed of his new circumstances, but Desi did not care. He hoped that before long they could save enough money to bring his mother over. He was confident that things would get better. They had to.

Desi's father had formed a business with other Cuban exiles to sell mosaic tiles imported from Mexico. They'd rented a small warehouse with nothing but a concrete floor, a washbasin, and a toilet in the back. One day, as Desi was stacking and arranging inventory, he spotted his father measuring out a small space near the washroom. He knew what his dad was thinking. He also knew that his father was too proud to ever be able to vocalize it. So he approached his father instead.

"You know, Dad, I don't think we should keep paying for the board-inghouse," Desi said. "We can close in a little place here and turn it into a perfectly good room."

Desi spun a picture in his head to make it all sound enticing. "We could put in a chest of drawers here," he said. "We could have a nice bedroom over there. We'll get a two-burner hot plate and some pots and pans. We'll really be in business! And the food—oh, the food would be way better than what they have at the boardinghouse."

For a long while, Desi's father said nothing. He had given his boy everything he ever wanted since the day he was born. Finally, he answered. "I don't want my son living in a warehouse."

"That's silly, Dad," Desi replied. "We'll be more comfortable here."

They moved in shortly thereafter. To save money, they shopped only for items on sale at the grocery store. When they got a deal on cartons of pork and beans, they ate it every day for weeks on end.

Desi's father tried to keep up a brave front, but Desi knew the situation was humiliating for him. One night, when Desi returned home after a date, he caught his father chasing rats with a baseball bat. To see his dad, the former mayor of Santiago, like this was just too much.

Quietly, Desi buried his head in his hands and sobbed. This was not the life he'd envisioned. For his father, or for himself.

Roney Plaza Hotel
Miami Beach, Florida
December 12, 1936

"No way my son is going to be a musician." His father's words echoed through his head as he peered through the curtains at the audience that had assembled to hear him. Being a musician was considered a lowly profession in Cuba and that tainted his father's opinion. But Desi harbored no such notions and jumped at the idea of a $39 a week salary.

Desi swallowed hard, adjusted his borrowed suit, and forced himself onto the stage. He was excited, but also very nervous. He'd never performed in front of a crowd before and his English was still barely passable.

The curtains parted and the penniless Cuban with the bongo drums strapped around his neck was transformed into a handsome and charismatic singing sensation. When he was finished, the applause from the crowd was almost deafening. Standing there, feeling loved and alive for the first time since the revolution, Desi Arnaz began to cry.

RKO Studios Commissary
Hollywood, California
May 12, 1940

The black Buick Roadmaster convertible rolled into the legendary RKO Studios lot. Desi Arnaz's initials were etched into the paint in gold. He had, both literally and figuratively, arrived—and he wanted the world to know it.

Desi's meteoric rise was miraculous, even to him. While 1940s Hollywood produced its share of overnight sensations, Desi's accession was still lightning fast. Movie producers, like the legendary and powerful Louis B. Mayer, were always discounting talent and experience in favor of personality and a pretty face.

But Desi Arnaz had all of it.

His current project, a film adaptation of a forgettable Broadway show called *Too Many Girls,* was typical Hollywood fluff. A rich debutante brings four bodyguards with her to college, each of them posing as football players. Desi's part, the one he'd been playing in performances on Broadway and in stage versions across the country, was of a handsome South American football phenomenon.

The debutante was being played by a twenty-eight-year-old acting veteran. Desi first saw her as she walked onto the set with a fake black eye and bedraggled clothes from a movie she was filming with her friend Maureen O'Hara. She looked like a washed-up mess.

"Who the hell was *that*?" Desi asked a producer after she walked by.

"That was Lucille Ball."

"*She's* going to be the ingénue?" Desi asked incredulously. He didn't see it.

On the second day of filming, Desi was at the piano, rehearsing his part, when he saw another woman pass by. She was dressed in a yellow sweater and tight beige pants. Her piercing blue eyes were in sharp contrast to her flowing reddish-blond hair.

"Who was that?" Desi whispered to the pianist.

"That's Lucille Ball."

Desi looked at her again. *Really? The same woman from yesterday? It couldn't be.*

"Man, that is one hunk of a woman," Desi raved in his unique pronunciation of the English language—*hunk* sounded like "hoonk" and woman came out like "woo-men." Despite his broken English, he had no shortage of confidence. In just a few years, he had developed a reputation as a notorious Latin lover, often seen in the company of any number of prominent leading ladies.

Lucille Ball was a renowned beauty who had starred in more than forty films by the time she walked onto that RKO stage. She didn't think too much of this particular play—but it was all in a day's work. Another forgettable film in the career of a woman who'd become known as the Queen of B-Movies.

"Meess Ball?"

Contrary to her public persona, Lucille was shy and introverted. She constantly struggled to come across as sophisticated and cool.

The young Cuban walking toward her was not the sort of person who would typically catch her eye. Always in search of father figures who promised stability, she had favored the company of older men: Broderick Crawford, William Holden, George Raft, and her current fiancé, Al Hall. Yet, for whatever reason, this man's mane of black hair, wildly expressive eyebrows, and chiseled chest made her instantly smitten.

"Why don't you call me Lucille," the starlet responded. "And I'll call you Dizzy."

"It's De-si," he replied, pronouncing it slowly. "Do you know how to rumba, Lucille?"

"No. I've never learned."

"Wouldya like me to teach you?" Desi asked. "It may come in handy for your part."

Her part didn't call for anything resembling a rumba, but she didn't know that yet. So they danced.

Two Years Later
Office of Louis B. Mayer
MGM Studios
September 3, 1942

Desi was furious. Not because Lucy had just signed a multipicture deal with Louis B. Mayer, the powerful head of MGM. People killed for contracts like that, and Desi was never jealous of his wife's success. What ticked him off was *how* she got the contract: with the help of producer Pandro Berman, a confidante of Mayer and, not coincidentally, Lucy's former lover.

But Lucy was not unfaithful. True, her contacts at MGM had helped her move ahead with the studio, but what, she asked her husband, was wrong with *that*? Besides, she made no secret of her desire to help him get a movie deal at the same studio—a deal that might keep him around the house and not on the road with his band, his drinking habits, and his adoring female fans.

Desi never understood his wife's preoccupation with his other women. Back in Cuba, his beloved grandfather had a mistress and his grandmother never said a word. Only in his old age did Grandpa settle down at home, telling young Desi with a wink that his "bird" didn't fly anymore.

It was for all those reasons that friends had given their marriage six months. Lucille jokingly gave it six weeks.

Desi knew he and Lucille shared qualities that caused friction: They were both headstrong; ambitious; and volatile. In most other respects they were complete opposites. Desi was charming and always looking for fun; Lucy was serious and did not laugh easily. He was gregarious; she was shy. He was always looking for the next big thing; she was cautious, conservative, reserved. But their love was passionate, enduring, and intense. They had already celebrated their second anniversary. Now they dreamed of working together in films and seeing their names sharing the same marquee.

Desi had cooled down considerably by the time Louis B. Mayer finally called him into the office. Known around MGM as L.B., the powerful cigar-chomping producer was an immigrant like Desi—he and his family had moved from Russia in the late nineteenth century. He built Hollywood's "star system" and had made a career out of turning young, attractive talents into household names. His success also made him wealthy, as Mayer became the first person in American history to make an annual salary of more than a million dollars.

"Something happens to you when you put that bongo drum around your shoulder," Mayer said. "Up until that point you're just another Mexican."

"Cuban, sir," Desi responded.

"Well, one of those Latin fellows. Now I want to see what we can do with you around here." He pressed the intercom button on his desk.

"Yes, Mr. Mayer?"

"See if Lana Turner is around. And send her on up."

When Mr. Mayer summoned an actress, she'd better be around. And of course Ms. Turner was. The voluptuous twenty-one-year-old with blond hair and smoldering eyes said hello to a starstruck Desi and then turned to the studio mogul.

Mayer sketched out a quick scene for the duo to play. Then he said, "Now, Desi, I want you to sweep Lana into your arms and kiss her passionately."

With no sign of reluctance, Desi did what he was told. And he did the same thing again minutes later when Mr. Mayer buzzed for another actress named Judy Garland. Mayer was impressed enough with the performances to offer Desi a contract for five hundred dollars a week.

What a sweet job, Desi thought. *Now my bird can really fly!*

Eight Years Later
CBS Television
New York, New York
Summer 1950

"I don't think people would accept it."

"He's just not right for the part."

"I'm not sure the audience would go for it."

Lucy was desperate. The executives at CBS were eager to have her adapt her popular radio show, *My Favorite Husband,* to television. The program, about a zany wife and her long-suffering husband, played by actor Richard Denning, was a surprise hit. She wanted to discuss an adaptation that would replace Denning with Desi, but now, as she met with executives across a long conference table at CBS headquarters, both sides expressed considerable reservations.

Lucy knew that starring in a television show might well be a death sentence for her film career. Television was the enemy of Hollywood. The rise of TV programs, shot almost exclusively in New York City, offered millions of people the chance to watch entertainment from their homes, rather than buying tickets at a movie theaters. Though some thought television was just a fad, others believed that it would doom the motion picture industry. Most actors with any hope of keeping their film careers alive wouldn't even dream of making a *guest* appearance on a television program, let alone starring in one.

But Lucy had a more pressing concern than her career: the state of her marriage. Only a few years earlier, after four passionate but stormy years together, Lucy and Desi had filed for divorce. Their different personalities and cultural backgrounds had, as so many predicted, made things untenable. He was on the road with his band, carousing with other women, and drinking constantly. She was hurt and angry, and largely alone at their "Desilu" ranch in Chatsworth, California. She wanted a family, but often remarked to friends, "You can't have children over the telephone."

Desi was simultaneously annoyed and baffled that his wife would have a problem with what he did when he wasn't at home. But they still loved each other. And the day before their divorce decree came down, they reconciled.

But things hadn't changed much in the six years since. Lucy still had no children, Desi was still drinking and flirting with admirers, and they were still apart for long stretches. Costarring in a television show would force them to live in the same zip code for a while.

CBS executives, however, were proving to be a problem. They didn't share her vision. Some of them seemed to have a problem with a Cuban on their airwaves in an interracial marriage with a redheaded American woman. Or at least they thought the rest of America would.

"People won't believe you're married," one of them protested.

"But *we are* married," Lucy snapped. "And I want him." She meant that in every conceivable way. She had almost lost her husband once; she was determined to keep him this time.

Desi was touched that his wife was fighting so hard for him. If she hadn't been so dogged, he might well have given up. But she believed in him, and in them as a couple, and that was enough.

At an impasse with the executives, Lucy, as usual, was extraordinarily direct. "If no one will give us a job together," she told them, "then we'll give ourselves one."

Desilu Ranch
Chatsworth, California
January 1951

Desi was overseeing the addition of an extra room to their home. After many years of trying, and at least one miscarriage, Lucy was pregnant. Nothing thrilled her more than the prospect of a child. She was nearing forty and thought her chance had passed.

For months Desi and Lucy had been on the road performing a comedy act together in an effort to prove to CBS that America would accept the idea of a Cuban singer married to a white American woman. Their original plot, with characters named Lucy and Larry Lopez, was based pretty closely on their actual lives. Both were successful entertainers: Larry a Cuban bandleader, and Lucy a well-known movie actress. The plot centered on the couple's desire to celebrate their anniversary privately and avoid showing up on the cover of *Look* magazine. The writers Desi had hired were talented, and the script was funny, but Desi saw a big problem: Few Americans were going to sympathize with their characters.

"Why are they so unhappy about *Look* magazine?" he asked the writers. "Who's going to care about that?" So they came up with another idea: Desi would still play a bandleader, but Lucy would be a wacky housewife determined to make it into show business, but lacking any real talent.

To finance the show, Desi and Lucy invested $5,000 in a start-up production company. Like their home, they named the company "Desilu," and Desi listed himself as president and Lucy as vice president.

A bongo player who had come to America with nothing but the clothes on his back had just created the first independent television company in America.

A Few Months Later

"CBS wants to do a pilot."

"That's great!" Desi replied to his agent. He was happy, but he wasn't surprised. Desi had approached CBS's main rival, NBC, about picking up the TV show. They'd even gone so far as to hire new writers to work out a pilot script. Once the press revealed that another network was interested in a show with Desi Arnaz and Lucille Ball, CBS suddenly became much more agreeable.

Desilu Ranch
Chatsworth, California
July 30, 1951

"All right, Desi," said the exasperated voice on the other end of the line. "You've got a deal."

He had been firm with the executives in New York: He and Lucy were going to stay in California. The whole point of doing the show together was so they could live at home together. And a now very pregnant Lucy wasn't about to relocate.

"You can't do the show on the West Coast," one of the show's potential advertisers told him. "It's impractical."

Desi found it hard to disagree. He hated watching the grainy TV broadcasts that most viewers in California were forced to watch. Nearly all television programs originated in New York, where they aired live, and were then fed to West Coast viewers through gray, grimy, and often garbled kinescopes. These poor-quality tapes were disastrous. What's more, they offered no ability to correct flubs from the live performances out east. Desi remembered watching one program in which an actor who played a corpse thought he was no longer on camera and could be seen getting up and walking offstage in the middle of a scene.

So, a few days earlier, he'd hit upon an idea: film. CBS could use the same high-quality film they used for Hollywood movies to tape broadcasts in Los Angeles. Then they could send those films to New York.

"How much is that going to cost us?" a skeptical executive asked when Desi first broached the idea.

"Five thousand an episode," Desi replied authoritatively. In truth, he had no idea how much it would cost. He'd never done any of this before. He had pulled the number out of thin air.

The show's sponsor, Philip Morris, agreed to chip in an extra $2,000 to defray some of the added expense. CBS upped their costs by $2,000 as well. As for the remaining $1,000, Desi had offered another out-of-the-ordinary idea: He and Lucy would take a $1,000-per-week pay cut for the first thirty-nine shows. With a draconian 90 percent federal tax rate on their marginal income in place, Desi figured he'd only see $4,000 of that $39,000 anyway. In exchange for the pay cut, he told his agent to get the network to agree that Desilu would own every show they produced, 100 percent.

After days of negotiation, the network finally agreed to Desi's unorthodox demands. The CBS executives figured Desi would eventually realize that filming a TV show was impractical and he and Lucy would come to their senses . . . and to New York. As for rights to the shows, that seemed like a no-brainer given that it would save them $1,000 an episode.

Besides, no one ever had any use for shows once they aired.

Desilu Studios
Hollywood, California
October 15, 1951

"I'm afraid the show can't go on tonight," the man told Desi.

The first episode of *I Love Lucy* had required months of careful planning and frustrating squabbles with CBS back in New York. Everyone thought the script was funny and the show had potential. Now it was falling prey to the most mundane problem of all: a toilet.

A sanitation worker from the California Health and Safety Department had visited the new soundstage at Desilu Studios and found a violation.

"What's wrong?" Desi asked. He'd been running around all day, dealing with writers, soundmen, lighting people, engineers, his fellow actors, and now this.

"Well, sir," the man replied, "California law requires that this building offer two bathrooms on the premises. One for men. One for ladies. You only have one available to the public." Moreover, the toilets had to be a certain distance away from where the audience was sitting.

"Can't we find a way around this?" Desi asked. Toilets? Were toilets really going to stop the show?

"Afraid not, sir."

At his own expense, Desi had found a large studio in California where they could stage the production. He'd accomplished it all by working eighteen hours days, seven days a week. There was absolutely no way that some trouble over a toilet was going to flush his show down the drain.

Desi found refuge in the same place he always had: with Lucy. He told her the whole story and shared the solution that one of the writers had proposed: letting the audience use the bathroom in her dressing room. It was the only other one in the building that met California code.

Lucy didn't see what all the fuss was about. "They just need a second bathroom?" she asked. "Well, that's no problem. Tell the ladies to be my guest."

Soundstages were always filled with adrenaline, but as Desi walked out in front of the studio audience, he found himself more emotional than ever. His mind began flashing back through his life and all that had transpired to bring him to this wonderful, improbable moment.

"Ladies and gentlemen," he began, as the last notes from the band faded away. "Welcome. I am Desi Arnaz." The audience cheered.

The television episode they were about to tape would be the first one to ever use multiple cameras with 35mm film and tape before a live studio audience. Up until that point, TV was almost exclusively taped with a single camera that would be moved around as necessary. By using multiple cameras, a far higher quality of film, and a real live audience, Desilu was completely reinventing how TV was produced.

Desi made it clear to everyone involved with the series that the real star of the show wasn't him; it was Lucy. He waved one of his arms toward the stage entrance. "And now, ladies and gentlemen, here's my favorite wife, the mother of my child, the vice president of Desilu Productions—*I* am the president—and my favorite redhead, Lucille Ball!"

As the crowd applauded, Lucy walked onto the stage and wrapped her husband in a warm embrace. "How ya doing, you gorgeous Cuban?" she asked. With a smile that belied how nervous she was, she blew kisses to the audience.

Within minutes, the actors took their marks. Someone yelled, "Action!" And a Hollywood legend was born.

Set of *Toast of the Town*
New York City
October 3, 1954

Desi and Lucy had flown to New York to be honored on Ed Sullivan's hit show, *Toast of the Town*. The couple seemed to be on top of the world. They now had two children, Desi and Lucie, a beautiful home, a hit TV show, and the love of a nation.

Desi, wearing a perfectly tailored tuxedo, stood up and scanned the studio audience in front of him. He glanced at Lucy, sitting to his right, just on the other side of Sullivan, then he turned to face the cameras. The cheering audience likely expected Ricky Ricardo to say something humorous. Instead, Desi's face was somber, his tone serious.

He nodded in the direction of his wife. "I think if it wouldn't have been for Lucy," he said, his voice quivering, "I would've stopped trying a long time ago because I was always the guy that didn't fit."

The long, circuitous journey from destitution and terror in Cuba flooded through his mind. With his eyes moist, he added, "We came to this country and we didn't have a cent in our pockets. From cleaning canary cages to this night here in New York, is a long ways. And I don't think that any other country in the world can give you that opportunity." He was choking on tears now. They would not stop. Emotion once again overcame him. "And I just wanna say thank you," he croaked.

"Thank you, America."

An applauding Sullivan rose to embrace Desi, who struggled to wipe the tears away. A similarly moved Lucy reached over and patted her husband on the arm. They had come a long way, indeed. But deep down, Desi was still haunted by the truth he'd vowed to remember while fleeing to Havana in the backseat of the car: Nothing good ever lasts.

Six Years Later
County Courthouse
Los Angeles, California
March 4, 1960

Few people in Hollywood were surprised by the breaking news: Lucille Ball was filing for divorce.

Friends had known that their marriage had become a façade for the last few years, breaking down over the same old problems: Desi's drinking, his womanizing, and the utter conflict between their personalities.

The gossipy tabloid *Confidential* came out with the headline-grabbing story that Desi Arnaz was cheating on Lucy. When an advance copy of the magazine circulated on the set, everyone seemed to freeze. Even though they all knew the story was true, no one knew how to react. One friend watched Lucy grab the magazine and hand it to her husband. "Oh, hell," she said. "I could tell them worse than that."

As their marriage crumbled, Desi's and Lucy's professional lives became even more successful. Three years earlier Desi had purchased RKO Studios, where he and Lucy had first met. He was now producing a new hit series, *The Untouchables,* starring Robert Stack, and Desilu had become a multimillion-dollar media empire.

As *I Love Lucy* ended its run in 1957—by then it had changed formats and been renamed *The Lucille Ball–Desi Arnaz Show*—their marriage was over in everything but name. On the last day of filming, there had been an eerie quiet. Lucy and Desi talked to each other like polite strangers.

Still, many in the cast and crew, like most Americans when they heard the news about the divorce, were heartbroken. They wanted a fairy-tale ending. Some, like *I Love Lucy*'s onetime director Bill Asher, believed right up to the end that things might turn around. "Maybe I'm a romantic," he said, "but there was a great, great love there."

Cast members remembered one particular scene from the show years earlier that hinted at what held the couple together. In the scene, Ricky Ricardo sings a song to Lucy after discovering for the first time that she is pregnant. The words Ricky sang to his wife were set to the tune of the show's iconic theme song.

Even as both Lucy and Desi knew their marriage was crumbling, they seemed to lose sight of their characters during the scene's first take. Overcome with emotion, they wept openly and held each other tightly. The director of the show had them do another take—this time with less visible emotion. But the studio audience insisted that they stick with the first take, the one that was real. Lucy and Desi agreed.

Unfortunately, the moment was fleeting. This second effort at divorce was going to stick.

Desilu Productions
Office of the President
August 17, 1964

After Desi's hit series *The Untouchables* was canceled, Lucille Ball was installed as the new president of Desilu Productions.

Desi was on a downward path. He was drinking again, off television screens, and seemingly adrift.

Lucy was now the sole manager of the Desilu empire. The company had sold the rights to *I Love Lucy* to CBS for $5 million, a whopping sum at the time. Lucy had also bought out Desi's share of the company for more than $2.5 million—thereby making her the most powerful woman in show business. Desilu Productions, with sixteen soundstages and one thousand employees, was also the busiest studio in Hollywood.

As a boss, Lucille Ball was nothing like Lucy Ricardo. She was serious, demanding, and a proud perfectionist. She had many friends and was a devoted, often overprotective mother. She was as tough in her job as any man. And she knew every detail about every lightbulb, screw, and bolt that made its way onto one of her sets.

The new Desilu Productions president had learned a lot from watching her husband all those years. She commanded her team to produce new and unique shows. Like Desi, she was also willing to go her own way and ignore advice from the so-called film and television experts in Hollywood and New York. One script that caught her attention was a show called *Mission: Impossible*. The production costs were high, but she thought it was worth the risk, so she signed the deal.

A script for another promising show now sat on her desk. This one had a confusing name—at first, she thought it involved sending celebrities abroad on USO tours. The script was filled with strange jargon, and the ideas seemed too highbrow for a general audience. Top officials at Desilu were not enamored with the concept, nor the expense that it would entail. They told her that even if they sold the show to a studio, it would cost Desilu more to produce it than they'd ever make in profit.

But Desi had taught Lucy to trust her instincts. This show seemed to her to be innovative and fresh and she felt like it could be bigger than anything the executives could put into their financial models. She also believed that, if it became a hit, they could monetize it in other ways—like merchandise—to offset the production costs.

After much deliberation, Lucille Ball gave the green light to *Star Trek*.

Twenty Years Later
Home of Lucie Arnaz Luckinbill
Los Angeles, California
May 1984

The California sun was less forgiving on Lucy than it was with Desi. As the two splashed in the pool, the water sparkling with reflected sun-

light, Lucy wore a white hat with a yellow ribbon that shaded her face
and complemented her modest yellow bathing suit. Desi was shirtless;
his bronzed, sun-starched skin topped off by a mane of silver hair.

Their daughter, Lucie Luckinbill, filmed them as they swam with
five-year-old Simon, their first grandson. It would be one more family
video to add to the yards of home movie footage Lucy had accumu-
lated over the years. It would also be the last time Desi and Lucy were
ever photographed together.

Ever the protective grandparent, Lucy clung to her grandchild tightly
while Desi circled them a few feet away. With his mouth, he made gur-
gling noises in the water, prompting squeals of delight from the boy.
Helping Simon to a seat on the edge of the pool, his grandparents sang
to him. Clapping her hands rhythmically, Lucy croaked, "Grand-pa-pa!
Grand-pa-pa! Grand-pa-pa!"

After bungling a few words to Simon in her ex-husband's native
language, she chided Desi, "All my life I've been telling you to speak in
Spanish!"

Desi stopped floating and shrugged in mock disgust. "All my life
you've been telling me I don't know how to speak English!"

Lucy reached over to Desi and tried to flatten his hair. It was a gesture both familiar and automatic. "I wanted you to speak Spanish to the
kids," she said.

He smirked. "They made fun of me!"

More than three decades earlier, Desi and Lucy had negotiated an
ownership interest in their pilot and then made the bold decision to
record it on film. In the process, they had invented the television rerun.

Now, together again, they were living a real-life one.

Lucy had remarried and Desi thought her new husband, Gary Mor-
ton, was a pleasant man. A stand-up comic with a perfectly adequate
act, if modest acclaim. He and Desi got along just fine. Gary never
seemed much of a threat. Desi liked to refer to him as "that guy."

As Desi sang "Babalu" to Simon, and Lucy laughed and clapped
along, it was—for just a moment—*I Love Lucy* again.

One last time.

Desi Arnaz Residence
Del Mar, California
November 1986

When she heard that the priests had been alerted, Lucy quickly called
a friend who then drove her over one hundred miles from Beverly Hills
to Del Mar. Pulling into her ex-husband's driveway, Lucy hurried into
his house. She had been told before leaving that he would refuse to see
her. Sixty-nine years old, and quickly dying of lung cancer attributed to
a lifetime of cigar and cigarette smoking, Desi was a shell of the man
he'd once been. Chemotherapy left him nearly bald. By some estimates,
he weighed less than one hundred pounds. No one was allowed to see
him in such a state. Any visitors would have to talk to him through
closed bedroom doors.

Of course, whenever Lucy called, which was frequently as his health
declined, he picked up the phone. On their last wedding anniversary
Desi sent her flowers, as he had done every year since their divorce.

Lucy, never one to play by the rules, was determined to see him. But,
just as she had been warned, he wouldn't let her into the bedroom. For
a while, Lucy yelled at him through the door, but finally, after much insisting and complaining and refusing to leave, Desi relented. She stayed
by his side talking to him for hours.

Lucy had come to gain a whole new appreciation for her ex-husband
and the dream they had shared together. Speaking to ABC's Barbara
Walters in a voice that had deepened considerably over the years due
to her smoking, Lucy had lamented. "We built up a lot of things. But
while we were building, they would not believe that *he* was doing the
building. He was doing the successful building of a very well-run
empire."

Returning to the car, Lucy was visibly shaken. As she had told Walters, "We certainly did have everything. Worked very hard to get it. Two
beautiful children. What else could you ask for? And I think if Desi
were here, he would agree that it was . . ." Her voice trailed off. Desi
wasn't there. Gambling, womanizing, and drinking had ruined him.

Now in her car, Lucy broke down, telling her friend, "That was the
one love. . . ."

Desi Arnaz Residence
Del Mar, California
November 1986

Desi knew he didn't have much time left. But he was determined to
write one last script before he died. It was to be a tribute, a short one,
and its subject was the love of his life. He had married again—his new
wife looking strikingly like Lucy. But it was still always Lucy first. Now,
as he lay in his home, nearly broke from gambling debts, and succumb-
ing to an illness attributed to a lifetime of smoking, he thought of her
again.

"Nurse," he called from his deathbed, "I need a pen and paper."

"But Mr. Arnaz," said the nurse as she walked into his bedroom,
"you are too weak to write."

"I'll talk," said Desi. "You write."

When his nurse returned, Desi lay silent for several minutes. He
thought of the first time he'd seen Lucy, with her fake black eye and
bedraggled clothes, on the set of *Too Many Girls*. He thought of all
the classics Desilu had produced over the years: *Star Trek*, *The Danny
Thomas Show*, *The Andy Griffith Show*, *The Untouchables*, *Mission: Impossible*, *Hogan's Heroes*, *That Girl*, *The Dick Van Dyke Show*, *Gomer Pyle*, *I Spy*,
and *My Three Sons*.

But, before long, his mind turned to his failures. As if the title of their
first movie had been an omen, there had indeed been "too many girls."
There had been too much drinking as well. He had been careless with
money. He had been hurtful to his family. And his recklessness had not
just cost him a media empire; it had cost him a marriage.

Desi regretted that he would be leaving his children a home he had
mortgaged to pay for his drinking and gambling debts. But his biggest
regret of all was losing Lucy.

She was to be honored the following month at the Kennedy Center
in Washington, D.C. President Reagan would be there with the First
Lady. So would a slew of television legends—some of whom Desilu's
Productions had made into stars.

The original plan for the ceremony had been for Desi to be a guest
speaker. The show's producers knew the ratings bonanza he would

bring. It would have been a very public, emotional reunion between two Hollywood legends. But Desi now understood he would never make it to Washington, even though he wanted to be there for Lucy. He felt like he was failing her—again.

Instead, Desi sent a message to be read at the Kennedy Center by Robert Stack, an actor who became famous playing Eliot Ness on Desilu's *The Untouchables*. Stack was a close friend and a kind man, but for the ceremony, as in Lucy's life, there was no good substitute for Desi Arnaz.

The question for Desi was what to say in a message that would likely be delivered after his death. He wanted to say "I'm sorry." He wanted to say "I wish I could go back and do a thousand things differently." He wanted to say that he wouldn't drink, he wouldn't cheat, and he wouldn't let anything or anyone come between him and the shy actress with the big smile and the bright red hair.

But he knew he couldn't write those words. He wasn't going to make this a speech about him—about his failings and his regrets. The ceremony at the Kennedy Center was about Lucy. And his message would be as well.

"I love Lucy," he said to the nurse, pausing just long enough for her to wonder whether Desi was making a declaration or dictating the beginning of the first sentence of his speech. "*I Love Lucy* had just one mission: to make people laugh."

As Desi spoke, the nurse wrote.

"Lucy gave it a rare quality," Desi continued. "She could perform the wildest, even the messiest physical comedy without losing her feminine appeal."

Desi paused. He had been bewitched by her feminine appeal for the past forty-six years.

"The *New York Times* asked me to divide the credit for success between the writers, the directors, and the cast," said Desi, still dictating. "I told them, 'Give Lucy ninety percent of the credit—divide the other ten percent among the rest of us.'" A tear came to his eye as he struggled to find the strength to say "Lucy . . . was . . . the show."

As selfless and generous as his words were, they weren't the whole truth. But precision wasn't his goal. This was a love letter. And he knew just how to end it.

"P.S.," he said, as tears trickled down his cheeks and memories of better days flooded his thoughts, "*I Love Lucy* was never just a title."

EPILOGUE

New York City
September 20, 2012

Speaking at the Goldman Sachs Communacopia Conference in New York, CBS Television president Leslie Moonves reflected back on the all but unbelievable success of one of its most beloved sitcoms. He stunned reporters by noting that even now, six decades after the show first aired, the Arnaz-Ball production was still a cash cow for the network.

By 2012, CBS, which had repurchased rights to *I Love Lucy* in 1994, was receiving $20 million a year in syndication revenue from the show. The sitcom was still being aired in seventy-seven countries around the world.

Desi Arnaz's unorthodox decision to take ownership of his show not only netted Desilu Productions millions of dollars, it also set a precedent for the generations of comedians who'd follow. Taking a page from Arnaz, *Seinfeld* co-creators Larry David and Jerry Seinfeld, for example, received around $400 million in syndication fees. And every major sitcom since *I Love Lucy* has seen new life in reruns—all thanks to the genius of Desi Arnaz, the inventor of the rerun.

In life, he "bestrode the flickering world of television like a colossus," the *Los Angeles Times* recalled in his obituary. But today—in a world of syndication, iTunes, and Netflix—the legacy of the rerun's inventor is bigger than ever. "It's well to remember that every evening we spend watching television," said the *Times*, "we are exposed to his influence."

6

The Muckraker: How a Lost Letter Revealed Upton Sinclair's Deception

Boston, Massachusetts
August 23, 1927
12 :20 A.M.

Bartolomeo Vanzetti entered the execution room calmly, though fear threatened to overwhelm him. His face was pale and drawn, a result of his six-year imprisonment.

Stemming back to colonial days, Massachusetts had been one of the first states to carry out executions. Hangings had once been common, but, since 1900, the electric chair had been the commonwealth's primary means of judgment.

Five minutes earlier, Vanzetti had heard his lifelong friend Nicola Sacco scream "Long live anarchy!" as the prison guards strapped him to the electric chair. Then the lights flickered, the machine whirred, and his friend's screams abruptly stopped.

Now it was Vanzetti's turn.

Having refused the chaplain's offer of a prayer and last rites, he walked up the steps to the chair and sat down. He watched as the guards tightened the leather straps around his ankles and wrists and

applied metal electrodes all over his body. Then, addressing his execu-
tioners, he said, "I wish to tell you that I am innocent, and that I never
committed any crime but sometimes some sin. I am innocent of all
crime, not only of this, but all.

"I am an innocent man."

He looked at the executioner and gave a solemn nod. It was time.

Boston, Massachusetts
August 23, 1927
6:30 A.M.

Boston was a city that prided itself on tradition, yet reveled in the rebel-
lion of the Boston Tea Party, the Boston Massacre, and the midnight
ride of Paul Revere. It was a city of privilege for America's first families,
known as the Boston Brahmins, and a vibrant hub for tens of thousands of Irish and Italian immigrants who had fled despair and famine
on the other side of the Atlantic. But, in the past few years, this once
harmonious melting pot had become a cauldron of racial tension and
anti-immigrant animosity.

At the center of the fray were two young Italians who had been convicted of armed robbery and murder. Their appeals had been going on
for six years.

Their prosecutors claimed they were terrorists. Their defenders
claimed they were scapegoats.

Their names were Sacco and Vanzetti.

The man with an oversize head, strong Roman nose, and fair skin without a trace of facial hair strolled up Beacon Hill at sunrise and reflected
on what had brought him to this crossroads of American history. Far
from his normally youthful, boyish look, Upton Sinclair now had dark
circles beneath his eyes, the result of marching all night with more than
twenty-five thousand Italian-Americans and other protesters who had
flocked to Boston over the news that Sacco and Vanzetti were about to
be executed.

The so-called trial of the century in Boston had captured the imagination of the American public. During the trial and the appeals process, protesters gathered in picket lines outside the courthouse. "If these men are executed, justice is dead in Massachusetts," one of their signs read. The plight of the two Italian anarchists had become a cause célèbre for many fellow intellectuals, socialists, and artists, from George Bernard Shaw and Albert Einstein to John Dos Passos and H. G. Wells.

Upton Sinclair was determined to outdo all of them. Never short on hyperbole, he dubbed the executions of Sacco and Vanzetti "the most shocking crime that has been committed in American history since the assassination of Lincoln."

He was angry, and, as America's foremost muckraking journalist, he was in a position to do something about it by writing the definitive account of their railroading due to political bias and anti-immigrant prejudice.

These anarchists, Sinclair believed, could be the face of the new American Revolution, one that would usher in a new era of socialism. While some saw anarchism as the antithesis of the top-down government control under socialism, Sinclair and other socialists around the world saw in Sacco and Vanzetti all the evidence they needed to prove the evilness and injustice of the capitalist system. "To the workers of the whole world," Sinclair told his friends, "it is a warning to get organized and check the bloodlust of capitalism."

But Sinclair thought some good might still come from the tragedy. In the two decades since the publication of his bestselling book, *The Jungle,* he had suffered a number of setbacks. He had been involved in various extramarital romances, survived a divorce from his wife, flirted with increasingly radical politics, and had built a utopian community in upstate New York called Helicon Hall. But he still had his pen and his zeal for justice. And he knew that was all he needed.

"What an ironic twist of fate," Sinclair muttered to himself, "that these Italian seekers of liberty should have been convicted within sight of Plymouth Rock, and killed on ground over which Paul Revere had ridden."

Now it was his personal mission to make sure their deaths were not

in vain. He had come to Boston sensing an opportunity to plunge a
dagger into the heart of the miserable country he believed America had
become—and that's exactly what he intended to do.

26 Years Earlier
Leek Island
Ontario, Canada
June 30, 1901

"Uppie, sit down," Meta Sinclair implored, sunlight shining through
the window on her long dark hair. The tone of his wife's voice was un-
mistakably grave, but her soft, gentle manner put young Upton Sinclair
at ease.

Meta beckoned Sinclair to the side of the bed. Their home, a rustic
cabin on a bend in the St. Lawrence River, was the young couple's refuge from the world—and from their parents' disapproval. Meta enjoyed
getting lost in the woods; it was one of the few places where she could
keep the voices in her head at bay. Upton found it a fine hideaway to do
his writing. The words flowed easier when there were no distractions.

"I'm—" She paused, her voice trembling. She tried again. "I'm, pr—"
She couldn't get the word out. She didn't have to. He knew. She broke
down in tears. He couldn't hold back his tears, either. This was what he
had been dreading. Indeed, it was his fear of fathering a child that had
led him to tell Meta that they should "live as brother and sister." That
hadn't lasted long.

The idea of fatherhood had never appealed to Sinclair. His memories
of his own father were vague. Time had blotted out much of the un-
pleasantness of the past. But he could still recall his teenage years living
with his father, a penniless liquor and hat salesman, in New York City
boardinghouses that reeked of booze and cheap perfume. Even when
his dad hit rock bottom he still possessed the airs of the southern aris-
tocracy to which he had been born: the sense of entitlement, the cold
arrogance.

Upton couldn't bear the thought of bringing a child of his own
into this world, let alone into the United States. Turn-of-the-century

capitalist America, he believed, was a land of exploitation, brutality, and class warfare. Only when the masses woke up and turned their factory tools into weapons might there be a future fit for raising a child.

There were other reasons, too—selfish ones: A baby's incessant demands for love and attention, along with its ceaseless wailing, would interfere with his crusade for social justice. He needed to concentrate on the works of Marx and Engels and to pour himself into his writing. He had a calling—and it wasn't fatherhood; it was to become a propagandist—a term he used proudly—for the cause of socialism, and to topple capitalism by educating Americans and persuading them to overthrow their government.

Sinclair was nothing if not a man with an outsize ego. Even though he had a series of literary flops that left him on the verge of bankruptcy, he was convinced that his gift for the written word made him the right man to lead the country into a new era of enlightenment and social equality.

But a child? That would ruin everything.

Leek Island
Ontario, Canada
August 4, 1901

Meta Sinclair flung herself from the bed, trying to slam her belly against the floor. She and Upton had debated whether to visit the local doctor, but an abortion would not only be illegal; it would also be dangerous. In the end, they decided to end the pregnancy themselves by attempting to induce a miscarriage.

Meta had foraged for herbal remedies, which she had ingested with food and drank as teas. She had exercised vigorously in the hope that the strain might prove too much for the child inside her. But nothing worked. This baby was determined to come into the world.

Whether his parents wanted him to or not.

Union Stock Yards
Packingtown, Chicago
October 8, 1904

A quiet rage seethed in Sinclair as he walked through the muddy streets around the stockyards. His gait was purposeful, his lips pursed as he took in the sights—and the stench—of his surroundings. He was glad to be away from the constant demands and distractions of his family. Meta was a gorgeous, sensual woman, but she had wild mood swings and fierce bouts of depression and rage. And, of course, he had no concern about not being around the son he never wanted.

At the age of twenty-six, Upton Sinclair was excitable and prone to working himself up into a righteous fury that would paralyze him with nervous tension, indigestion, and migraines. But today his mind was clear. He was armed with his lunch pail and his powers of observation. None of his previous writing projects had achieved the success he sought, but he had every confidence that this one would be different. In fact, *Appeal to Reason,* the nation's leading socialist weekly newspaper, had already agreed to serialize his reporting from Packingtown, home of the Union Stock Yards.

Built over a swamp in South Chicago, the Yards could accommodate more than 75,000 hogs, 21,000 cattle, and 22,000 sheep at any one time, making it the meatpacking center of the world, the Capital of Slaughter. The railroads brought ten million animals to the Yards each year to be slaughtered, their parts processed and shipped to consumers from San Francisco to New York, to London and beyond.

But it wasn't a sense of empathy for the animals that filled the young writer with anger. He seethed because the men and women who worked there were pawns of capitalists and business tycoons who profited handsomely from the bloody, dangerous work their underlings performed each day. This was slavery for a new generation.

He knew how that sounded. Yes, he supposed, it was true that these workers hadn't been pulled from their homes by force. They had, in fact, flocked here by the thousands from eastern and southern Europe in search of jobs. Sinclair also knew that these workers wouldn't be beaten or killed if they tried to leave. Still, he reasoned, they were slaves nonetheless. Slaves to their own desperation. Slaves to a system that rewards the wealthy few at the expense of the desperate, starving many. These men were barely paid. They were stripped of their dignity, void of their very humanity.

"Wage slavery" is what Sinclair called this new kind of bondage propagated by greedy capitalists. And he was resolved to end it by writing a book that would expose the scheme and provoke enough outrage to inspire a new revolution. He intended for his book to do for organized labor and the socialist movement what Harriet Beecher Stowe's *Uncle Tom's Cabin* had done for the cause of abolition before the Civil War.

It would be called *The Jungle*.

Packingtown, Chicago
October 14, 1904

The metallic smell of blood invaded Sinclair's nostrils. He walked down the center aisle of the hog room past hundreds of hanging carcasses. This was where the whole hogs were hung and split down the backbone with a two-foot blade. Even at this stage, after the fatal hammer blow to the head, slit throat, and severed major arteries and veins, even after the entrails were removed and the carcass was hung on hooks, there was blood. It caked the floor and spattered the walls.

This was industrial-age killing, an assembly line of meat production. Or, as Sinclair liked to think of it, a "disassembly line." The process of slaughtering an animal and packing up its meat involved eighty separate jobs. There were the knockers, the leg breakers, the rippers, and the gutters. Hooks moved the animals through the factory to the smokers, the salters, the picklers, the canners. And those were just the workers who dealt with the meat. There were also workers who turned the organs, the bones, and the fat into lard, soap, and fertilizer.

A satisfied smile crossed Sinclair's lips. He had managed to convince the plant foreman that he was a Polish immigrant needing a job inside the Armour meatpacking factory. He marveled at his own gift for duplicity and the ease with which he could fool others. Of course, he

didn't dare bring his reporter's notepad with him. Instead he memorized everything he saw and then rushed back to his room across the railroad tracks to write it all down.

This is how he would make his mark. His father had gone in and out of this world without making any impact—other than depriving it of a few barrels of whiskey.

But not him.

The Jungle, he knew, would make him a legend.

The White House
Washington, D.C.
April 4, 1906

The hulking man pulled the spectacles off his nose. A less imposing figure might have looked small behind the massive desk in the Oval Office, but not the barrel-chested Theodore Roosevelt. Five years earlier, at just forty-seven years old, he had become the youngest president ever to assume office. Roosevelt carried himself with the youthful vigor of a man many years younger. A writer of considerable talent, he fancied himself a man of letters, which was one of the reasons why he had invited Upton Sinclair to the White House.

Teddy Roosevelt prided himself on his ability to accurately size people up. As he looked at the young man who entered his office, he sensed that the fellow was a bit of an upstart, brimming with a little too much self-confidence. But the president also got the feeling that the man's heart was in the right place.

Roosevelt had made something of a career out of assailing monopolies, often to the detriment of customers and workers. He also liked to see his name in the newspapers. When he was governor of New York, he often held press conferences twice a day, making sure reporters would have ample opportunity to learn of his successes and giving himself a chance to rail unchallenged against those he deemed corrupt.

For these and other reasons, the president was receptive to Sinclair's book, *The Jungle.* Assuming office after the assassination of President William McKinley, Roosevelt was a forceful presence on the national stage. He was eager to use his power to bring America's enemies to heel, whether they be recalcitrant heads of state or capitalists at home who needed to have their heads knocked together.

Roosevelt agreed with Sinclair's conclusion that avaricious capitalist meatpackers were colluding to form a monopoly and take advantage of the working class. He reasoned that these arrogant, wealthy industrialists needed to be put back in their place, just as he, the trust-busting president, had done with the railroad barons and with John Rockefeller and his Standard Oil monopoly. Roosevelt was also not an idiot when it came to politics: He saw the wisdom of supporting a book that had quickly won national acclaim and press attention.

Over the past year, Roosevelt and Sinclair, two self-described crusaders for justice, had exchanged long letters, the last of which had ended with an invitation from the president. "If you can come down here during the first week in April," Roosevelt wrote, "I shall be particularly glad to see you."

The majesty of the president's office, the living, beating heart of the American capitalist system, impressed even a skeptic like Sinclair. The office had been refurbished only a few years earlier as part of the effort to build a suite of executive offices for Roosevelt and his staff. It would eventually become known as the West Wing.

As the president rose and extended a hand to Sinclair, the author noted that a dog-eared copy of *The Jungle* was conspicuously displayed on Roosevelt's desk. Sinclair knew that Roosevelt was a speed-reader with a reputation for consuming books with enthusiasm and vigor. He was said to read a book before breakfast and as many as two or three more by dinnertime. Once asked by a friend to recommend a book, Roosevelt had suggested a hundred, all of which he'd claimed to have read in the previous two years.

"Welcome to Washington, my boy," the president said affably. He gestured to a chair, urged Sinclair to sit, and took a seat across from him.

An aide opened the door to the office. "Some cookies and tea, sir?" he asked.

"None for me," Roosevelt responded, patting his stomach. "I'm trying to get back into shape for tennis season now that the weather is turning bearable again. But Mr. Sinclair here will have some."

Roosevelt had mastered the politician's skill of studied sincerity. He also had a habit of getting right to the point. "I want to thank you for bringing these problems in Chicago's stockyards to my attention—"

"*America's* attention, Mr. President," Sinclair interrupted.

Roosevelt nodded vigorously. "That's right. America's attention. We're going to be sending a team of investigators—the best of the best—to take a look into the allegations—"

"They're not allegations," Sinclair interrupted again. If the president thought he was going to dominate a conversation with someone of Sinclair's intelligence and stature, he was very wrong.

Teddy Roosevelt wasn't used to being interrupted. The atmosphere in the room quickly chilled.

"But, Mr. Sinclair, by your own admission, you have written a novel. And surely, like all novelists, you have taken some creative license."

"No, everything I wrote in *The Jungle* is the truth. It's the truth about what goes on in those infernal factories, and what happens to the people who spend their lives working in them. My book is an exact and faithful picture of the conditions that exist in Packingtown, Chicago, down to the smallest details. It is as true as a study written by a sociologist."

Sinclair's cheeks reddened. He was working himself into a lather again.

"Then, why, dear sir, is your publisher billing *The Jungle* as a novel?" the president asked.

Sinclair struggled to maintain his composure. In his mind, both his reporting and his very integrity were being questioned.

He stammered indignantly, "Why, why, yes of course I've taken some liberties here and there to dramatize and interpret what I saw. That's necessary to hold people's attention."

Roosevelt nodded with satisfaction. "So then you understand why I must send our investigators to validate what you've written—"

"If you send those investigators it will be like sending burglars to the crime scene to deliver a verdict on their own guilt!"

By the time the meeting ended, neither man was very impressed with the other. Sinclair now viewed the president as an appalling clown and dupe. *Even the unabashed trust-busting progressive Teddy Roosevelt is a pawn of the industrialists, his entire government well fed with bribes,* he thought.

Roosevelt was equally unenamored with Sinclair. Writing to a friend, the president noted, "I have an utter contempt for him. He is hysterical, unbalanced, and untruthful. Three-fourths of the things he said were absolute falsehoods. For some of the remainder there was only a basis of truth."

13 Years Later
R Street NW
Washington D.C.
June 2, 1919
11 :13 P.M.

Carlo Valdinoci walked down the quiet cobblestone streets of George-town. Wearing a new fedora purchased at Philadelphia's Italian Market, he was dressed to the nines. He strode confidently in his new black suit, a colorful checkered dress shirt, and a bright blue polka-dotted tie.

He ambled a bit awkwardly, however, due to the Smith & Wesson revolver and Colt automatic concealed in his clothes and the heavy leather satchel jammed with twenty pounds of dynamite he had slung over his shoulder.

Despite his awkward gait, Valdinoci soon reached his destination: the home of Attorney General of the United States A. Mitchell Palmer, a southerner who had been appointed earlier that year by President Woodrow Wilson. Valdinoci gingerly mounted the front steps, planning to leave his deadly package by the front door. Its blasting cap was set to detonate a few minutes after he made his escape.

Everything was going smoothly until he reached the top step. Only then did the weight of the mini-arsenal he carried begin to swing to one side. Valdinoci swung his weight the other way to compensate, but he overdid it. He began to wobble, and then lost his balance com-pletely.

He tripped. He fell. And then he exploded.

In a blinding flash of light, the would-be assassin instantly burst into thousands of pieces of bone and flesh. Pages of anarchist literature fluttered in the grass.

The concussive force of the blast shattered nearby windows, including those of the house across the street, where Assistant Secretary of the Navy Franklin Delano Roosevelt lived. Five doors down, part of Valdinoci's spinal column crashed through a window and landed in the bed of a sleeping fourteen-year old.

In response to the attack on his home, Attorney General Palmer ordered the FBI to conduct a series of raids along the East Coast against the ring of primarily Italian anarchists believed to be responsible for the bombing of his home, along with a string of other bombings around the United States that had left dozens dead.

Palmer believed that these people were the same kind of fanatics who had plunged Europe into a world war five years earlier after the assassination of Archduke Franz Ferdinand. He was determined to stamp them out.

The first U.S. war on terrorism had begun.

South Braintree, Massachusetts
April 15, 1920
3:02 P.M.

The four-story redbrick building that housed the Slater-Morrill shoe factory looked just like the hundreds of other factories that dotted the suburban landscape around Boston.

Frederick Parmenter, the company's paymaster, and Alessandro Berardelli, a security guard, were getting set to hand out the weekly payroll. The 9:18 train from Boston had brought the cash to the office that morning, and now the paymaster and guard were carrying the two heavy boxes containing more than fifteen thousand dollars from the main office to the factory on Pearl Street.

•   •   •

Two men slouched against the iron fence outside the shoe factory, the brims of their hats low on their foreheads. They nervously fingered the weapons concealed in their jackets. Maybe this is what martyrdom felt like, they thought. Their friend Valdinoci had not thought he would die that night outside Attorney General Palmer's house. But they knew his death had not been in vain: The first acts of terrorism in America had put the anarchists on the map and signaled that the revolution had begun.

The revolution would go nowhere, however, without cash. Anarchists were being rounded up and jailed, and the cause was in desperate need of money. And that was why these two men now stood outside the shoe factory.

Parmenter and Berardelli got to within a few feet of the men before the gunshots rang out. The paymaster and security guard fell to the ground, the heavy payroll boxes making a loud clang as they hit the ground.

A dark blue Buick pulled up to the scene. The two killers grabbed the boxes and jumped into the backseat as the car screeched away.

As they drove away, the two men looked up and saw Slater-Morrill employees peering out from the grimy windows. The killers opened the side windows, stuck their guns out, and opened fire, watching as the workers ducked to avoid the bullets and shattering glass.

Nicola Sacco and Bartolomeo Vanzetti ducked back inside the car and smiled. The fewer witnesses the better.

U.S. Courthouse
Dedham, Massachusetts
July 13, 1921

Sacco and Vanzetti sat silently in their cage as the trial that had captured the attention of the nation—and much of the world—played out before them. They had maintained their innocence from the moment they were questioned. They had never wavered. The real killers, they claimed, were still at large.

Their lawyer argued that the only culprits in the Dedham courtroom were xenophobia, paranoia, and a biased and broken system of justice.

"What is your full name?" asked the prosecutor.

"Lewis Pelser," the witness replied.

"Where do you live?

"Two eighty-seven Centre Street, Jamaica Plain."

"And what is your occupation?"

"Shoecutter."

Pelser's testimony went on for half an hour. He explained how he had been at the shoe factory the day Berardelli and Parmenter were gunned down. He had looked out the window and seen two men fleeing the scene.

"Do you see in the courtroom the man you saw shooting Berardelli that day?" the prosecutor asked him.

"Well, I wouldn't say it was him, but he is a dead image of him."

"Who is the man you are referring to?"

"The fellow on the right here." He pointed at the man neatly dressed in a white shirt and black tie, with a prominent jaw, notched chin, and bushy eyebrows. It was Nicola Sacco.

"Are you ready to proceed, Mr. Moore?" Judge Webster Thayer asked from the bench.

Fred Moore, the lead attorney for the defense, had been waiting for this moment his entire life. It was the trial of the century, and this, his closing argument, would be his starring role in the proceedings. Moore was a well-known socialist lawyer who had previously represented members of the Industrial Workers of the World and other radicals.

"If it please the Court, Mr. Foreman and gentlemen of the jury, I know of no time when a lawyer quite as keenly feels his responsibility as he does at the conclusion of a capital case."

For the next forty-five minutes, Moore examined the evidence and the witnesses presented by the prosecution and raised doubts about their credibility.

"In the course of the arguments had in this case, attention will be directed, I take it, to the peculiar type of mind represented by the defendant, to the fact that the defendant has opinions and ideas foreign

to the opinions and ideas of the vast majority of the American citizenship."

Moore ended with a final plea to the nine stone-faced jurors. "We of
counsel and the Court cannot divide or assume your responsibilities.
You are the responsible men. You are the judges of the facts. The Court
gives you the law, but you, only you, can pronounce the verdict upon
facts, and when you pronounce the verdict, gentlemen, remember that
you are duty bound to give it in accordance with the facts as you believe them to have been found on the witness stand."

The jury ultimately did just that. After deliberating for only a few
hours, their verdict was unanimous.

Six Years Later
Moscow, Russia
August 25, 1927

Joseph Stalin was enraged at the news that Sacco and Vanzetti had been
executed two days earlier in Boston. Six years of appeals and delays had
exhausted the doomed pair's legal options. They were gone, but they
would not be forgotten—not if Stalin had anything to say about it. On
his orders, the Soviet navy christened one vessel the *Sacco* and another
the *Vanzetti*. Streets in every major city in Russia were renamed for the
men. *The Letters of Sacco and Vanzetti,* a book that collected their numerous writings from jail, was immediately translated into Russian and
sold hundreds of thousands of copies.

Just outside Moscow, the Sacco and Vanzetti pencil factory was built,
Every one of the hundreds of millions of pencils it produced would be
emblazoned with the names of the two martyrs. The pencils would be
distributed to schools around the Soviet bloc so that students learning
spelling and math would also learn that America was a horrible, unjust
place where innocent men were executed for their political opinions.

Boston, Massachusetts
October 1, 1928

Upton Sinclair had a lot in common with Joseph Stalin: Both men viewed America as the greatest force of evil in the world; both saw capitalism as slavery; and both were willing to do just about anything to further the cause of global socialism.

That's what made them revolutionaries.

In recent months, Sinclair had been hard at work on his new novel, *Boston,* about the trial of Sacco and Vanzetti. He was confident that his research would prove that the executed anarchists had been innocent—meaning the American government had been wrong and the Soviet government had been right. He was pursuing leads and interviewing witnesses, much as he had done twenty years earlier in the Chicago stockyards.

Trying to obtain a transcript of the court proceedings, Sinclair had written letters to dozens of lawyers, including future Supreme Court justice Felix Frankfurter, who had become a prominent advocate for Sacco and Vanzetti. He pleaded with Frankfurter to send him his copy of the transcript: "Perhaps a thousand times as many people will read my novel as will ever look at the official record."

Modesty had never been one of Upton Sinclair's strengths, but in this case, his belief in the size of his readership was well founded. *The Jungle* had been a national bestseller. He knew that *Boston* would be as well. After all, he was Upton Sinclair, America's foremost truth teller, a man of unimpeachable integrity, a writer of guts and grit willing to trudge through blood and muck to find a kernel of truth. The public *needed* to know how capitalist titans and corrupt politicians and a perverted justice system chewed their citizens up and spit them out!

That's how his readers saw him.

That's how he saw himself.

Denver, Colorado
October 27, 1928

Upton Sinclair and Fred Moore sat alone in a hotel room across from
the Denver train station. The literary giant intended to get answers to
his questions and finally put his mind at ease.

Several days earlier, Sinclair had telegraphed Sacco and Vanzetti's
lawyer asking if he, Sinclair, could stop in Denver on his way home
to Los Angeles in order to interview Moore for his forthcoming book.
Something had been eating at Sinclair. When he had pored over every
detail in the case and completed his research, he sensed that something
was amiss—and it bothered him. No one could say that Sinclair didn't
have a discerning eye for detail.

As he'd read the cross-examination of Sacco, he found a discrep-
ancy in the defendant's alibi. Seven defense witnesses had testified
that Sacco was at the U.S. passport office in Boston at the time of the
murder and far from the shoe factory in Braintree. But Sacco's own testimony on cross-examination contradicted important details in those
witnesses' testimonies.

Sinclair had already asked several of the witnesses what they made
of the contradiction. A number of them had admitted that Sacco's
testimony had been concocted to conceal his role in various 1919 terrorist attacks, such as the one targeting Attorney General Palmer. Still,
the defense witnesses had all insisted that Sacco was innocent of the
Boston murders.

So now Sinclair had turned directly to Fred Moore for answers.

"Fred, tell me the whole truth about the case," Sinclair begged.

Moore stared at him for a long moment. "First," Moore replied, "tell
me what you have got."

Somewhere in the Rocky Mountains
October 28, 1928
3:08 A.M.

Sinclair tossed and turned in his narrow bunk as the train crossed the Continental Divide and steamed down the western slope toward California. He couldn't stop thinking about what Fred Moore had told him.

At first, Moore hadn't wanted to talk. But Sinclair tricked Moore into thinking that he already knew the important facts, so Moore eventually opened up. He started talking. And talking. And talking.

Before long, Sinclair was sorry he'd gotten Fred Moore started. Because Moore told him something he didn't want to hear.

The question now was what to do with the information. A million thoughts flooded through Sinclair's mind as the train sped through the night, but none more important than what Moore's revelation might mean for the future of socialism. Sinclair's life had been spent in service to an ideological cause. Nothing mattered more to him than the fight against capitalism. Not his wife. Not his son. Not the applause and accolades that came from his fans' embrace of *The Jungle*. Nothing.

Of course, there was no denying that all of the attention was nice. He hadn't expected to enjoy it so much, and when he began working on *Boston,* he hadn't expected to have such a strong desire to experience it again. Gradually, the need for accolades became more than a bonus; it became a need.

And so, as he listened to the rhythm of the train's wheels against the tracks, the question that had been foremost in his mind drifted away. Of course he continued to think about what Moore's secret would mean for socialism, but he also began to ask a much more personal question: "What does Moore's revelation mean for me?"

Los Angeles, California
January 27, 1929

Sinclair beamed with pride. The first edition of *Boston* was an instant bestseller. As he felt the book's smooth pages and green cover, he marveled at his writing and the important message of socialist revolution that it offered to his fans and followers.

At the climax of the story, the book's narrator summarizes the inspiration that Sinclair hoped Sacco and Vanzetti would provide to millions in the aftermath of their execution.

> *To a hundred million groping, and ten times as many still in slumber, the names of Sacco and Vanzetti would be the eternal symbols of a dream, identical with civilization itself, of a human society in which wealth belongs to the producers of wealth, and the rewards of labor are to the laborers.*

As much as Sinclair enjoyed reading—and rereading—his soaring rhetoric, he enjoyed hearing the liberal intelligentsia's reaction to it even more. They didn't just like it, they *loved* it. They didn't just admire him, they *worshipped* him. *Boston* was greeted by Sinclair's fans as some combination of the Gospel according to St. Marx and the Stone Tablets brought down from Mount Socialism. The *Nation* compared him to Charles Dickens. The *New York Times* praised the book as "a literary achievement . . . wrought into a narrative on the heroic scale with form and coherence." Noted playwright George Bernard Shaw told Sinclair, "When people ask me what has happened in my long lifetime, I do not refer them to the newspaper files and to the authorities, but to your novels."

Sinclair memorized every positive review and every letter of praise. He repeated them in his head—and to anyone who would indulge him in conversation. The book had accomplished exactly what he'd hoped by giving inspiration and ammunition to budding socialists everywhere, and, as a side benefit, it brought him more of the praise and applause to which he had become addicted.

Boston was another milestone in Upton Sinclair's storied literary career. The doubts he'd entertained on that sleepless train ride through the Rockies were long behind him. Upton Sinclair thought little anymore of Fred Moore or the secret he'd shared.

Now, with the sound of a nation's applause ringing in his ears, Upton Sinclair slept like a baby.

39 Years Later
Bound Brook, New Jersey
November 26, 1968

Upton Sinclair—labeled by the *New York Times* as a "crusader for social justice"—died in his sleep at ninety-years-old. The obituary in that morning's paper quoted no better expert on Sinclair than Sinclair himself, who once offered what the *Times* called "a moment of proud self-assessment toward the close of his life":

> *The English Queen Mary, who failed to hold the French port of Calais, said that when she died the word "Calais" would be found written on her heart. I don't know whether anyone will care to examine my heart, but if they do they will find two words there—"Social Justice." For that is what I have believed in and fought for.*

The *Times* noted Sinclair's most famous works, such as *The Jungle,* and made a special note of *Boston,* which they called "one of the best of his social novels, which told the story of the Sacco-Vanzetti case."

But not, as it turns out, the *whole* story.

EPILOGUE

27 Years Later
Irvine, California
December 2005

Strolling past boxed documents at an auction house, one of them in particular—Lot 217—caught Paul Hegness's eye.

Hegness, a collector of rare books and first editions, found in that auction lot a letter addressed to a man named John Beardsley. It was signed by the great author Upton Sinclair.

As Hegness read through the letter, the last paragraph caught his attention. "This letter is for yourself alone," Sinclair wrote. "Stick it away in your safe, and some time in the far distant future the world may know the real truth about the matter. I am here trying to make plain my own part in the story."

Hegness turned back to the beginning of the letter and read with rapt attention as Sinclair revealed the details of his fateful meeting in Denver with Fred Moore.

When Moore had asked Sinclair to reveal what he already knew about the famous case, Sinclair thought he might get better answers from Moore if he pretended to have already learned of Sacco and Vanzetti's guilt.

"Look, these two men are guilty as sin," Sinclair had said. "You and I know both know they were guilty of the holdup and they killed those two men at the shoe factory."

If Sinclair's assertion offended the defense attorney, Moore didn't show it. "Since you have got the whole story," Moore said simply, "there is no use in my holding anything back." Moore wasn't going to lie to a respected man like Upton Sinclair. Maybe, he hoped, the world-renowned truth teller would keep silent in the interests of their shared political beliefs.

For hours that night, Moore spilled every detail of the case. He told Sinclair how he had ginned up a set of alibis for both Sacco and Vanzetti. He disclosed that they were in an active terrorist cell that had been buying dynamite and working to attack politicians and Wall Street bankers. And he revealed that the pair had previously performed a number of other payroll holdups in order to fund the acquisition of dynamite and weapons.

On his train ride to California, Sinclair had pondered his predicament. He had already announced to the world that he was going to write a book setting the record straight about Sacco and Vanzetti. Parts of it had, in fact, already been published in a leading literary journal. Fans assumed that the book would exonerate the martyred anarchists. But, after learning of their guilt from Fred Moore, Sinclair was faced with three options, none of them good.

First, he could rewrite the book, revealing Sacco and Vanzetti's guilt. That story would have the benefit of being true, but it could have horrible repercussions. It would set back the cause of socialism and, perhaps even worse, it would alienate Sinclair from his fans. They would stop buying his books. They would reject him and ridicule him as a sellout to the capitalists.

Second, he could drop the entire project. It was a better option than the first. The problem was that he was on the record as having praised both Sacco and Vanzetti. Thousands of words had already been printed. He had been convinced that the men were pacifists, not violent radicals who believed in "direct action"—the euphemism of the day for terrorism. Any decision to abandon the book now would telegraph to his fans that he had changed his mind and had concluded Sacco and Vanzetti were guilty. And then he'd be no better off than if he had simply written the truth.

The third option offered the path of least resistance: write the book he had always intended to write, and disregard what he had learned from Fred Moore as the ramblings of a delusional, scorned defense attorney who had lost the case of the century for his clients. Sacco and Vanzetti would still be the victims of class warfare. The capitalists who had rushed to judgment and denied them a fair trial would still be the real criminals. The book would still become a bestseller. Sinclair would still make money and win all the accolades and applause he coveted. And the cause of socialism would still be one step closer to winning the war for the hearts and minds of the American people.

In the end, Sinclair treated the truth the same way he had treated his son—as a valueless distraction from the cause of socialism and his ever-growing ambition. By the time he died, the Sinclair who had spent a sleepless night on that train was long gone. All that remained was the confession Paul Hegness had accidentally stumbled upon in an old box of letters.

Why did Sinclair write the letter? It's unclear—but one thing is certain: The day he wrote it was the only time in his life when he was willing to admit that *Boston,* one of his great works, was a lie.

Note: The entire text of Sinclair's extraordinary letter to John Beardsley can be found in the appendix at the end of this book.

7

Alan Turing: How the Father of the Computer Saved the World for Democracy

50 Miles off Cape Hatteras, North Carolina
March 29, 1942
12 P.M.

The SS *City of New York* cut through the waves as it barreled northward toward the port that bore its name. Over the last week the ship's officers had received radio reports filled with SOS signals from merchant vessels being sunk up and down the Atlantic Coast by Nazi U-boats. Most of the passengers had heard rumors about the onslaught, but they had no idea that these were not really rumors at all.

Those oblivious to the imminent danger included the ship's doctor, Leonard Conly. The voyage to East Africa and back was his first journey at sea. Even now, after four months of sailing, life hadn't improved much. He spent a good part of each day retching in his cabin as the swells pummeled the ship's sides. Today seemed particularly rough. As he kneeled by the toilet, he closed his eyes and thought of his wife and one-year-old son back in Brooklyn. He would see them both again in just a few days.

He heard the ship's bell summoning the passengers for lunch, and the thought of food made him retch again. It was Palm Sunday, the day of Jesus's entry into Jerusalem. But for Leonard Conly and the 144 souls aboard the ship, the day did not bring salvation.

The SS *City of New York* descended into its watery grave faster than anyone anticipated. Just as the passengers were sitting down to lunch, a crew member saw a periscope protruding above the water, followed by the unmistakable wake of a torpedo.

Everyone on board felt the explosion that followed.

It all happened so fast. The crew quickly evacuated the passengers to lifeboats. Dr. Conly stayed close to a blond, blue-eyed pregnant woman and helped her aboard. Now, hours later, they were at the mercy of the sea, drifting north in lifeboats in the waters of the Gulf Stream. The brutal cold had already taken the life of one of the survivors, his body cast off to sea.

But Leonard Conly had more immediate problems: Desanka Mohorovicic, the pregnant woman he'd escorted to safety, was about to give birth aboard a violently pitching lifeboat in fifteen-foot swells with a dozen shivering fellow survivors inches away.

The night was jet black and Conly could hardly see a thing. His two cracked ribs—broken when he slipped while jumping into the lifeboat—didn't help matters, either. He might as well have been delivering the baby on board a roller coaster back on Coney Island.

Mohorovicic screamed in pain. This was the moment. Conly winced as he reached out to her and took a healthy, eight-pound baby boy into his hands.

March 30, 1942
4:30 A.M.

The destroyer USS *Jesse Roper* plied the inky black waters of the Atlantic Ocean looking for any more survivors from the sinking of the *City of New York*. The captain knew that the odds were long.

In the first six months of 1942, five thousand people, many of them

Americans, were killed and 397 ships were sunk or damaged by German U-boats in the waters off American shores. That list included the *Jesse Roper*'s sister ship, the USS *Jacob Jones*. Almost all the sailors on board had perished.

The *Jesse Roper* had found a few lifeboats scattered like buoys across the Nazi-infested Atlantic, their beacons signaling SOS in bright white lights. As the destroyer pulled alongside another, the crew saw a woman inside cradling a newborn baby.

The child was named Jesse Roper after the ship that saved him. The press soon dubbed him "the baby Hitler couldn't get." As news of the rescue spread across America, spirits and morale rose.

While the country did not yet know it, the rescue of Baby Jesse was not the only reason to celebrate: The British were taking on the fearsome U-boats—and winning.

And leading the charge was a most unlikely chap.

St. Leonards-on-Sea, England
April 9, 1919

The six-year-old boy's hay fever was the worst at this time of year.

St. Leonards-on-Sea, a small, quiet town on the southeast coast of England, was a safe place. Safe enough for a boy to stroll down the street alone without his parents worrying about him. Not that Alan Turing's parents even knew what he was up to; they were thousands of miles away in Madras, India, where Mr. Turing served in the Indian Civil Service. Alan's parents were members of the British upper class who embraced the "white man's burden" of empire building, leaving mundane matters, like the raising of children, to servants back home in England.

Alan's allergies didn't keep him from his daily stroll. There was not much that could deter this stubborn boy when he set his mind on something, and he loved to wander around by himself and daydream.

Today's perambulation was typical in many ways. For starters, Alan was, as usual, a mess. His sailor's outfit, standard attire for young boys at the time, was stained with fruit juice and his shirttail was untucked. His sailor's cap sat askew atop his disheveled dark hair.

Carefree as he rambled between neighborhood gardens and houses, young Alan became entranced by the bees buzzing around him. *Where, he wondered, is the nest for all the bees that are out today?* He began observing, plotting the intersection of their flight paths in his mind, and following the likely path. He found the hive minutes later. Nothing was more fun for him than solving problems.

As he turned back toward home, Alan stopped to read the serial numbers stamped into the iron lampposts. He didn't realize it yet—at least not consciously—but what attracted him most to numbers was that they always obeyed their own rules. They had a code, and they were true to it. That was the kind of world that the precocious boy wanted to live in.

North Wales
December 25, 1924

Alan couldn't sleep. It was well past midnight, and he would celebrate Christmas morning with his older brother and parents, who were visiting from India, in just a few hours. The twelve-year old couldn't wait to run downstairs to the parlor of his family's vacation home. If his wish came true, the crucibles and test tubes of a chemistry set would be waiting for him under the tree.

In the meantime, he sat in bed reading E. T. Brewster's *Natural Wonders Every Child Should Know* by candlelight. Its first chapter was titled "How the Chicken Got Inside the Egg" and, from cover to cover, the book made science approachable and exciting by defining life as the product of scientific processes.

Brewster's book taught that the body was a machine made of living bricks. Alan's favorite section was about poisons. "The life of any creature—man, animal, or plant—is one long fight against being poisoned," Brewster wrote. With his homemade fountain pen, Alan had underlined "one long fight against being poisoned." It was heady, somewhat morbid, and occasionally inaccurate reading material, but he stayed up all night revisiting his favorite passages and wondering about their implications for life in general—and his life in particular.

In this way, Alan was a most unusual boy. But when Christmas morning finally arrived, there was nothing unique about the joy in his bright blue eyes when his parents let him open his gift.

It was a chemistry set.

10 Years Later
German Countryside
June 7, 1934

A madman had taken over Germany, but like his many of his country-men, Alan Turing was too apolitical and naïve to realize it. Therefore, it was far from extraordinary that upon his graduation from Cambridge with a degree in mathematics, he chose to go on a cycling holiday in Germany. It was a chance to celebrate his selection as one of the youngest dons in Cambridge's modern history and to get away from his little corner of the world—a corner defined mostly by mind-bogglingly complex mathematical inquiries.

Alan's cycling trip through Germany should have taken his mind off work, but even on vacation he couldn't escape the pull of mathematics. In fact, a few days of isolation made him realize that he didn't actually *want* to escape.

As he cycled from Cologne to Göttingen, which just so happened to be the math capital of the world, the five-foot, ten-inch mathematician with the bright blue eyes, unkempt hair, and omnipresent five o'clock shadow thought back to a puzzle that had attracted his attention in his last year of college. It was called "the decision problem" and the basic question it posited was whether a single mechanical method exists that could always correctly decide whether a mathematical assertion was prov-able. In other words, was it possible to design a set of principles that, if applied correctly, could serve as a lie detector for mathematical theories?

Three decades earlier, David Hilbert, the godfather of Alan's genera-tion of mathematicians, had hypothesized that the answer was "yes." Alan Turing disagreed.

Alan had fallen in love with the predictability and reliability of numbers, but he never presumed that their dependability precluded the value of new ideas. He didn't think that any single mechanical method could account for the infinite possibilities of numbers. And because man can manipulate numbers creatively, man needs creativity to prove the assertions he makes with those numbers. There is—*there must be*—Alan thought, a perpetual need for more intuition and innovation than any one single mechanical method could ever provide.

Far from using the trip as an escape from math, Alan spent the hours on his bicycle pondering the decision problem. He found himself enjoying the journey from town to town and feeling disappointed when he arrived at hostels and pubs at the end of the day. While he was bighearted and quick to share a laugh with those he knew well, he was uncomfortable around strangers. He despised small talk because he never knew what to say. That generally led him to say whatever was on his mind, which, unintentionally, often bored, insulted, or baffled his listeners.

Alan disdained pomposity and hierarchy of any sort. He never suffered fools or foolishness gladly. That attitude didn't fit well in Nazi Germany, where it was dangerous to speak one's mind. Alan didn't go around purposely insulting the Führer, whom he viewed as more idiotic than evil, but he was unwilling to acknowledge "Heil Hitler" salutes. Nazism, with its inane slogans and silly salutes, seemed especially foolish to him.

English-speaking foreigners who refused to play by the Nazis' rules were occasionally beaten up or harassed, but Alan skated by without any real trouble. For all of his short life, he'd been playing by his own set of rules, and so far, his luck had held out.

It never occurred to the absentminded soon-to-be professor that his good fortune wouldn't last forever.

Cambridge, England
March 15, 1935

The twenty-two-year-old Cambridge don had added marathon training to his other hobbies, which included tennis, competing in bridge
tournaments, and going to the cinema. Of course, he still pursued his
interest in codes and amateur cryptography. But of all these pastimes,
running was his favorite. It afforded him an opportunity to be alone, to
release pent-up energy, and to daydream among the natural wonders of
England's rolling hills and glistening rivers.

As usual, today's early-morning run began along the beautifully
manicured quad of King's College, then through the school's ancient
gates, down its cobblestone streets, past the towering spires of England's seven-hundred-year-old university, and across the River Cam
and Bourn Brook. Alan started relatively slow but increased his speed
with every mile. By the time he had hit the ten-mile mark he felt like he
was flying.

His wide, looping route eventually brought him back to within ear-
shot of the university's bell towers. He stopped in a quiet meadow just
outside the Cambridge city limits in a little village called Grantchester.
The dew was still on the grass, and Alan lay flat on his back staring at
the sky.

Imagine a machine that could read instructions, he said out loud to himself.

I think a machine like that, he continued, a bit unsure of how far he
could take this line of thought, *could be the answer to the decision problem.
It could disprove Hilbert's hypothesis.*

Alan paused. His speech had a natural hesitation to it, as if the words
on his lips were having a hard time keeping pace with the thoughts in
his head. At times like this, he wanted his speech to match the precision of his mind.

He continued thinking out loud. *The machine would scan a tape, and the
tape would have a numeric code on it. The code tells the machine what to do, and
the machine does it.*

With that, the pace of his thoughts picked up, and the tone of his
voice reflected a budding confidence. *At any given moment,* he contin-

ued, sitting up now and barely unable to contain his excitement, *the machine is reading one space on a tape, which moves backward and forward across the machine's eye, and based on what the tape tells it, the machine will write more things on the tape. Imagine it! Numbers that talk to a machine, and a machine that talks back—with new and different numbers!*

The part of the tape that the machine isn't currently reading would be like our memory, he continued. *It would be the machine's memory. And anyone who writes code for the tape could add to the machine's memory. Anyone who writes a proper code can instruct the machine to do almost anything.*

His arms were waving, and he was growing increasingly animated. He began to think of the possibilities. *With the right code, the machine could play music! Or chess! It could add numbers! It could process words! It would be like a phonograph and an adding machine and a typewriter—all in one single machine! It could hold the answers to countless questions, and the only thing you'd have to do to find out the answer is ask the question in a language the machine can understand!*

By now, he was bubbling over with excitement, pacing around the meadow as a cool breeze blew his sweat-streaked hair from side to side. He remembered a line from Brewster's *Natural Wonders Every Child Should Know:* "The body is a machine." If that were true, then why couldn't the inverse be true? Why couldn't a machine be a body—or at least have a mind of its own?

Alan Turing quickly realized that his concept of this machine would allow him to prove he was correct about the "decision problem," because he could use it to illustrate that, in mathematics, there is always room for more intuition and innovation than any one single mechanical method, or machine, can provide. But there was much that he did not yet realize. He didn't yet know, for example, that he'd just given birth to the concept for history's most powerful and transformative machine. He didn't yet know that the codes he imagined would be the backbone of what we now call software. Nor did he know that the machine he imagined would one day be called a computer. Instead, alone in an English meadow, Alan Turing became the first person to not just dream of a machine with the capabilities of the computers we now know, but to actually put together in his mind the technical elements of how that machine could be built.

Cambridge, England
October 28, 1938

Alan had seen countless comedies, mysteries, westerns, and dramas at Cambridge's Regent Street Picture House, but he had never seen anything quite like this: a full-length animated feature film called *Snow White and the Seven Dwarfs*.

Alan's head bobbed along to the song "Whistle While You Work," and he laughed at Snow White's little friends, who were almost as eccentric as he was. But his favorite scene by far was one of the creepy moments of the film that juxtaposed cruelty with kindness, monstrous ugliness with angelic beauty, and death with life.

Alan sat with rapt attention as the cackling queen on the big screen dipped an apple in poison. As the chemicals covered the skin of the fruit with a skull and crossbones, the evil queen—disguised as an elderly hag—commanded her pet raven: "Look at the skin: a symbol of what lies within." Then she ordered the apple to "turn red to tempt Snow White, to make her hunger for a bite."

In between bouts of maniacal laughter, the queen explained to the raven, "When she breaks the tender peel, to taste the apple from my hand, her breath will still, her blood congeal. And then *I'll* be the fairest in the land!"

For whatever reason, Alan loved Walt Disney's *Snow White and the Seven Dwarfs*. Perhaps it was his lifelong interest in poisons. Maybe it was simply the eccentric, Peter Pan element of his personality, which had never warmed to the protocols and rigid expectations of English adults. Or, perhaps, it was a soft spot for the poison's romantic antidote: "The victim of the sleeping death," chanted the wicked queen, "can be revived only by Love's First Kiss." In the case of Snow White, that meant Prince Charming.

After seeing the movie, Alan made a habit of eating an apple every night before bed. Throughout the fall of 1938, while Britain's prime minister Neville Chamberlain appeased Hitler, and Molotov began the Soviet Union's negotiations with the German Reich's von Ribbentrop that would eventually culminate in the Nazi-Soviet Non-Aggression Pact, the young Cambridge don who had solved the decision problem and invented the idea of the computer could often be heard quietly singing to himself his favorite couplet from the evil queen's incantation: "Dip the apple in the brew. Let the sleeping death seep through."

Cambridge, England
September 3, 1939

The prime minister's voice came crackling over the radio at 11:15 that morning. Alan listened alone from his untidy Cambridge apartment.

"This morning," Neville Chamberlain declared, "the British ambassador in Berlin handed the German government a final note stating that, unless we heard from them by eleven o'clock, that they were prepared at once to withdraw their troops from Poland, a state of war would exist between us."

And then came the announcement Chamberlain had worked so hard at Munich to avoid making: "I have to tell you now that no such undertaking has been received, and that consequently this country is at war with Germany."

It would mean a blockade of their island. It could mean an aerial bombardment of London. It might even mean the first successful invasion of Great Britain since William the Conqueror had landed in 1066, not far from the seaside town where Alan Turing grew up.

"You can imagine what a bitter blow it is to me," said Chamberlain, "that all my long struggle to win peace has failed." But Hitler's invasion of Poland—unlike, by Chamberlain's shortsighted reckoning, Hitler's remilitarization of the Rhineland, annexation of Austria, and conquest of Czechoslovakia—"shows convincingly that there is no chance of expecting that this man will ever give up his practice of using force to gain his will. He can only be stopped by force. . . . I know that you will all play your part with calmness and courage."

Calmness and courage had never been in short supply among Englishmen—or in Alan Turing. He had complete confidence in himself and his country, along with complete contempt for the German Führer, whose capacity for evil he had clearly underestimated. Even before Chamberlain's three-minute speech was over, Alan knew exactly how he could best play his part to help save England and defeat Hitler.

"You may be taking your part in the fighting services or as a volunteer in one of the branches of civil defense," said Chamberlain. "If so you will report for duty in accordance with the instructions you have received."

Alan didn't expect his service to include an assignment to a branch of the armed forces or the civil defense, but he knew he would serve His Majesty's Government somehow.

"Now may God bless you all," concluded Chamberlain. "May He defend the right. It is the evil things that we shall be fighting against— brute force, bad faith, injustice, oppression, and persecution—and against them I am certain that the right will prevail."

The next day, Alan Turing reported for duty, which, like so much in his life, would not be conventional at all.

Bletchley Park
September 4, 1939

Alan left the living quarters he was assigned at the Crown Inn at Shenley Brook End and rode his bike to his new place of business: a large, garish manor house that had been redecorated too often by too many owners with more money than taste. Both the exterior and interior of the house incorporated design elements from five different periods: Romanesque, Gothic, Tudor, Neo-Norman, and Victorian. The result was an expensively redesigned eyesore. Alan's first impression of the house was that it was proof of Leonardo da Vinci's axiom: "Simplicity is the ultimate sophistication."

The manor house stood on a hill overlooking the grounds of Bletchley Park, the new home of the Government Code and Cipher School. The school—which would never have any real students and which was less a "school" than a laboratory for code-breaking—had recently been moved out of London in order to protect its secrecy, and because its most important staff would be drawn from the faculties of Oxford and Cambridge.

Bletchley Park was a natural choice for a location because it sat on a rail line halfway between the two universities. Its isolation in the English countryside would minimize the number of nosy neighbors, and its sprawling grounds and somewhat elegant ambiance might reduce the natural stress of those who chose to accept its mission: breaking the secret code used by every Nazi field commander, air traffic controller, and U-boat captain trying to blockade Britain and starve its citizens into submission.

Alan arrived at the manor house, parked his bicycle, and proceeded to an elegant meeting room. He took his seat at a small antique table surrounded by seven men with a professorial air about them. Standing at the head of the table with a slide projector screen behind him was Bletchley Park's director, Commander Alastair Denniston.

"The Nazi code-making machine is called the Enigma," Denniston began. "The purpose of this orientation session is to tell you how the Enigma works.

"Secret codes have been used by militaries for millennia. Julius Caesar used to write orders in which each written letter would represent the letter that was three letters before it. So, if he wrote 'Jdxo,' it meant 'Gaul.' Pretty simple, right?"

Alan had been fiddling with codes more complicated than that since he was a boy in St. Leonards-by-Sea. He knew that code-writing had come a long way since Caesar's campaigns.

"Well," continued Denniston, "the German code is trillions of times more complicated than Caesar's. Imagine that someone in Berlin wants to send a message to a U-boat in the North Atlantic. The person in Berlin writes a message by hand in plain German. It might say, 'das wetter ist trübe,' which means, 'the weather is cloudy.' He then types the message on an Enigma machine, which looks a little like a typewriter. Take a look."

A picture of an Enigma machine flashed on the projection screen.

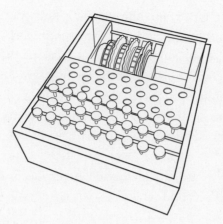

"And here's where the magic begins," continued Denniston. "The Enigma machine changes each letter in the message. It might change 'das wetter ist trube' into 'b-t-t o-o-f-d-s-e e-i-c g-t-t-a-i.' The message is now encoded, and that's what is sent to the U-boat via the wireless telegraph. Is everyone following me so far?"

Alan already had about a thousand questions, but he chose not to interrupt.

"Now," said Denniston, "the person in the U-boat receives the encoded message, and he types it into his own Enigma machine, which changes every encoded letter back into its original plain German letter."

"I suppose," asked Gordon Welchman, who taught math at Cambridge with Alan and had come with him to Bletchley Park, "we have no idea how the Enigma does what it does?"

"Actually," replied Denniston, "that's not correct. Thanks to our friends in Poland, we know *exactly* how it works. While England was burying its head in the sand for the past decade, Poland was preparing for war. Just before the first German tanks crossed their border, our Polish friends explained to us that they had not only figured out the Enigma's wiring, they'd even built one of their own."

"So why do any of us even need to be here?" asked John Jeffreys, another mathematician from Cambridge. "It sounds like the Poles did our work for us."

"Hardly," said Denniston. "There's more to the Enigma than its wires. Each letter typed into the machine first goes to a plug board that sits between the keyboard and the user. It works like a telephone switchboard, and an operator randomly selects new settings for it every day. So, on Monday, it might turn the letter 'a' into 'b,' and 'b' into 'a'; on Tuesday, it might turn 'a' into 't,' and 't' into 'a'; and on Wednesday it might keep 'a' as 'a.' Even though we know how the wiring works, we don't know which setting the Germans have chosen for any particular day."

Denniston now flashed a picture of three wheels, each labeled with letters, onto the projection screen.

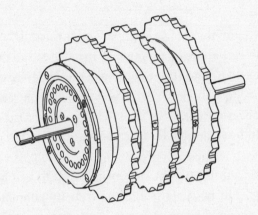

"These are the Enigma's rotors," he explained. "The signal for each individual letter is carried by electric current to a rotor sitting above the right side of the keyboard. The right rotor changes the letter into a new letter, and then sends the letter to an adjacent rotor in the middle. The middle rotor changes the letter again and sends it to the left rotor, which changes the letter yet again and sends it to a reflector. The reflector changes the letter for the third time and sends it back to the left rotor, which changes the letter and sends it back to the middle rotor, which changes the letter and sends it back to the right rotor, which sends the letter back to the plug board for one last switcheroo.

"Here's an illustration of the process, but for the sake of simplicity, it leaves off the plug board." Denniston flipped a switch and projected his final slide:

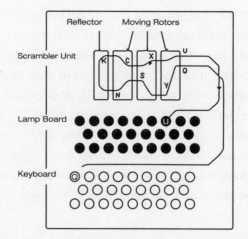

"By the time the plug board and the rotors have done their work, the original letter could be anything! The final, encoded letter appears on a board of little lamps, each labeled with a different letter. The lamp board looks like a keyboard, but with little lamps instead of buttons on a keyboard. The user simply writes down each letter on a piece of paper after the Enigma produces it."

"How long does all this letter-switching take?" asked Jeffreys.

"It all happens in less than a second," said Denniston. "And the trickiest thing is that the rotors are always moving. Once one letter goes through this process, one of the rotors turns a notch, which means that if 'q' became 'u' the first time you pressed 'u' on the Enigma—as in the example on the screen—then 'u' might become 'z' the next time you press 'u,' even if it's just a moment later. Even though certain settings only change once a day, the alignment of the rotors is constantly changing. In fact, the alignment changes after every letter of every message, which means the code changes after every letter of every message."

"Bloody hell!" said Welchman, looking stunned. "We're supposed to crack this code? By my estimate, there are over 17,000 possible combinations produced by the rotors. That isn't so bad, but there are 150 trillion ways of connecting ten pairs of letters on that blasted plug board. And I assume the Krauts randomly change the starting position of each rotor every day, just like the plug board? So every day is a new day of trillions of new possible combinations."

"Quite right, Mr. Welchman," replied Denniston. "It's actually 17,576—but, believe it or not, it's much worse than that. The Germans choose three rotors every day out of a stock of five possible rotors. That means there are sixty possible rotor combinations. In other words, the number of potential combinations is 60 times 17,576 times 150 trillion.

"The U-boat version of Enigma is even more complicated. Its user selects three rotors from a stockpile of eight possible ones. That means there are 336 possible rotor combinations, making it 336 times 17,576 times 150 trillion."

"So, that's almost a sextillion combinations," Alan said, speaking up for the first time. "885,376,800,000,000,000,000 by my calculations. If we tested a possible combination of rotors and plug board settings every second of every day for 28 trillion years, we'd still have 55 billion combinations untested. And even if we were somehow able to decipher a single letter in a single word, after 28 trillion years, we'd have to start all over again for the very next letter, because the Enigma's rotors spin after each one."

Alan looked around the table and saw stunned expressions on his colleagues' faces.

"Yes," said Denniston, "that's quite right."

"I have only have one question, Alastair," said Alan, who was dismissive of protocol even when his mind *wasn't* consumed with mathematical puzzles; it never occurred to him to refer to his superior by rank.

"Yes, Turing," said Denniston, clearly irked that a subordinate was addressing him by his first name, "what's your question?"

Alan knew he'd never be the life of a cocktail party or set a marathon record, although he had almost qualified for Britain's Olympic team. He knew he'd never write like Keats or speak like Churchill. But he understood more about mathematics and probability than anyone in England. From the moment he had heard about the Enigma, he never doubted his ability to build and program a machine—an electronic brain—that could outguess any machine the Nazis could come up with.

It would be like tackling the decision problem.

It would be fun.

"My question is," said Alan Turing, "when can I start?"

Bletchley Park
October 26, 1940

Alan sat alone in his office, his fingers stained with fountain pen ink, a week's worth of dirty clothes flung haphazardly around the spartan room, and a notebook before him filled with almost illegible scribblings. Hundreds of pages were covered with algorithms, German phrases, pages-long equations, and dozens of diagrams with arrows pointing in a seemingly infinite number of directions, connecting a seemingly infinite number of signs and symbols.

Alan had slept until noon, and now, nine hours later, he still looked as if he had just woken up. Despite the three-mile bicycle ride to Bletchley Park from his room in Shenley Brook End, he hadn't bothered to change out of his pajamas. Alan had met his professorial comrades' informality and raised it, throwing in a few Turingesque eccentricities for good measure.

To prevent the symptoms of hay fever, he biked to work wearing a gas mask. To keep his oversize trousers up, he used a string of yarn around his waist instead of a belt. To protect his finances, he had bought and buried bars of silver that would likely hold their value even in the worst-case scenario of a successful German invasion, although in his absentmindedness, he had already forgotten the exact spot in the woods where he'd buried them.

Perhaps oddest of all was Alan's decision to chain his coffee mug to a radiator in his office. He didn't require much, but he needed his black coffee. And coffee cups, which were difficult to come by in war-torn England, were prime targets for petty thieves.

"Turing!" shouted Alastair Denniston, barging into Alan's office uninvited and unwelcomed. "Why weren't you in your office this morning?"

"I was."

"What do you mean you were? I was here at nine o'clock, and you were nowhere to be found."

"I'm afraid you just missed me," Alan said, smiling. "I left my office at three o'clock in the morning."

"Very funny," said an unamused Denniston. "Look, I'm not here to talk about your work hours or your unprofessional appearance for that matter. Heaven knows you put in as much time as anyone else here, even if you have unorthodox ways of doing it. My concern, rather, is what you're working on."

"The U-boat Enigma?" asked Alan.

"Quite right," said Denniston. "In case you haven't noticed, the Krauts are bombing London to smithereens. They've already marched through Poland, Denmark, Norway, Holland, Belgium, Luxembourg, and France. We might bloody well be next. Seven thousand civilian fatalities in London last month alone."

"Why," Alan asked calmly, trying and failing to mask his annoyance with this seemingly pointless interruption, "are you telling me things I already know?"

"Because," Denniston bellowed, "I'm not sure why you're spending so much time on the U-boat Enigma, which hardly anyone believes can be broken, when you could be spending more time on the version of the Enigma being used by the German army and Luftwaffe.

"You know, Turing, no one ever surrendered to a ship. But if the Luftwaffe pummels us into submission and the German army gets a foothold in Britain, it's Katy-bar-the-door. Then you'll really need that silver bullion you buried and lost!"

"Yes," Alan replied, still trying to keep a lid on his rising temper, "but we've already made great strides against the army and air force Enigma. Thanks to the tireless work of the few mathematicians you finally hired last September we're deciphering the army's and the Luftwaffe's encrypted messages faster than ever."

"I'm not trying to detract from the great work you've done," said Denniston, trying to offer an olive branch to his star code-breaker. "Everyone knows that you're the most technically gifted cryptographer at Bletchley, and without you, our deciphering mechanisms would be a hundred times slower than they are. I'm only asking why you wouldn't keep working to make them *another* hundred times faster. The intelligence loses its value with every hour that passes between our receiving

it and our deciphering it. Shouldn't you be working on *that*? Everyone
who isn't named 'Alan Turing' thinks there's only a one-in-a-million
chance of anyone being able to break the U-boat Enigma. You're tilting
at windmills!"

"Frank Birch doesn't think I'm Don Quixote," Alan shot back.

"Birch doesn't understand your fancy math any better than I do!"
Denniston retorted, his anger returning and his face becoming a
deeper shade of red with every word. "That is to say, he doesn't know
an algorithm from an allergy. Birch is the head of the Naval Intelligence
Section, and the only reason he believes the U-boat Enigma can be
broken is because he thinks it *needs* to be broken!"

"Damn right it needs to be broken!" Alan could no longer contain
his anger. "Listen, Alastair. The U-boat Enigma is the whole ball game.
Cracking it is what mathematicians and logicians would call 'necessary
but insufficient' to our survival. It's 'insufficient' because Britain can
still lose the war if it beats the U-Boat Enigma. Even if we manage to
feed our people and arm our soldiers, we might still lose the war. But
it's 'necessary' because Britain cannot win the war *without* beating it. If
we can't feed our people or arm our soldiers, we absolutely *cannot* win
the war."

Alan felt like he was gaining some rhetorical momentum and he
wasn't about to stop. Denniston was in the military chain of command,
but Alan was still a civilian. He was free to speak his mind, which he'd
never had much of a problem doing.

"In case you haven't noticed," Alan continued, "we live on an island.
The food we eat, the raw materials that make our tanks and planes, it
all comes from what we so magisterially refer to as the 'Empire.' That
means cargo ships have to travel thousands of miles across U-boat-
infested waters if we want to eat, put bullets in rifles, and pump gas
into fighter planes. So long as we don't know where those U-boats are,
our ships can't dodge them, and in that case, the demise of the United
Kingdom is a question of when, not if."

"Yes, yes, I know all this, but—"

"But nothing!" said Alan. "We lost two hundred thousand tons of
cargo last month, and as the Germans build more U-boats—which
they are doing as we speak—that tonnage of sunk cargo will double

and triple and quadruple. If this continues we'll never be able to amass the tanks, planes, and men to launch an invasion across the Channel to liberate France. Never mind that—we won't even be able to feed ourselves! Is that what you want?"

"Well, no," stammered Denniston, "but—"

"Then leave me alone," said Alan. "I'll work when I want, how I want, wearing whatever I want! And I'll do what no one else on this island can do: I'll break this infernal code."

Alan stopped, tempted to leave it at that, but he couldn't resist a grand finale. "Archimedes said, 'Give me a lever long enough, and I'll move the world.' Well, if you'd just give me a little time and space, I'll move Hitler's armed forces right back to Germany, and then into history."

Denniston decided to throw in the towel. There was no point in arguing with Alan Turing. He was too smart. And too stubborn. "You're a messy, frustrating man, Turing," Denniston said, turning to leave.

"Well, it's a messy, frustrating world we live in, Alastair," Alan replied, turning back to his notebook of diagrams and equations, and repeating, in a whisper, the couplet that he'd first heard at the Regent Street Picture House. For whatever reason, it always seemed to bring him a degree of comfort and serenity: "Dip the apple in the brew. Let the sleeping death seep through. . . ."

Bletchley Park
January 7, 1941

Alan Turing had invented a machine that contained dozens of smaller machines, each designed to replicate the work of a real Enigma. With dozens of replicated Enigmas, the machine made guessing mechanical, which allowed it to work at superhuman speeds.

But even that wasn't nearly fast enough. Instead of taking trillions of years to decipher a U-boat Enigma code—as random guessing by hand would have done—Alan's machine would take months, possibly even years. That was still way too long for the intelligence to have any value.

Alan hadn't slept all night. Haggard and still wearing a wrinkled robe, he burst into Denniston's office first thing in the morning. "The keys," he exclaimed, "are the common words that the Germans use in many of their messages. Military ranks. Weather forecasts. 'Heil Hitler!' We can look for these words by looking for clumps of letters that resemble them."

"But how can any clump of encoded letters resemble a word?" asked Denniston. "Isn't every encoded letter randomly generated by the Enigma?"

"Not quite!" Alan said excitedly. "There's one thing about every letter that isn't random. Because of the Enigma's reflector, no letter is ever encoded as itself. Sure, a letter might remain the same after first entering and exiting the plug board, but once it has gone through the rotors, no letter is ever encoded as itself. The real letter 'c' is never encoded by the Enigma as 'c.' The real letter 'd' is never encoded as the real letter 'd.'

"All you have to do is find a commonly used word, like 'Admiral,'" Alan explained. "Write it out. Now slide it along the encoded text. We're looking for a seven-letter combination in the encoded message that does *not* have 'a' for the first letter, or 'd' for the second letter, or 'm' for the third letter, et cetera—all the way through the seventh letter.

"If you find a seven-letter combination without those letters in those places, then there's a good chance that those letters are the encoded word for 'admiral.' The longer the word—let's call it our crib—the longer the crib, the more likely that this process will work. For example, the phrase 'continuation of previous message,' which the Germans use hundreds of times a day, would be a perfect crib."

"Okay," said Denniston, "but how does that help you decipher the rest of the message?"

"That's where a machine comes in, Alastair. We just have to reprogram the electronic brain we've already built." Alan was smiling at the thought of it. In 1935, he'd first dreamed of what the math world was currently calling "Turing machines." Although the device he now imagined was far less universal in its capabilities than a "Turing machine," the principle of using a machine to imitate the mind of a man was the same.

"I'm not sure I follow," said Denniston.

"You don't have to," Alan replied. "Just tell the big man on Downing Street that I know how to build a machine that will break the U-Boat Enigma. Once it's built, we'll be deciphering thousands of messages every day, not after weeks and months of analysis of a single message, but after a few hours. By this time next year, convoys will know where every U-boat is and how to dodge them from New York to Southampton. We'll go weeks without so much as a single successful U-boat attack!"

Of course, the machine would always be a work in progress, as code-breakers discovered more and more cribs, and as Bletchley adapted the machine to changes in the Nazi code-making schemes. Some weeks and months would be much better than others. But the ever-evolving machine soon proved far faster than anything else at breaking codes, and time, as Alan knew, was of the essence.

And not just in the waters surrounding the United Kingdom.

New York City
November 13, 1942–March 23, 1943

As Alan's ship sailed into New York Harbor, he thought about the Anglo-American alliance. For the first two years of the war, the British had fought without their American cousins. Against all odds, they had survived. Then, after the Japanese forced the United States into the war by bombing Pearl Harbor in December 1941, the alliance that would eventually win the war was born. It was at that "very moment," according to Winston Churchill's later reminiscences, that he "knew that the United States was in the war, up to the neck and in to the death" and that, as a result, "Hitler's fate was sealed."

Since then, the British had grown accustomed to the new reality that Americans were assuming greater influence and power, but that didn't mean the British had nothing to teach their American allies—especially when it came to battling the Nazi U-boats that were sinking American ships. Hundreds of those ships littered the depths of the Atlantic along America's eastern shore. Now, more than a year into the Atlantic Alliance, both sides were undertaking an unprecedented sharing of intelligence based on their common enemy.

That collaboration of intelligence had taken Alan from his embarkation in New York City to meetings in Washington, D.C. There he shared his code-breaking insights with American cryptanalysts at "Communications Supplementary Activities," the U.S. Navy's code-making and code-breaking service.

About two months later, Alan returned to New York, where he spent most of the next two months in a large building at 463 West Street, near the city's piers, and under whose roof some of the best scientists on the continent were working twelve-hour days to design the devices the Allies needed to win the war. It was called Bell Laboratories.

On his first day at Bell Labs, Alan was shown a huge, climate-controlled room with thirty different machine components—mounting bays—each one seven feet long. "This machine," said Frank Cohen, the scientist giving Alan his orientation tour, "is what will soon make it possible for my president to speak to your prime minister without the German Führer knowing what they say."

Alan inspected the thirty large, rectangular mounting bays. "Secret speech?" he asked. "You mean it will scramble a transatlantic phone call like we scramble transatlantic telegrams?"

"Exactly," said Cohen. "We installed an experimental model in November, and now we're building an operational one. You're the first Englishman to set eyes on it."

As if on cue, Alan's bright blue eyes glowed with excitement. Men had been encoding the written word for millennia, but a machine that could easily and reliably encode the spoken word would be revolutionary.

"Of course," continued Cohen, "there are dozens of kinks in the system that we're still trying to solve. To be perfectly candid, some of us are feeling a bit stumped. We were hoping you could lend us a hand."

Alan stared in wonder at the machine and nodded in assent. It was clunky, fragile, and not even operational, but, to Alan Turing, it was beautiful—another testament to what the creative mind of man could build.

"Well, when can you start?" asked Cohen.

Alan smiled, still staring at the machine.

"I already have."

Normandy, France
D-Day: June 6, 1944

Fifteen months after Alan returned to Britain from the United States—
where he had helped make the secret-speech machine operational,
contributed to a host of other projects at Bell Labs, and taught his
American counterparts in Naval Intelligence what he knew about the
Enigma and code-breaking—the Allies launched the largest amphibi-
ous invasion in the history of warfare.

"You are about to embark upon a great crusade," General Dwight D.
Eisenhower had told the men of his mighty armada. "The hopes and
prayers of liberty-loving people everywhere march with you."

With them were tanks, artillery, planes, and an arsenal that matched
the German Reich's mighty war machine gun for gun and shell for
shell.

Almost every element of the arsenal, including one hundred thousand American and Canadian soldiers, sailors, and airmen, had crossed
a once-perilous ocean—an ocean that Alan Turing, more than any
other man, had made safe from Adolf Hitler's Nazi U-boats. He had
cracked the Enigma machine, which not even the genius code-breakers
at Bletchley Park had thought was solvable. Alan Turing had not only
been important in bringing about Germany's defeat, but absolutely essential.

For his indispensable efforts, His Majesty's Government awarded
him the Order of the British Empire.

Eight Years Later
Manchester, England
February 7, 1952

"But how do you know the name of the man who robbed your house?" asked the incredulous policeman standing in the messy living room of Manchester University's most distinguished computer scientist. The police officer had never met a computer scientist, let alone seen a computer, and after arriving at Alan's house for the first time yesterday, he hadn't particularly warmed to this one.

"I just know, okay," replied Alan. He was already exhausted by the stress of his home being burglarized a week earlier and the news he had received three days earlier that a former fling was in cahoots with the robber. Yesterday he had made a halfhearted attempt to report the crime without revealing that the burglar's accomplice was an acquaintance of his.

"Well, that's not what you told us yesterday," said the gruff, overweight bobby. "We checked out the story you gave us yesterday and it was full of holes. How do you actually know the name of your burglar?"

"Fine," said Alan, "I'll tell you truth."

He hated lying. He had no talent for it. It was out of character for him to be anything less than brutally honest, and he felt relieved by his instantaneous decision to come clean about the false story he had concocted yesterday.

"I was at a bar," Alan began. "And a man sat down next to me. He wasn't a particularly bright man, or even an especially good man. He'd been in and out of jail for some petty larcenies. Against my better judgment, we became friends. And that friend later met another man in another bar. And that other man was the one who robbed me."

"That makes no sense at all," the policeman said, confused. "How do you know the man your friend met is the man who robbed you?"

"A couple of days after the burglary," explained Alan, "I met my friend again, the one from the bar, and he told me the name of the burglar, who apparently assumed that even if I knew his name, I'd never report him to the police."

"And why on earth would he assume that?"

"Because, if you must know, my friend was more than a friend," said Alan. "We were romantic friends." And then, just to make sure the slow-witted officer knew what he meant, Alan added, "It was an affair. This man and me, we had a brief . . . regrettable . . . affair."

Alan thought it felt good to get that off his chest. His life's work had been a series of searches for the truth, and it had gone against every bone in his body to hide the truth when telling the police how he came to know the name of the man who'd robbed his house. Honesty had always been, if not convenient, at least instinctual for him. In Germany, he hadn't pretended to admire the Führer. At Bletchley Park, he hadn't pretended to respect Denniston. And now, today, in his own living room, he wasn't about to pretend anything. The representatives of His Majesty's Government at Bletchley had almost certainly known he was gay when he was breaking the Enigma code, and he saw no reason why the representative of the government who was investigating the burglary of his home shouldn't know it as well.

But as soon as he saw the antagonistic expression on the policeman's face, Alan regretted his candor. Everyone knew there were gay people in England, and English society was not, by the standards of some countries, aggressively hostile toward them. Alan had never gone out of his way to hide his sexual orientation. But nevertheless, it was most unconventional to come right out and admit it.

It was also illegal.

"Well," said the policeman contemptuously, "if that's the case, you'll have to come down to the station with me. You've just confessed to the crime of 'gross indecency.'"

"Now wait just a moment! I'm the one who got robbed here!"

"And that'll be dealt with, don't you worry," replied the cop. "But we've got to deal with you, too, Mr. Turing. Your robber's problem is his problem. And your problem is your problem. And the law is the law."

"The police actually *arrest* people for this? Who are you, Oliver Cromwell?!"

"Never was one for history, Mr. Turing," said the officer. "Not sure I follow you. But what I need now is for *you* to follow *me* downtown. You're under arrest."

The ironies were not lost on Alan. He had answered his prime minister's war cry in 1939 to defend "the right" against bad faith, injustice and persecution, and yet now his decision to call a blackmailing burglar's bluff was about to land him in jail, courtesy of the government he had served indispensably.

Manchester, England
June 7, 1954

Alan sat alone in bed, staring at the apple on his nightstand. It was half past one o'clock in the morning, right around the time he'd done some of his best work at Bletchley Park.

The Government Code and Cipher School seemed like a distant memory to him now. He had gone from cracking Nazi codes to writing computer codes. In the seven years since the war ended, Alan and a small team of mathematicians and engineers at Manchester University had designed the blueprint for what he called an "electronic brain," but what his colleagues called a "Turing machine." Outside of academic circles it was becoming known as a "computer." These were heady, exciting times for him. But it all came crashing down after the police officer in his living room put him under arrest.

To avoid prison, Alan had pleaded guilty and accepted a reduced punishment: a cocktail of chemicals unlike any he'd experimented with as a boy on Christmas morning or as a student playing with iodates at secondary school. The primary ingredient in the compulsory cocktail was estrogen, which was supposed to eradicate his libido.

In effect, it was a successful nonsurgical form of sterilization. But it had embarrassing side effects: It made the marathon runner fat. Worse than that, it caused him to grow breasts. The physical deformities on his chest were like a scarlet letter, a constant reminder to everyone of his punishment for a sex crime.

There were other changes in his life that were less obvious to observers, but even more painful to Alan. He had always been discreet, and although he wasn't ashamed of his private life, he was horrified at seeing its details splashed across the pages of local newspapers. Even more difficult to bear was the reaction of his brother John. Upon receiving a letter from Alan explaining the arrest, John made it clear that Alan repulsed him and deserved the government's punishment.

Perhaps most troubling of all was the scrutiny he received from Britain's national security apparatus, which viewed men who committed crimes of "moral turpitude" as security risks. Because Alan's work at Bletchley had given him access to some of the nation's most closely guarded secrets, officials in London required him to keep them apprised of his whereabouts. They were particularly concerned about his trips abroad to countries that allowed sex criminals to visit.

He may not have become a "different man," but his life was certainly very different now.

After the arrest, the public humiliation, and the exacerbation of a loneliness he had felt for most of his life, Alan didn't have as much to lose as most men. Certainly, he felt, he didn't have as much to live for as the man who was protected by the police and whose government repaid his selfless service with something better than persecution, forced sterilization, and feeble attempts at social engineering. Two years after his arrest, the simple fact was that Alan no longer wanted to be surrounded by a society of simpletons.

"Dip the apple in the brew," he whispered, sitting on the side of his bed. "Let the sleeping death seep through."

When his housekeeper arrived the next morning, she found him lying in bed—asleep forever.

Beside him was an apple with a single bite taken from it.

It had been dipped in cyanide.

EPILOGUE

There is a modest tribute to Alan Turing at Manchester University, where he spent the final nine years of his life. It is a bronze statue of him sitting on a bench, staring into the distance and holding an apple.

Turing's accomplishments will also undoubtedly receive a new wave of attention later this year when *The Imitation Game*, a major motion picture about his role in breaking the Enigma codes, opens in theaters.

But the true Turing monument is the world we now live in: a world free of the fascism that he, perhaps as much as Patton or Bradley or Eisenhower, helped to defeat. And in a world where Windows means more than framed glass apertures in buildings, where Deep Blue can compete with Russian chess master Garry Kasparov, and where a lovely female voice on your phone can tell you anything from the name of Britain's prime minister to the winner of last year's Super Bowl.

Every time a computer searches the Internet, plays music, or processes words by retrieving an encoded application from its "memory," a small tribute is made to the man who imagined tape with an ever-changing code that a machine can read, rewrite, and obey.

Perhaps the most striking, if possibly coincidental, memorial to the man who invented the first computer is that anytime someone looks at an iPhone, iPad, or MacBook they find the image of an apple on the back.

It is missing a single bite.

8

The Spy Who Turned to a Pumpkin: Alger Hiss and the Liberal Establishment That Defended a Traitor

I had attacked an intellectual and a liberal. A whole generation felt itself on trial.

—Whittaker Chambers

Yalta, Soviet Union
February 4, 1945

While the barrel-shaped British prime minister droned on, the American diplomat stole glances at the magnificent view outside the windows. The Black Sea looked menacing and cold from the warmth of Livadia Palace. With antique mirrors, crystal chandeliers, and the finest in Soviet hospitality, the palace was a grand setting. The American figured it was the perfect place for leaders seeking to carve up the world to meet. It was here, he recalled, where the last Russian czar and his family enjoyed many summers, basking in their decadence while their people starved. At least until Soviet communists rose up and conquered them.

The Soviets were now using the same apartments in the same decadent palace for themselves. That irony did not even cross the mind of the forty-year-old American diplomat, Alger Hiss, who viewed the communist leadership as a force for good.

The three titans of the world—Winston Churchill, Joseph Stalin, and Franklin D. Roosevelt—along with their respective military brass and diplomatic corps, had cause to celebrate. After five years of grinding war, it was finally coming to an end. The fascists were all but defeated. The only question left was how to divide up the spoils.

"These are among the most important days that any of us shall live," Prime Minister Winston Churchill thundered. Hiss rolled his eyes. It wasn't even noon and he was convinced that Churchill had already downed one too many Johnnie Walkers. He had a penchant for grandeur, hyperbole, and self-importance. Someone ought to just tell the senile old man he was losing his empire.

Then it was the Soviet leader's turn. Hiss fixed his eyes on the commanding presence of the mustachioed Stalin. It was the first time he had been in a room with the powerful Soviet leader, and he wasn't disappointed. Stalin had nearly ended his monologue, which had been accentuated by the loud pounding of his fist on the table, when the English translation began:

For the Russian people, the question of Poland is not only a question of honor but also a question of security. Throughout history, Poland has been the corridor through which the enemy has passed into Russia. Poland is a question of life and death for Russia.

Hiss thought that Stalin was a man of strength and composure. The Baltics. Poland. Eastern Europe. Stalin insisted on having it all. Soviet blood—20 million martyrs—had earned it. Meanwhile, the Brits and Americans had been content to fight from afar, letting the Soviets do the hard work against Hitler.

Across the round table, Churchill looked irritated. Hiss knew what he must be thinking: *Wasn't this precisely the reason the Allies had entered the war? To preserve the freedom and independence of nations like Poland?*

The stage was now set for the third member to speak, a man Hiss had gotten the opportunity to observe closely since being assigned to the Yalta delegation by the State Department. The crippled, ailing

American president looked unperturbed. Gaunt and drawn, Franklin D. Roosevelt turned his head and beckoned Hiss to come closer.

Hiss revered the old man. Though FDR was a capitalist, he had done his best to promote social justice for the masses, a new social construct. Roosevelt always thought the best of people, and that included Stalin. But Hiss could see that Stalin's expansive demands to control all of Eastern Europe seemed extreme, even to Roosevelt.

"Mr. Hiss," Roosevelt asked, his voice stronger than his body, "what are our objections on Poland?"

Hiss leaned forward, whispering into the commander in chief's ear. "None really, Mr. President. The Soviets have assured us they will hold free and fair elections in whatever territory they are currently occupying. What we need is Soviet agreement on the creation of the United Nations." The UN was FDR's passion, the diminished heir to the grandiose League of Nations for which his predecessor Woodrow Wilson had vainly given his life.

Roosevelt took a drag on his long cigarette. "Very well," he said.

Hiss leaned back in his chair and did his best to suppress a smile.

16 Years Earlier
Cambridge, Massachusetts
June 14, 1929

Commencement exercises were under way and Alger Hiss could not help but feel a moment of validation. Not only for the stellar grades he'd received at Harvard Law School, although even he had to admit they were impressive, but rather because he had survived it all: his father's suicide when he was just two years old; his sister's suicide twenty-two years later; the death of his brother from Bright's disease; and the sad, dreary existence of growing up in a Baltimore neighborhood that seemed to be in a constant state of decline.

Hiss scanned the crowd of beaming, proud parents. In their top hats, morning coats, and exquisitely crocheted lace dresses, this was a portrait of privilege. Adams. Cabot. Choate. Eliot. Lowell. Putnam. Weld. Williams. Winthrop. They were all there. They had sent their children to Exeter and Andover. Then to Princeton and Yale. Now, with Harvard Law degrees in hand, these children would be unleashed into the world to become industry magnates, bankers, and governors. Hiss knew it wasn't because they worked harder or were smarter; it was because they happened to have names that usually traced back to the *Mayflower*.

His mother sat a dozen or so rows back, stone-faced and grim. In the creased lines of her face were the unmistakable signs of suffering, although you would never know it from talking to her. She was the one who had taught her children to rise above their circumstances. Forty years ago, she might have fit in here. She had grown up with wealth but, without a husband to provide income for the family, her inheritance had dwindled to nothing. A widow with five children to raise, Mary Lavinia Hiss had good reason to be mad at the world, but had never shown an ounce of it. She taught Hiss and his siblings that self-pity was for the weak.

Perhaps more so than his brothers and sisters, young Alger took his mother's advice to heart. He'd been a scrapper for much of his life—aided by a keen mind, a natural charm, and appealing looks. Few knew that he lived a nearly penniless existence, even selling spring water from his little wagon to earn money when he was a boy. From an early age, he'd learned to ingratiate himself to get ahead. He was the kind of guy who was everyone's best friend, and was named the "most popular" student while earning top marks at Johns Hopkins. He also learned to look the part. Hiss realized that if he surrounded himself with people of wealth and taste and status, then others would assume he had it as well.

"Hiss," the dean called out, shaking Alger from his childhood memories and his resentment for just about every other student sitting alongside him on the stage. Hiss stood and strode with purpose to the podium. He forced a smile when he caught the eye of Professor Felix Frankfurter, sitting in the first row.

Professor Frankfurter had known how far Alger's talents could go, even if he wasn't from one of New England's wealthiest families. Hiss had been introduced to the revered liberal law professor by a mutual friend and had quickly become a regular at the Frankfurters' Sunday teas—which featured the professor's favorite authors, friends, and fashionable leftist views on issues of the day. Hiss and Frankfurter saw most of these issues the same way. For example, they shared the firm belief that anarchists Nicola Sacco and Bartolomeo Vanzetti had been falsely convicted at their famous Boston murder trial.

When the ailing Oliver Wendell Holmes Jr., the legendary jurist appointed to the bench by Theodore Roosevelt, had delegated the selection of his law clerks entirely to Professor Frankfurter, it came as no surprise to anyone that his top recommendation was his protégé, Mr. Alger Hiss.

Now, at twenty-four years old, with a tall, lean frame, wavy dark hair, large ears, and expressionless eyes, Hiss had not only attained a coveted law degree from Harvard, but he was about to clerk for the most famous and esteemed Supreme Court justice.

As he stood at the podium looking out at the crowd, Hiss realized just how far from his humble Baltimore roots and life of small-bore tragedies he'd come. He also knew that it was only the beginning.

Washington, D.C.
April 8, 1930

Alger Hiss watched as Oliver Wendell Holmes bristled at what he clearly viewed as an impertinent and unprofessional suggestion.

"It won't work," he told his young clerk. "It's too personal."

Hiss was undaunted. He wished to achieve a higher level of intimacy with Holmes, one that would distinguish him from the other clerks, all of whom had sterling pedigrees similar to his own.

When he first met the justice, Oliver Wendell Holmes had already been on the bench for twenty-seven years. His health was clearly on the decline—there was no doubt about that—but he still had the finest mind of anyone on the Court. Even as he completed his ninth decade, Holmes was so proficient at expediently turning out stunningly lucid and scholarly opinions that Chief Justice Charles Evans Hughes sometimes withheld work from Holmes to save his slower colleagues the embarrassment.

But Hiss could see time had caught up with him. Now, at eighty-eight years old, Holmes's eyesight was failing. Before his beloved wife,

Fanny, died earlier that year, she had taken to reading him literature out loud. But now, with her gone, Holmes missed the enjoyment of a good book. Seeing an opening, the ambitious Hiss saw an opportunity.

"Mr. Justice, it would be an honor if I could read to you," Hiss suggested to him one evening. Holmes rejected the idea out of hand. A clerk spending hours alone with him was far too much of an imposition. It was also inappropriate and much too personal—which is exactly why Hiss wanted to do it.

He saw himself becoming a confidant of the justice, learning from him, sharing his secrets. Holmes could also help him strengthen his façade of established wealth, breeding, and social class. But, if he really examined himself, and if he were willing to admit it, there was more to it than that. In Holmes, Hiss saw the wise, revered fatherly figure that he'd lacked all of his life.

One didn't push Oliver Wendell Holmes, and one certainly didn't pester him. So Hiss devised a different strategy. "Mr. Justice, the decision is yours, of course." Hiss was always unfailingly polite, but he did note to the jurist that there was an existing precedent. "But, sir, in case you were not aware, Esme's secretary reads to him."

Hiss knew that Sir Esme Howard, the British ambassador, was one of Holmes's favorite visitors and a man Holmes very much admired. If he knew that the respected Sir Esme had his secretary read to him, Hiss figured that Holmes might reconsider.

And he was right. Holmes soon relented and let Hiss read to him almost every weekday. Of course, Hiss did not mention to Holmes what might have been a useful fact: Sir Esme's secretary did indeed read to him, but that was because the secretary was also his son.

How easy it was, Hiss thought, to get what one wanted with nothing other than a simple omission of a key fact or two.

16 Years Later
Washington, D.C.
January 22, 1945

Two days after being sworn in for an unprecedented fourth term as president of the United States, Franklin Roosevelt arrived at the Bureau of Engraving and Printing. Underneath the building was a secret rail line where his specially outfitted private train car, the *Ferdinand Magellan,* was waiting to take the wheelchair-bound president on the first part of a long, arduous trip that would eventually culminate in Yalta on the Crimean Sea. There he would meet with Soviet premier Joseph Stalin and British prime minister Winston Churchill to plan for the aftermath of what was now an inevitable Allied victory over Hitler's Germany.

Among the American delegation that accompanied Roosevelt was the elegant and erudite Alger Hiss. Since joining the federal government in 1933, Hiss had excelled in his career. This was not all that surprising given that he had arrived brimming with qualifications and endorsements from men like Justice Felix Frankfurter—appointed to the Supreme Court by FDR in 1939—and the late Oliver Wendell Holmes.

Hiss was a perfect match for what many called "the striped pants set" at the State Department compound popularly known as "Foggy Bottom"—young men with Ivy League degrees, great self-assurance, and occasionally batty ideas about the world. The previous spring Hiss had become special assistant in the new Office of Special Political Affairs within the State Department, where he spent most of his time on postwar planning. He wasn't that concerned about the Soviet Union— he believed they would continue to be a key American ally after the war; but he *was* concerned about Great Britain attempting to protect what was left of its empire.

Hiss was enthusiastic about his next assignment. He had been tasked with preparing all of the background material to be used by the U.S. delegation at the Yalta Conference, even for matters outside his department. It was clear to anyone paying attention that Hiss's career was on an impressive trajectory—one with seemingly no limits. The establishment didn't just embrace him; they admired and even loved him. He felt like nothing could stop his ascent.

Nothing, that is, except for one little secret.

U.S. Capitol
Washington, D.C.
August 3, 1948

The freshman Republican from California had been in Congress for less than two years. He'd been sent to Washington through the hard work of small-business owners, ranchers, and bankers who had drafted him to run and represent California's 12th District.

He was an odd choice. He certainly did not look the part of a typical congressman. His most noticeable features were his prominent jowls, bushy eyebrows shadowing his small darting eyes, and an omnipresent five o'clock shadow.

But Richard Milhous Nixon was a bright man, and an ambitious one. He was looking for a chance to excel and move up the ladder. Sitting on the House Un-American Activities Committee, which was set up to investigate whether communists had infiltrated the U.S. government, Nixon thought he might very well have found that chance.

Along with the rest of the country, Nixon had been startled by allegations made a few days earlier by Elizabeth Bentley, a former Soviet spy. The attractive blonde testified that she had been a courier for a Communist Party spy ring in the 1930s and 1940s, and that the ring included key members of the U.S government. She said that her involvement with the Soviet espionage ring was so integral to their plans that the Soviets had made efforts to take her life. Her testimony caused a sensation in the press, emboldened congressional investigators convinced that communists had infiltrated the government, and put the administration of Franklin Roosevelt's successor, Harry S. Truman, on the defensive.

Nixon, like other members of the committee, knew they needed a second source for the allegations. Bentley had, after all, admitted to being a communist herself, so her credibility was very much in doubt.

At today's hearing, Nixon believed they just might get that corroboration.

Whittaker Chambers was not an ideal witness. He was short and plump and unattractive. He was also an admitted communist, though he told the committee that he had broken with the ideology in the 1930s, at which point he had defected to U.S. authorities. Now, working as an editor for *Time* magazine, Chambers had a reputation for being intelligent and accomplished. Sitting in front of the committee, he corroborated Bentley's testimony and provided further names.

Among those names was one in particular that shocked the committee: Alger Hiss, a former State Department official currently serving as president of the Carnegie Foundation.

The story Chambers told was persuasive: Shortly after moving to Washington following his graduation from Harvard, Hiss had become a member of a discussion group organized by Harold Ware, a member of the Communist Party. But, in reality, Chambers told investigators, it was much more than a discussion group; it was also engaged in advancing the communist agenda. Although Ware died in a car crash, the group's activities continued and, according to Chambers, involved individuals in numerous federal agencies. Chambers claimed that he got to know Hiss and his wife, Priscilla, while living rent-free in an apartment owned by Hiss.

Chambers acknowledged he previously had given names of communists to federal authorities after his defection to the United States.

"Did you name Hiss?" Richard Nixon asked.

"Yes," Chambers replied.

"Mr. Chambers, were you informed of any action that was taken as a result of your report?"

"No. There was none."

The revelation infuriated Nixon. It was clear to him that the State Department and the Washington establishment had been protecting Alger Hiss all along. He was, after all, one of their own.

A Few Hours Later
Washington, D.C.
August 3, 1948

"I don't know Chambers."

Learning of the allegations made against him, Alger Hiss was indignant—and convincing. "There is no basis for his statements about me," he told reporters who called after the hearing.

Sitting in his office and contemplating his course, he barely had a moment of quiet to think things through. The phone rang constantly. His many friends in Washington were calling to check in. Former Undersecretary of State Dean Acheson and former first lady Eleanor Roosevelt had rung. Now his old mentor, the man to whom he owed his entire career, was on the line.

"Let the matter drop. If it was a lie, then why should you address it and give it more credibility?" asked Justice Frankfurter. Hiss knew he had a point. Everyone else who had been named as a communist had pled the Fifth and declined to testify.

Hiss said, "I have no reason to beat around the bush. That's what guilty people do. I'm an innocent man. I don't know who this Whittaker Chambers is and why he has gone to such lengths to smear me. He's a troubled soul, that much is obvious. But I cannot tolerate such things being said about me."

"Well, Alger, whatever you need, know that I will always vouch for you," Frankfurter reassured him.

After they hung up, Hiss dashed off a telegram to be wired to the committee immediately:

I DO NOT KNOW MR. CHAMBERS AND, SO FAR AS I AM AWARE, HAVE NEVER LAID EYES ON HIM. THERE IS NO BASIS FOR THE STATEMENTS ABOUT ME MADE TO YOUR COMMITTEE. . . . I WOULD FURTHER APPRECIATE THE OPPORTUNITY OF APPEARING BEFORE YOUR COMMITTEE.

It was not long before his request was granted.

U.S. Capitol
Washington, D.C.
August 5, 1948

It had been just forty-eight hours since Whittaker Chambers had sworn an oath and made his allegations. Hiss was eager, even thrilled, to be given the chance to respond. He would show his accusers that the reputation he had worked so hard to build could not be pulled apart by a former communist with a clear agenda.

Alger Hiss walked into the hearing room looking like a poster child for establishment elegance. Dressed in a gray suit and dark tie, a white pocket square carefully tucked into his breast pocket, he stood up straight and walked with a purpose. He knew that his résumé had entered the room before him and would underscore every word he'd utter. Johns Hopkins University. *Harvard Law Review*. A Supreme Court clerk, New Deal lawyer, and senior official in the U.S. Department of State. Now he was the president of the Carnegie Foundation for International Peace and, according to some whispers, a future candidate for secretary of state.

With a studied sense of command, impeccable manners, and graceful carriage, Hiss made it clear that he had come this morning before the HUAC to rebut the allegations made by this Chambers character, a man who, he repeatedly assured his questioners, he had never known.

Karl Mundt, a forty-eight-year-old Republican congressman from South Dakota, administered the standard oath to Hiss, asking if he would tell "the truth, the whole truth and nothing but the truth."

"So help me God," Hiss replied. Then, with a voice that had the power of a thunderclap, he said those words again.

"So help me God."

Hiss knew how to take over a meeting, and this one would be no different. As he settled into the witness chair, behind a pair of large microphones, his voice was assured, confident, and resolute. He had worked on his opening remarks with his brother and several prominent Washington attorneys, yet the illusion was what was most important. These were meant to be the indignant words, all but spontaneously uttered, by the wrongfully accused.

Hiss was so confident in himself and his message that he appeared before the HUAC without the benefit of counsel. He sat alone to face the lions—though, he thought, if they were lions, they were toothless ones. He could not have been less intimidated by the blowhard members of the HUAC; he'd had tougher bouts with faculty members at Harvard. In fact, the committee itself had been under pressure from the media and the left for months, most recently over its clumsy investigation into Hollywood. According to reports, Truman's White House counsel already had a bill in his desk drawer to abolish the committee if the Democrats reclaimed the House in the 1948 elections. HUAC needed a win, and they believed that Whittaker Chambers's bombshell of testimony a few days earlier would help them get it.

But the doughy, tentative Chambers was not the sort of witness who would have carried much weight at the Carnegie Foundation, or before the Supreme Court, or at Harvard. Hiss almost felt sorry for him. His allegations would collapse so long as Hiss looked forthright and credible. He'd been impressing sharper, more important men than the ones on this committee all his life.

"I am not and never have been a member of the Communist Party," he said firmly. Nor, to the best of his knowledge, were any of his friends or his wife. "I think I would know," he added.

In regards to Whittaker Chambers, Hiss reiterated that he'd never even *met* a man going by that name, but insisted that he would like the opportunity to do so. "The very name of Whittaker Chambers means nothing to me," he assured Robert Stripling, the committee's chief investigator.

Mundt seemed particularly concerned about the prominent role Hiss played at the Yalta Conference, which had become a political hot potato. According to one theory, pro-communist advisors had manipulated the sickly, weak president to further their agenda. If Hiss was, in fact, a communist, that would explain a lot—such as why the United States had agreed to surrendering half of Europe to Soviet influence. But Hiss did not take the bait, instead making it clear to Mundt that he shared some of the congressman's anger over the fruits of Yalta.

As for Chambers's allegations, Hiss's rebuttal consisted of a powerful, sweeping set of denials to each and every charge hurled against him. He expressed his disappointment that the committee did not interview him privately before the ridiculous accusations were made in public. "Denials do not always catch up with charges," he gently reminded them.

As his testimony continued, Hiss noticed that Congressman John McDowell of Pennsylvania was among the first to begin looking sheepish. His reelection was not going well. The embattled congressman apologized for any damage done to Hiss, a man whom "many Americans, including members of this Committee, hold in high repute." Chairman Mundt also made the point of expressing his appreciation to Hiss for cooperating in such a forthright fashion.

Not to be outdone by either McDowell or Mundt, Mississippi Democrat John Rankin rushed from behind the dais and pushed his way through the crowd that had gathered around Hiss immediately after the committee adjourned. "Let me congratulate you on a performance unlike any we've seen in a decade," Rankin told Hiss, shaking his hand admiringly.

Hiss squeezed Rankin's hand firmly. Running over simple-minded politicians was as easy as he thought it would be.

Moments Later
U.S. Capitol
Washington, D.C.
August 5, 1948

Away from the microphones, there was no hiding from the truth: Richard Nixon knew that the hearing had gone terribly and that his colleagues on the committee were panicked.

Alger Hiss had, in a calm, controlled, and humorous demeanor, clearly carried the day inside and outside the committee room. He'd come off as a man with better things to do, yet someone who still performed his civic duty admirably.

Karl Mundt was among the first to buckle. "We've been had," he said, with a loud sigh. "We're ruined."

"We should just wash our hands of the whole mess," Louisiana

Democrat Eddie Hébert advised. "Cut our losses now. Let the Justice Department handle the cleanup."

Nearly all of the committee members agreed. Alger Hiss had gotten the best of them, and they knew they had better find something else soon to distract the public from this fiasco. It was the prevalent view, but it was not the only one.

Nixon had a different impression of Hiss's appearance than other committee members. He found the Ivy League elitist to be insolent and condescending. He was preoccupied with Hiss's answer to what seemed like a simple question: Who, Nixon had asked him, was involved in getting you to come to Washington in the first place?

Hiss's response had been smug: "I would rather limit myself than use names loosely before your committee as so many witnesses do."

After going back and forth with him on the point, Nixon had finally said, "I would like to have a direct answer to the question."

Hiss reluctantly complied, naming several members of Washington's establishment, including Justice Frankfurter. It had mollified Nixon, but only for the moment. Nixon believed that Hiss was playing with him. He could have answered the question easily the first time, but instead he seemed to enjoy making Nixon work for it. The man was so smug, so sure of himself, so utterly unfazed by the accusations against him, that it was all a little too perfect. Sure, there was manufactured outrage, he'd hit all the right notes, but none of it seemed quite real. There was, of course, also the matter of Whittaker Chambers's assertions. Everyone on the committee now seemed to be discounting them, but Chambers himself did not back down from his allegations in the slightest.

One of these two men—Chambers or Hiss—Nixon realized, was an accomplished liar. It gnawed at him that the Washington establishment was so quick to absolve a man who was part of their clique. How did they know with such conviction that Hiss was the one telling the truth?

"I understand the concerns being expressed," Nixon told his colleagues. "But retreating now would only make the committee look worse." He volunteered to personally take the lead on the investigation.

At this key juncture, with the future of the committee hanging in the balance, Robert Stripling, the committee's veteran investigator, spoke up and backed Nixon. Either Hiss or Chambers had lied under oath to a committee of the United States Congress. Stripling, like Nixon, strongly believed it was Hiss. There was something about the way he'd handled the questions, curiously hedging so many of his answers.

With Stripling's backing, Mundt agreed to take the freshman up on his offer to lead the investigation. Nixon's colleagues were visibly pleased by the decision, but Nixon knew they were thinking about themselves, not him. Nobody cared about throwing the ambitious but unknown young Californian to the wolves.

Roosevelt Hotel
New York City
August 8, 1948

It was troubling news. There was no doubt about it. If what Nixon's colleague from Wisconsin, Charles Kersten, had told him was true, then Nixon's hopes for the investigation, and his moment in the spotlight, were sure to be dashed.

A day earlier, Kersten learned that members of the Carnegie Foundation board were pressuring John Foster Dulles to issue a statement in support of Mr. Hiss. A titan of the Wall Street legal community, the Republican Party's éminence grise on foreign affairs, and a close advisor to the Dewey campaign, Dulles was widely expected to be sworn in as secretary of state once New York governor Thomas Dewey trounced Truman in the November presidential election. If Dulles came out in support of Hiss, it would mean the end of the investigation. No Republican in Congress would want to tangle with a party leader of Dulles's stature or come crosswise with the Dewey administration.

On the train from Washington to a New York City hotel, where they were set to meet with Dulles, Nixon and Kersten had fretted. What would they say to persuade him to stay out of this? What would they do if he refused?

In his suite at the Roosevelt Hotel, which served as "Dewey for President" headquarters, Dulles, joined by his brother Allan, welcomed the congressmen warmly and showed Kersten and Nixon to their seats. The Dulles brothers listened to Nixon's concerns carefully, and then both reviewed the transcripts of Chambers's original testimony.

Nixon and Kersten waited patiently on the sofa in silence. Minutes passed, then minutes more. Finally, John Foster Dulles put down the papers, rose from his chair, and folded his hands behind his back. Then he paced back and forth in front of the fireplace with his head down for what seemed like an eternity.

At last he stopped, his careful eyes turning toward Nixon and Kersten. "There's no question about it," Dulles concluded. "It's almost impossible to believe, but Chambers does appear to know Hiss."

Dulles told Nixon that he would not write a letter in support of Hiss and that it was, in fact, clear there was a real case against him. "In view of the facts Chambers has testified to, you'd be derelict in your duty as a congressman if you did not see the case through to a conclusion."

Nixon exhaled and smiled broadly. He was back in business.

Commodore Hotel
New York City
August 16, 1948

Situated conveniently adjacent to Grand Central Terminal, the Commodore was impressive in both scope and grace. One end of the hotel was specially stocked with telephones, stock tickers, even stenographers—everything busy men of affairs required.

Room 1400 of the Commodore became the HUAC's New York City headquarters. There, the Nixon subcommittee met, far away from the D.C. media frenzy, to further their investigation into Alger Hiss.

The first step, Nixon knew, was to prove that Hiss had lied in his August 5, 1948, testimony about ever knowing Whittaker Chambers.

Under questioning, Chambers gave Nixon and his colleagues extensive details about his relationship with the Hisses. He told them all about the times he had stayed with the family and he knew details like family nicknames, loan balances, and personal hobbies. He could even describe the cars parked in their family garage. The details about Hiss were so extensive that Chambers was either telling the truth or was a complete and total psychopath. Nixon talked with him long enough to conclude the latter wasn't likely. Sure, Chambers was an odd duck, but he didn't seem insane or delusional.

As Hiss entered the hotel room and sat before members of the subcommittee, Nixon still saw the same smug, self-satisfied man who'd bested them days earlier. But this time, Nixon was determined to reach a different outcome.

As the subcommittee grilled Hiss on the details that Chambers knew about him, Hiss began to backtrack ever so slightly. Now that he thought about it, he acknowledged, Nixon might be describing a man he had known as George Crosley when he'd been on detail from the Department of Agriculture to a U.S. Senate committee. But this Crosley, Hiss said, was nothing but a passing acquaintance. And Hiss would have to see him in person to know for sure if it was the same man.

Nixon watched as his colleague, John McDowell, leaned forward. "Mr. Hiss, have you ever seen a prothonotary warbler?"

It was not every day that a United States congressman asked a suspected communist about the sighting of a rare songbird, and Nixon was curious to see if Hiss would dodge it. "I have," Hiss replied, politely. "On the Potomac."

Nixon struggled to keep his expression blank. What Hiss did not know was that Chambers had told the committee that Hiss and his wife were bird-watchers who had gotten very excited about seeing that particular warbler—one of the rarest, most prized sightings by mid-Atlantic birders. Only someone very intimate with Hiss and his wife—certainly more intimate than a passing acquaintance like "George Crosley" had been—would have known this and many other small details about Hiss's private life.

Nixon marveled that even as Hiss's lie about Chambers began to unravel, he remained a picture of absolute grace and calm. He seemed wholly unflappable—and that gave Richard Nixon an idea.

24 Hours Later
Commodore Hotel
New York City

For once, Alger Hiss could not conceal his fury. The bastards had lied to him! They were trying to trap him. Someone—probably that beady-eyed character Nixon—had already leaked his testimony to the morning's newspapers, all carefully slanted to make his answers look suspicious.

Hiss had been called back to the Commodore less than a day after he'd spoken with the subcommittee to meet privately with Nixon, McDowell, and one other person. Perhaps, Hiss surmised, this was an effort to apologize for the leak and to make some sort of amends.

Hiss entered Room 1400 and stopped dead in his tracks. In the suite were investigative staff members, plus a stenographer to transcribe every word he uttered. The congressmen hadn't told Hiss he'd actually be returning for a formal appearance. Nor had they mentioned that the "other person" in attendance was in fact Whittaker Chambers himself.

Almost before he knew what was happening, Hiss was formally sworn in again.

Nixon explained that it was important to the subcommittee to determine whether Chambers and Crosley were one and the same person before proceeding any further in a public forum.

"I'm not prepared to testify," Hiss protested. He lashed out at the congressmen, accusing them of leaking his previous day's testimony to the press. He was so animated that at one point, a committee staffer, concerned Hiss might strike Chambers, grabbed him by the arm.

After much back and forth, Hiss finally acknowledged that he did know Chambers, but only as George Crosley. In response, Chambers replied that he had never assumed such an identity.

When Chambers identified Hiss for the record as the man who he had known as a member of the Communist Party, Hiss took the opportunity to go on the offensive. He knew that Chambers had been given immunity for his testimony to the committee and he used it against them.

"May I say for the record at this point, that I would like to invite

Mr. Whittaker Chambers to make those same statements out of the presence of this committee and without those statements being privileged from a lawsuit for libel." Then his eyes locked directly on to his accuser. "I challenge you to do it, and hope you will do it damned quickly."

U.S. Capitol
Washington, D.C.
August 25, 1948

The morning portended another Washington summer scorcher. The mercury already registered 93 degrees and, although Congress had long since recessed for the summer, the Caucus Room was packed. The Chambers-Hiss duel had won national headlines, with supporters on both sides of the case absolutely convinced of the others' mendacity. Twelve hundred people watched the hearing live, while many others lingered in the hallway, hoping to overhear scraps of testimony.

In the middle of everything, like a conductor and his orchestra, was the freshman congressman Richard M. Nixon.

At 10:30 A.M., the committee was gaveled to order. Unlike his earlier appearance, this time Hiss arrived with his lawyer. He and Chambers were asked to rise and face one another. Hiss, clad in an impeccably tailored light gray suit and a striped tie, could not hide his disdain.

Stripling asked Hiss whether he had ever seen Chambers. Hiss replied that he had known Chambers, but only as "Crosley," and had not seen him since 1935.

Stripling then turned to Chambers. "Have you ever seen this man?" the investigator intoned. Chambers identified Hiss and said they had last seen each other in 1938.

With that, both witnesses were asked to sit.

The hearing quickly turned into a detailed examination of leases and automobile loans as the committee tried to ascertain how well Hiss had really known Chambers. Hiss, who had not been able to identify anyone else who had known Chambers as "Crosley," objected. "The important charges are not questions of leases, but questions of whether I was a Communist," he said.

But Nixon refused to let Hiss set the terms of inquisition. Not this time.

"The issue in this hearing today is whether Mr. Hiss or Mr. Chambers has committed perjury before this committee, as well as whether Mr. Hiss is a Communist," Nixon retorted. If Hiss had lied about such details, it would of course raise serious questions about what he was attempting to cover up.

Some committee members could barely contain their incredulity over Hiss's story. Eddie Hébert, the Louisiana congressman who had previously wanted the committee to cut its losses, now wondered aloud how Hiss could claim to barely know "Crosley" when the testimony clearly showed that Hiss had had a close relationship with him.

Congressman Mundt was even more direct. "You knew this man," he told Hiss. "You knew him very well. You knew him so well that you even trusted him with your apartment; you let him use your furniture; you let him use or gave him your automobile. You think you *probably* took him to New York. You bought him lunches in the Senate restaurant. You had him staying in your home . . . and you made a series of small loans to him. There seems no question about that."

Hiss's defense rested chiefly on the opinions of others. He produced the names of thirty-four patriotic Americans in good standing who had volunteered to testify as to his impeccable character and loyalty. On the list were two members of the Senate and three former secretaries of state. Hiss reminded the HUAC that Chambers, by contrast, was "a self-confessed liar, spy and traitor." Hiss then read a number of questions regarding Chambers's background that he hoped the committee would ask. Finally, he repeated his previous challenge to Chambers: *Level your allegations outside of a setting in which you are immune from prosecution, so that I can sue you for libel.*

Despite Hiss's attempts at regaining control, the hearing went terribly for him. This time it was Chambers who supplied the steady, calm presence. Hiss was a devoted and "romantic communist," Chambers told the HUAC. No, he did not hate Hiss; in fact, Hiss had been the closest friend he'd had in the Communist Party.

"We are caught in a tragedy of history," Chambers told the committee. "Mr. Hiss represents the concealed enemy against which we are all fighting. I have testified against him with remorse and pity, but in a moment of historic jeopardy in which this nation now stands, so help me God, I could not do otherwise."

As candid as Chambers had been with the HUAC, he had not told them everything he knew.

Not even close.

Washington, D.C.
September 3, 1948

Alger Hiss had no choice. Once Whittaker Chambers publicly accused him of being a communist on a television program, he had to make good on his threat.

Hiss informed his attorney to file suit against Chambers for libel. He then immediately made his lawsuit public. Would a guilty man really file suit against his accuser?

As part of the lawsuit, Hiss's lawyers requested any documents sent by any member of the Hiss family to Chambers. It was an audacious move designed to further demonstrate his legendary self-confidence—after all, if he was requesting these documents then could they really contain anything nefarious?

But somewhere in his back of his mind, even Alger Hiss wondered if this was a step too far.

Alexandria, Virginia
December 1, 1948

As his wife packed for their upcoming vacation in Panama, Richard Nixon caught sight of a column in the *Washington Post*. "Startling" information had apparently been unearthed and handed to investigators that would reveal which party in the Hiss-Chambers affair was lying.

Nixon picked up a telephone and reached Stripling. "What the hell is this about?" He told Stripling he was heading into the office right away. Chambers had been a cooperative witness, and Nixon had de-

fended attacks on his credibility, but Nixon sensed he was holding
something back.

Nixon met Stripling right at the front door to their office. "What the
hell does Chambers have?" Nixon snapped, tossing the *Post* on the desk.

Stripling's face was white. "I've been asking around. Looks like
Chambers left out some very material facts in his testimony before us."

"Like what?"

"Like that Hiss was a lot more than just a communist; he was a
spy—and he took documents." He paused. "Maybe you better put your
vacation plans on hold, Dick."

Nixon scowled, immediately recognizing their dilemma. Chambers
told the committee he had never committed espionage against the government. But if he had taken possession of classified documents stolen
from the U.S. government and worked with Hiss as a courier, that
would turn out to be a lie and damage his own credibility. On the other
hand, if Chambers's paperwork proved that Hiss was giving secret
documents to the communists, Hiss would be on the hook for treason.

As the two men deliberated their next steps, they were visited by
Nicholas Vazzana, a lawyer for Whittaker Chambers. He had seen the
paper, too, and wanted to have an opportunity to speak for his client.

"Congressman Nixon," Vazzana said, "I'm here to help clarify a few
things on Whittaker's behalf."

Nixon turned to the lawyer in a fury. "Is this story true?" he demanded. "What's your client been holding back from us? What the hell
is going on?"

"There are documents pertaining to the case," Vazzana said in a calm
and deliberate voice. "I'm afraid I'm under an admonition from the Justice Department not to discuss their contents."

Nixon and Stripling would have none of that, and for over an hour
they kept pressing the lawyer to divulge more.

"Well, Congressman, the fact of the matter is that Mr. Hiss's lawyers
demanded that my client provide proof of his accusations."

"Well, we've all demanded that!" Nixon countered.

"The lawyers also asked Mr. Chambers specifically if he had any
documents in his possession." Vazzana paused. "No one on the committee asked my client that question."

Stripling looked incredulous. "Oh, that's bull!"

"But the answer to that question," Vazzana continued, "is yes." The documents had, in fact, been turned over to the Truman Justice Department weeks earlier. The department had done nothing with them. In fact, someone had leaked to the press that Justice was preparing to drop their inquiry into the allegations against Hiss altogether. *Those deceitful bastards!* Nixon raged. *It's a classic cover-up!*

Nixon was furious. Chambers had lied to him. And he was a damned fool for giving the documents to the Democrats. "Does he have anything else? What the hell do we do now?"

"I don't know. You'll have to talk to my client."

Stripling and Nixon drove in almost complete silence to meet with Chambers. Nixon wasn't sure what he was going to say to Chambers when he saw him. He was so sick and tired of the case—the heat he'd taken from the press and the Democrats, the bullshit answers he was getting from Hiss, and now Chambers. Part of him wanted to throw in the towel, but something convinced him to pay Chambers one more visit.

They arrived at his house in Westminster, Maryland, sixty-five miles from Washington, D.C. Chambers greeted them politely, but Nixon was in no mood for small talk.

"I can't believe you gave all your documents to the Democrats," Nixon thundered. "How could you be so foolish? They'll probably destroy them!"

Chambers tried to calm him. "I'm not so stupid," he replied. "I only gave them copies. And I also didn't give them everything I have."

"What do you mean?"

"I have other documents. Important ones," Chambers said. "I held on to them just in case the department decided to suppress the ones I gave them."

On the drive back to Washington from Chambers's farm, Nixon turned to Stripling. "Well," said the congressman, "what do you think he's got?"

"I don't know," said Stripling, "but whatever he has will blow the dome off the Capitol."

New York City
December 3, 1948

Richard Nixon arrived in New York for another hearing with Whittaker
Chambers.

Stripling had sent two HUAC investigators to Chambers's farm,
where Chambers showed them what he had not disclosed to Hiss's
lawyers, or to the Justice Department. In the darkness of the late
evening, guided only by the dim glow of his porch lights, Chambers
led the investigators to a strawberry patch that had a pumpkin vine
growing across it. Chambers crouched down and examined a pumpkin, and then another, until he found the one he had hollowed out
the day before. Pulling its top off, he said, "Here is what you're looking for."

Inside the pumpkin, protected by wax paper and metal cans, were
rolls of microfilm containing additional State Department and Navy
Department documents—documents that Chambers said Hiss had
provided to him. Fearing that Hiss's legal team or communist allies
might raid the farm, Chambers had been moving the microfilm from
one hiding place to another until he had finally settled on the inside of
a pumpkin.

The revelation propelled Nixon to the forefront of media attention.
Before hordes of photographers, he and Stripling were photographed
looking at the film with a magnifying glass. The photo had been
staged—it was impossible to read the film with a magnifying glass—but
that didn't matter, the public was hooked.

Grand Jury Room
U.S. Courthouse
Foley Square, New York City
December 15, 1949

The Justice Department could no longer ignore Alger Hiss. He had
been summoned multiple times over the previous week to testify before a grand jury looking into claims of espionage. The FBI had found

Hiss's old Underwood typewriter, and now their expert was telling the grand jury members that it was the exact machine on which the stolen documents had been typed.

When asked how it came to be that secret U.S. government documents that had been typed on the machine in question had fallen into Chambers's possession, Hiss's charm and eloquence finally seemed to fail him. "Until the day I die," he said, "I shall wonder how Whittaker Chambers got into my house to use my typewriter."

Two Years Later
Federal Detention Center
New York City
March 22, 1951

Alger Hiss arrived at the same federal courthouse where he had been tried and convicted on two counts of perjury. It had been more than a year since he'd been sentenced, but he was allowed to remain free while his appeal worked its way to the U.S. Supreme Court.

Ten days earlier, the same Court for which Hiss once clerked had denied his final appeal, exhausting his legal remedies.

Hiss managed a smile or two, but otherwise showed little emotion as federal marshals placed handcuffs on him and led him away to his new life behind bars. He planned to maintain his complete and total innocence and continue to insist he was just a scapegoat. That was essential to his post-prison plans for rehabilitation and also part of his strategy for surviving his sentence. Hiss knew that his audience was no longer the public, or a jury, but an altogether different constituency—one where communist spies were not looked upon favorably.

Arriving at the federal detention center in New York City, where he was to be held and processed before arriving at his final destination at the United States Penitentiary in Lewisburg, Pennsylvania, Hiss felt like an animal in a zoo. Iron cages with bars on the sides and top. Double-decker bunks with naked lightbulbs protruding from the ceiling. It was just like in the movies.

It was here that Hiss soon met a man he knew only as "Danny F."

Neither Hiss nor Danny enjoyed the casual chatter of the lonely men who would talk to anyone about anything, so they wound up mostly talking to each other. A member of an organized crime syndicate, this was not Danny's first time in prison, and he imparted lots of advice to Hiss about relating to the other inmates. But of all the tips he gave Hiss, one would stand out as the most important of all: "When you get to Lewisburg, ask for Mike M.

"Tell him I sent you."

Lewisburg Penitentiary
Lewisburg, Pennsylvania
Spring 1951

Nestled near Bucknell University on 950 rolling acres of central Pennsylvania farmland, Lewisburg Penitentiary was a massive brick structure with thirty-foot concrete walls and watchtowers at each corner. Alger Hiss was allowed, as all inmates with good behavior generally were, to reside in an "honors" section where cell doors were unlocked, allowing free movement within the block.

Danny's instructions to Hiss to introduce himself to "Mike M." became a "survive in jail" card. Mike, it turned out, was one of Lewisburg's leading inmates, and the head of the Italian-American population there. Hiss carefully observed him and the other Italian-American inmates, most of whom were incarcerated for activities related to organized crime. Their general attitude reminded Hiss of what he knew about prisoners of war: Once released, they'd go right back to the same thing they were doing before their imprisonment. Jail was merely an occupational hazard.

Just as if he were walking into the Carnegie Foundation's boardroom, Hiss went to work immediately. First, he ingratiated himself with the organized crime community. He was also unfailingly respectful and polite to prison authorities, as well as to fellow prisoners. He avoided discussing his own case and avoided other "political" prisoners, such as those sentenced under the Smith Act, which made it illegal to advocate for the overthrow of the United States government. By design, he would become a regular guy, never complaining and taking his sentence like a man. Hiss knew that shifting audiences meant shifting tactics.

Hiss was also extremely generous with his time. He tutored one inmate to read and, as a lawyer, he was in constant demand from others to render advice and review legal documents. This put him in some jeopardy with prison authorities, but Hiss generally managed to stay on their good side by charming them as successfully as he had charmed most of the powerful people he'd encountered in his life.

Mike eventually asked for Hiss's legal advice, and then ended up trusting him so much that he referred Hiss to mob boss Frank Costello. Once Hiss met with Costello he cemented himself with the Italian-Americans—and that relationship paid off quickly. When a prison guard suggested to a couple of them that someone should "do something" about that traitor Hiss, Mike made sure that no one acted on it.

Hiss also enjoyed showing off his well-honed oratory talents. Inmates at Lewisburg were given the opportunity as part of their rehabilitation to take part in debates with local college students. Hiss trounced his Bucknell opponents so soundly that they barred him from any further appearances.

Lewisburg Penitentiary
Lewisburg, Pennsylvania
November 27, 1954

It had been three and a half years since Alger Hiss first entered the Lewisburg Penitentiary. Some days had been better than others, but today—his last as a federal prisoner—was the one he had been looking forward to for all that time.

"I am very glad to use this chance," Hiss said to a crowd of about seventy reporters who were waiting for him just outside the prison walls, "to reassert my complete innocence of the charges that were brought against me by Whittaker Chambers." Already beginning to cast himself as a political martyr, he added, "I have had to wait in silence

while, in my absence, a myth has been developed. I hope that the return
of the mere man will help to dispel the myth."

In a sense, Lewisburg had been a test run for Alger: an experiment of
sorts. He had learned to develop a persona that would keep him safe in
federal prison. Now he would develop a persona that would convince the
public he was exactly the opposite of what he really was: a man who had
spied on his country on behalf of one of history's most brutal and totali-
tarian dictatorships. Hiss knew this would require showing people what
they wanted to see, and telling them what they wanted to hear. And he
would need plenty of allies. His family, friends, and any others he could
recruit would all need to become accomplices to his grand scheme.

Upon his release, Hiss's wife, Priscilla, wanted them to move away.
Change their names. Forget their past. But Alger was not about to lie
low and fade away into history.

The case of Alger Hiss had ended in the American legal system. But
in the American political system, it was just beginning.

Princeton University
April 26, 1956

The public interest was intense. When five hundred press credentials
were requested, the university intervened, declaring that Alger Hiss's
talk would last thirty minutes, including questions, and that only two
hundred students and fifty reporters could attend.

This was to be Hiss's first public appearance since being released
from prison, and every reporter in America seemed intent on being
there. It was just as Hiss had guessed. He had lost his law license,
and was effectively blackballed from meaningful work, but he saw the
Princeton invite as an opportunity to begin propelling his rehabilitation
strategy forward.

The invitation from Princeton came from a student group that
had invited a number of widely known public figures to address "The
Meaning of Geneva," a reference to the 1955 U.S.-Soviet disarmament
conference that had taken place in Switzerland. When the group announced that Hiss would attend its meeting, there was a hue and cry

from the Princeton faithful. *A convicted perjurer is attempting to use Princeton's prestige to restore his reputation!* The university's administration, while opposed to the appearance, defended the right of its students to invite Hiss, despite alumni displeasure.

Hiss dined at the home of his friend, Princeton history professor Elmer Beller, before the address. After supper, Hiss, Beller, and a few others followed a police escort through a horde of protesting American Legion members and alumni to Whig Hall. Papier-mâché pumpkins, anti-Hiss signs, and other artwork decrying the "Traitor Hiss" had decorated the campus all day.

When it was all over, not much had changed. Hiss knew his remarks that evening had been fairly dull. He was frustrated; his plans for a comeback had not progressed at all in the short time since his release. The conditions were not right, he reasoned. The court system had afforded him due process and Hiss had been convicted. Authorities and "the system" were still respected in America.

But he knew that would change. It always did. And once that happened, he would be ready to take full advantage.

18 Years Later
Baltimore, Maryland
May 21, 1974

Standing before the crowd at Johns Hopkins, Alger Hiss was resplendent in a three-piece suit. Carrying an unlit pipe in his hand, he was in a buoyant mood—and not just because he was being well received by his alma mater.

Richard Nixon, his old nemesis, was now knee-deep in a scandal of epic proportions. Nixon's veracity and credibility were being questioned—and not just over Watergate, but over everything in his life, including his legendary prosecution of Alger Hiss. In a sense, the Hiss case became a cause célèbre among liberals eager to further demonize Nixon and the Republicans. Alger Hiss had protested his innocence from the outset, never wavering. Now more and more people were beginning to believe him.

Hiss spoke at Johns Hopkins for forty-five minutes—touching on revelations from newly released tapes in which President Nixon talked to aide John Dean about his case. "Then we worked that thing," Nixon told Dean. "We then got the evidence, we got the typewriter, we got the 'pumpkin papers.' The FBI did not cooperate. The Justice Department did not cooperate."

Some who heard Nixon's words believed he was reveling in past triumphs. But to others, especially to those who were inclined to suspect the worst about everything Nixon said, the president was all but confessing that he'd tampered with the Hiss case for political fame.

Hiss, of course, preferred the latter version of events, and he worked the partisan crowd, filled with antiwar and anti-Nixon lefties, to that end. He was a victim of government persecution, he claimed, "forgery by typewriter." Nixon was a modern-day Inspector Javert, determined to ruin a good man.

When asked if he was bitter toward Nixon, Hiss took the high road. "No one who did unkind things to me was the cause for bitterness," he said. "Chambers was out of his head and Nixon was a man on the up escalator."

Then, in a clear, steady voice, he added, "None of what went on was justified. It was all hyped up for political purposes. There was certainly no domestic threat of communism."

Alger Hiss left the stage that night more triumphant than he'd been in years. Things were finally going his way.

Boston, Massachusetts
August 5, 1975

A unanimous decision by the Massachusetts Supreme Judicial Court concluded that, despite his conviction for perjury, Alger Hiss had demonstrated the "moral and intellectual fitness" required to be an attorney at law. Supported by prominent leftists across the country, he was readmitted to the Massachusetts bar.

Hiss was the first lawyer to have been reinstated in the commonwealth's history. More important to him, however, was the tacit nod of approval this action gave to his character. It was, to Hiss, one more important rung in his climb back to social prominence.

Pittsburgh, Pennsylvania
October 8, 1975

"I was just the right size," Hiss told students at the University of Pittsburgh, nodding in agreement, as he outlined the conservatives' conspiracy against him. "I had been at Yalta, which people regarded as very sinister. I had worked in the United Nations. I also think some of the people who found me a communist thought I was Jewish."

There was no question about it any longer: Thanks to Richard Nixon, Alger Hiss was a hit on college campuses.

Brimming with confidence, Hiss needled Nixon's successor, whose approval ratings had plummeted after issuing Nixon a pardon over Watergate. Hiss claimed he had contacted the *New York Times* to offer a statement: "If Mr. Ford is so handy with pardons, I'd be glad to get one—not on the basis of clemency, but on the basis of miscarriage of justice."

17 Years Later
New York City
October 29, 1992

The polished voice of Alger Hiss had not waned after eighty-two years. And he still had much to say. "It won't settle things for people I've regarded as prejudiced from the beginning," he told a reporter, "but I think this is a final verdict on the thing."

The report from General Dmitri Volkogonov, chairman of the military intelligence archives of the new post-Soviet government, was unequivocal: "Not a single document—and a great amount of materials have been studied—substantiates the allegation that Mr. A. Hiss collaborated with the intelligence services of the Soviet Union." Volkogonov added that the espionage accusations against Hiss were "completely groundless."

Some Americans found the revelation as shocking as it was curious.

How could one man have possibly seen all of the intelligence of the bureaucratic and bloated Soviet government that had been gathered over six decades?

Hiss had little interest in questions like that. He was surprised and delighted by the unexpected stroke of good luck. "Rationally, I realized time was running out, and that the correction of Chambers's charges might not come about in my lifetime," he said. "But inside I was sure somehow that I would be vindicated."

That feeling did not last for long.

New York City
October 23, 1993

Maria Schmidt, a Hungarian historian who had been researching the work of the dreaded Hungarian secret police, turned over the documents to Cold War scholars. Looking through the once-restricted files of the Interior Ministry, she discovered a thick dossier of documents that included the statements of a Soviet spy named Noel Field.

According to the documents, Field, an American who had worked with Alger Hiss at the State Department, told Hungarian authorities that Hiss had recruited him as a spy. Field had called Hiss a friend and trusted confidant, one of his greatest accomplices in the communist underground. Another document described Field's view of Hiss's self-assured testimony to HUAC:

> *Alger defended himself . . . with great intelligence. He had been trained as a lawyer and knew all the phrases and tricks. I, on the other hand, had no such experience. . . . I did not trust myself to stand before my accusers and shout "innocent" in their faces. . . . I also understood the same from a short letter from Hiss, who obviously could not write openly.*

The revelations stunned even the most hardened Hiss defenders, especially as another major defender of the story began to crumble. General Dmitri Volkogonov, who had offered confident assurances of Hiss's innocence only a year earlier, was now changing his tune. He had only seen selected archives, he confessed, explaining that many other files probably had been destroyed in the Stalin era.

But the new allegations did not faze Alger Hiss. He continued to proclaim his innocence to anyone who would listen. The Field documents, Hiss claimed, were invalid because Field, who was in Hungarian custody during the Stalinist-era purges, had made his statements under obvious duress.

EPILOGUE

New York City
November 15, 1996

Alger Hiss died at the age of ninety-two, but that did not stop the debate over his guilt—especially in the media. In its eulogy, the *New York Times* labeled Hiss "the erudite diplomat and Harvard-trained government lawyer." It called his conviction for perjury "one of the great riddles of the Cold War."

The Associated Press published an obituary that cited General Dmitri Volkogonov's earlier proclamation of Hiss's innocence, without noting that the general had later backtracked on his statements. *NBC Nightly News* followed suit, with Tom Brokaw saying, "Hiss considered vindication a declaration by a Russian general, who controlled the KGB archives, saying that Hiss had never been a spy. Alger Hiss, dead tonight at age 92."

Media aside, all reasonable questions about Hiss's guilt were laid to rest right alongside him. In 1994, the State Department had made public an internal security probe of Hiss done nearly five decades earlier. The probe found that he had taken highly classified documents on matters of national security that were of great interest to the Soviets, for which he was not authorized. Hiss had quietly resigned after the investigation was completed.

Earlier in 1996, the National Security Agency made public a decrypted transcript of a Soviet cable describing a Soviet spy serving in the American delegation known as "Ales." But it was the agency's three-word annotation that garnered everyone's attention: "Probably

Alger Hiss." The transcripts were from a large collection of coded Soviet cables, known as Venona, which the NSA had broken years ago,
but which were not declassified until the 1990s. All told they identified
349 citizens and others legally residing in the United States who had
worked for Soviet intelligence. "Ales" was prominent among them, and
the details about this man's activities and life fit Hiss's nearly perfectly.

Not only had the U.S. government *not* framed Alger Hiss, but it had,
in fact, covered up the most damning evidence against him for at least
twenty-five years after making the determination that "Ales" and Hiss
were the same person.

Until Venona, Hiss had been able to use others as a shield. He
claimed their class prejudices, their political views, their family ties, all
blinded them to the overwhelming evidence of his innocence. But as
the *Wall Street Journal* noted, after Venona, the only people still proclaiming Hiss's innocence were those who would not be convinced
even had he personally confessed.

New York City
April 2007

On its website, CBS News trumpeted the headline "Author: Hiss Innocent of Espionage." The network, long suspected of left-wing bias, had
covered a daylong symposium at New York University, where one panelist
claimed Hiss had been confused with another State Department official.

Alger Hiss's stepson, who was also on the panel, claimed that there
was another motive entirely for Chambers's accusations against his
stepfather. "It is my conviction that Whittaker Chambers was in love
with Alger Hiss, that he was rejected by Alger Hiss and he took that
rejection in a vindictive way."

He offered no discernible proof for the assertion.

The willful suspension of disbelief over the motivations and
dangers—even the very existence—of America's sworn enemies continued virtually unabated, a trend that would continue to pose serious
threats to America's safety in the years ahead.

9

The City of Tomorrow:
Walt Disney's Last and Lost Dream

If I could live for another fifteen years, I could surpass everything else I'd
ever done.

—Walt Disney, 1966, days before his death

Anaheim, California
July 18, 1955

It was a disaster.

Horrified, Walt Disney read through review after awful review of the
private opening of the Disneyland Theme Park in the morning papers.
The complaints went on and on: Oppressive heat had caused women's
heels to become stuck in the newly poured asphalt; the roads around
the park were gridlocked for hours; some newspapers even accused
them of turning off the water fountains so that visitors would have to
buy Pepsi, one of the park's sponsors.

That last charge, in particular, infuriated Walt. The truth was that
they'd run out of time to connect all the water lines. The engineers told
him that he had to make a choice: the toilets or the fountains. "People
can buy Pepsi Cola but they can't pee in the street," Walt muttered
aloud as he read.

He closed his eyes and rubbed his temples. He had been so busy scurrying from one part of the park to the other that he hadn't noticed any of the glitches the critics were now having so much fun with. He could barely stand to read any more. *Oh, how the board must be loving this,* he thought. *Lillian, too. Even Roy. They'll all say "I told you so."*

But, of course, they would all be wrong. Walt knew that. Deep inside, he knew it. Yes, there were problems, but he had seen the wonderment in the eyes of the kids, and, more important, in the eyes of their parents.

So yes, some things needed to be fixed, but the park was inviting, friendly, and clean. No cigarette butt lasted thirty seconds on the ground before an employee swept it up. He saw to that. And the atmosphere of the place—magical, infused with a sense of optimism and idealism—was the embodiment of the American Dream itself.

No. He wasn't going to let some two-bit critics get to him. It was easy to hide behind a printing press, but the only people that mattered were the families who would visit. This, after all, was for them. "Disneyland is *your* land," he'd said to the crowd in his opening address. "Here, age relives fond memories of the past, and here youth may savor the challenge and promise of the future. Disneyland is dedicated to the ideals, the dreams, and the hard facts that have created America, with the hope that it will be a source of joy and inspiration to all the world."

It wasn't just a speech—he truly believed those words. Even after the previous day's fiasco, he was more certain about Disneyland than he ever had been before.

But somewhere in the back of his mind, Walt knew that Disneyland, even once perfected, wouldn't be quite enough. The park personified the dream of a utopia but, more and more, Walt Disney wanted to build a real one.

40 Years Earlier
A Farm near Kansas City, Missouri
1915

Farming did not come naturally to Walt. The imaginative teenager found the work to be monotonous and the isolation to be difficult.

Then there were the animals. He kept growing attached to the pigs and cows that were soon to be slaughtered.

But worst of all was his very own father, Elias. Sure, Walt wasn't the best farmer. His mind was not always on the corn that needed plowing, or the cows that needed milking—but none of that justified his father's bursts of violence against him.

The only thing that thirteen-year-old Walt looked forward to during his days on the farm was that he had plenty of time to think. And to dream. He used the long hours to imagine a place as different from the farm as possible.

Walt picked up the bucket of fresh milk and walked toward the barn door.

"Hey, brother."

Lost in his own thoughts, the voice jolted him back to reality. Roy stood in the doorway, his features darkened by the bright sun behind him.

Although Roy Disney was nine years older than Walt, his features very much resembled his younger brother's—both had long, narrow faces and eyes that almost hid in a squint. But, unlike Walt, Roy was reserved, always quiet and low-key. Though his devotion to his family home was questionable—Roy had run off to work at a bank in Kansas City as soon as he could—his love for his little brother was not. And now he had come home to pay him a visit.

"Roy!" Walt dropped the milk bucket and embraced his older brother. They spent the next hour sitting on hay bales in the barn reminiscing about better times as young kids, buying ice cream and soda pop on Main Street in their hometown of Marceline, Missouri.

"*Walt!*"

Both boys recognized the bellow of their father. It was clear from his tone that he was agitated. Probably drinking again.

"Oh, no," Walt murmured.

"Walt, get your butt over here!"

Elias had found out that Walt, after reading in a magazine about a better way to cool milk, had packed the day's haul with the wrong amount of ice. Elias wasn't interested in trying anything new or novel. It was exactly this type of thing that set off his notorious temper.

The boys heard their father as he headed toward them in the barn. He was like a summer thunderstorm that formed quickly and without warning.

"Walt, go to the basement," he called out as he entered the barn, his red cheeks standing in stark contrast to the dirty blue overalls he wore each day. "I'll meet you down there. If you're lucky, I'll only use my belt."

Roy stayed quiet as Elias erupted with rage, but once their father had left he offered his brother some advice. "He's got no reason for hitting you," Roy said. "You're fourteen years old. Don't take it anymore."

Walt went down to the basement where his father was waiting. Elias Disney, still in a frenzy, impulsively grabbed a hammer. Walt's eyes filled with fear. Elias clenched the hammer and swung it at his son.

The hammer closed in on its target with brutal force. But then something strange happened, something that had never happened before: Walt grabbed the hammer midswing.

His father looked at him with eyes full of surprise. Walt yanked the hammer free and tossed it aside. Elias reared back and lined up a fist aimed at the left side of Walt's face. Walt grabbed it. And then he grabbed his father's other fist.

He and his father stood there like that for what seemed like an eternity. A boy on the verge of manhood holding his father's fists of fury. A father realizing for the first time that his boy was no longer a child.

Then Elias Disney started to cry.

That night, Walt fell asleep thinking about his hometown, Marceline, some 125 miles away, where he and Roy had been so happy. Leaving there after the failure of the family farm and the long stares from neighbors over their father's embrace of socialism was painful for Walt. He remembered perfect streets, friendly people, and happy faces. He remembered the feeling of security, of possibility and of adventure.

What a world he had found in Marceline. What a world he might find again.

Walt Disney Estate
Los Angeles, California
December 4, 1952

It had been an exasperating year for Lillian Disney. Her husband's mind seemed to be elsewhere. He was easily distracted. Of course, she was used to that after nearly thirty years of marriage. And in some ways it was a good thing. Lillian saw that Walt had a level of passion for his work that matched the days when he'd geared the whole studio up for *Snow White,* the world's first feature animated film. But that was nearly twenty years ago. Disney was no longer just a start-up, but now a major movie studio. Walt told her that they'd fallen into a rut and he wanted to do something entirely different.

Lillian watched him become absorbed with all of his various projects—from *The Adventures of Pinocchio* to *Cinderella* and now *Peter Pan,* which was set to be released early the following year. She'd never had much patience or interest in her husband's childish larks. In fact, despite her husband's creation of iconic film characters, she only had allowed one piece of Disney art in the entire house—and it was tucked away in their girls' bedroom.

Still, Walt's preoccupation with his work wasn't all bad. After all, it had made them wealthy and turned "Disney" into a household name. But his latest obsession—building a small town with a castle and an island and a lake—was driving Lillian crazy. She knew that if she didn't rein him in, this would be Walt's Waterloo: the end of his successful career, and the beginning of their financial ruin.

"But Lilly, dear, there's nothing like it in the entire world," Walt said as he sketched away on a notepad in bed.

Lillian rolled her eyes and kept brushing her hair in the mirror.

"It's unique," he continued. "I know, because I've looked everywhere for something like it! It's a new concept in entertainment altogether. I think—I *know*—it would be a success!"

When Walt had first outlined his vision of a place where families could immerse themselves in the stories of Disney with life-size characters, rides, entertainment and—above all—a sense of community, Lillian struggled not to laugh. She thought the idea was just plain silly.

She ignored it, hoping it would find the discard pile along with so many of his other ideas. But that never happened. This utopian town had become more than a conversation topic; it had become an all-consuming obsession. Walt had spent the next decade or so dragging her and their two girls all over America and Europe, looking at fairs and amusement parks. Most were grimy and unwelcoming. He'd even visited zoos to see if perhaps they had cracked the code—but he found most of them filled with dirty, unkempt animals.

"Walt, if you are going to look at more zoos," Lilly had warned, "I'm not going with you!"

He came away from all of their field trips realizing that there was no precedent for anything like what he envisioned anywhere in the world. The only place that had even come close to matching his dream was Tivoli Gardens in Copenhagen—a wide-open space that boasted music, food, drink, entertainment, and unfailingly polite employees.

"This is what a park should be!" Walt had exclaimed to her, smiling the whole flight home.

Burbank, California
March 1953

"I believe the ayes have it."

Roy Disney rubbed his dark horn-rimmed glasses with a hand-kerchief as the final tally was taken. The Disney board had heard the proposal many times, discussed it for months, and now Roy, as co-chairman of the board, was satisfied with the final vote. He watched the board members carefully. Polite. Stone-faced. Complacent.

Walt's older brother had always been seen as the more serious of the Disney brothers—and certainly as the more practical. Even now, as he helped Walt realize his plans for a vast amusement park, he shared the board's grave doubts. Many didn't seem to have any idea what Walt was talking about, although they all smiled politely and indulged what they saw as another of their founder's endless flights of fancy.

While his brother undoubtedly had a tendency to dream big, Roy knew that these were never really just *dreams*. They were plans. And Walt was dead serious about them. As if right on script, he was now nearly dancing with delight.

No one had ever done anything on a scale as large as the one his brother now contemplated. Ever the pragmatic, numbers-based executive to his brother's dreams, Roy calculated that millions of visitors would have to come to the park each year to keep it in the black, and then come back year after year, thereafter. It seemed impossible.

But Walt had surprised him before.

Later that day, a gleeful Walt Disney sat in his office at WED Enterprises, a new spinoff that Walt had total creative control over. Roy had negotiated that with the board, knowing that they would not want to cross the man who'd made them all a fortune. Board members knew how impossible it was to deal with Walt, especially when he was on one of his crusades. "If you give him this," Roy had told them, "he'll be out of your hair." And, besides, Roy reminded them, Walt was going to find a way to do what he wanted anyway—so why not be supportive?

Walt's office was tucked inside an old bungalow on the edge of the Disney lot, as far from the rest of the studio, and its shortsighted bureaucrats, as possible.

All around him were trappings of his past successes: stills of Mickey Mouse, Donald Duck, and Goofy. But he knew there was much more yet to come.

He had the board out of his way. He had his team lined up. Now all he needed was one thing more: cash.

As usual, he had an unorthodox idea about how to get it.

Disney Studios
Burbank, California
September 23, 1953

Standing before the fledgling staff of WED Enterprises, Roy Disney was not happy.

"I need to *show* them something," he told Walt. "It can't just be talk anymore."

His tone wasn't exactly desperate, although it might well have been. The sad truth was that Roy's attempt to fund Walt's dream was creating a fiscal disaster. Walt had borrowed $50,000 from the bank. He had sold his house to raise additional cash and then corralled a few investors to scrape together more. To Lilly's horror, Walt had even borrowed $100,000 from his life insurance policy.

But it still wasn't enough. Not even close. A park like the one Walt envisioned would cost millions—as much as $5 million by some estimates—and there was no guarantee it would ever make money. In fact, the opposite was true: Roy increasingly feared it could be the biggest financial boondoggle in their history.

Walt, however, had a plan. He always had a plan.

"Television," Walt said to the assembled staff. "Television is the answer." He had never shared the traditional view of other studio heads that television was the natural enemy of motion pictures. He thought they could feed into each other. His attitude was simple: Go wherever the public is. Every chance you could find to emblazon the Disney brand on the public's consciousness, do it. That's how he'd made Mickey Mouse a household name in spite of others telling him it was a waste of time.

Roy Disney knew television executives well enough to realize that flying to New York merely to talk to them about grandiose plans for some amusement park would not go well. He was meeting with investors on Monday, and he needed something tangible to put in front of them that they could get excited about.

The only problem was that he had nothing.

Herb Ryman had hurried to the studio as soon as he'd hung up on the phone call from his old friend and colleague Dick Irvine.

Walt greeted him at the studio gate, a wide smile on his face. "Herbie, we're going to build an amusement park."

"That's interesting," Ryman said. "Where are you going to build it?"

"Well, we were going to do it across the street, but now it's gotten too big. We're going to look for a place."

"What are you going to call it?"

"Disneyland."

"That's as good as anything."

"Look, Herbie, my brother Roy is going to New York Monday to line up financing for the park. I've got to give him plans of what we're going to do. Those businessmen don't listen to talk, you know; you've got to show them what you're going to do."

"Well, where is the drawing? I'd like to see it."

"You're going to make it."

"No, I'm not," Herbie replied. "This is the first I ever heard about this. You'd better forget it. It'll embarrass both you and me. I'm not going to make a fool of either one of us."

"Herbie, this is my dream. I've wanted this for years and I need your help," Walt pleaded. "You're the only one who can do it. I'll stay here with you and we'll do it together."

And that's exactly what they did. For the next forty-two hours, Ryman worked side by side with Walt to bring his vision to life on paper. In the end, the drawings amounted to a large triangle with a castle at one end and a Main Street that would funnel in visitors at the other. Various segments of the park were described in some detail: True-Life Adventureland had a botanical garden; Fantasyland featured Disney characters like Snow White, Peter Pan, and Alice in Wonderland; the World of Tomorrow included an industrial exhibit, a monorail, and a moving sidewalk. There were even tracks for a small railroad.

On another page was a note outlining in writing for the first time what Walt had been dreaming about for years:

Sometime in 1955 Walt Disney will present for the people of the world—and children of all ages—a new experience in entertainment. Disneyland will be something of a fair, an exhibition, playground, a community center, a museum of living facts, and a showplace of beauty and magic. It

will be filled with accomplishments, the joys and hopes of the world we
live in. And it will remind us and show us how to make those wonders
part of our own lives.

Walt sent the drawings to Roy and sat by the phone, eager for his
brother's reaction. When it finally came, it was quintessential Roy.
"I guess these will have to do."

New York City
September 28, 1953

"Looks like we may have a deal."

Roy was excited, but he tried to keep his voice on the telephone
measured so that Walt's mind didn't start racing before he could even
finish with the update.

Roy explained that CBS had flatly said no. Its executives wanted to
see a pilot of Walt's proposed television program first. "We don't do
samples at Disney," Roy had told them—and that was that.

NBC was interested in both the show and the amusement park, but
Roy couldn't finalize a deal with them. The legendary and influential
General David Sarnoff, leader of NBC's owner, RCA, was enthusiastic.
But the executives and lawyers beneath Sarnoff proved to be frustrat-
ing, bureaucratic, and time-consuming.

ABC was a long shot. They were far behind the other two in the
ratings—the network didn't have a single show on the air that rated
among the top twenty-five. In the end, that worked to Roy's advantage.
Unlike the others, ABC was willing to do whatever it took to get Disney
on board. They understood the power of the Disney name and they
desperately needed something that would make an impression with the
audience.

After long discussions with network executives, Roy managed to get
ABC to agree to a deal in principle: Disney would provide a one-hour
weekly TV series to them in exchange for $500,000 paid directly to the
park, and loan guarantees of up to $4.5 million to finance the rest.

"They bought an amusement park," Roy said, shaking his head in disbelief, "so they could get a TV show."

Despite Roy's attempts to relay the deal matter-of-factly, Walt was exuberant on the other end of the phone. Roy was excited as well, but, unlike his brother, he couldn't stop worrying about one small wrinkle in their plan: He and Walt had absolutely no idea what the TV show was going to be about.

Burbank, California
October 28, 1954

Reviews from the previous evening's debut episode on ABC flooded in. Walt Disney's secretary sifted through various newspapers, telegrams, and phone messages.

From his desk, Walt could see that his show had exceeded everyone's expectations—ABC's, the Disney company's, Roy's, their sponsor's, heck, even his own. The overnight ratings were astonishing: The program had beat every show on television, except for *I Love Lucy*—and they'd even given that a run for its money.

Ratings aside, the show itself was a huge win for Walt. *The Disneyland Show* was basically an hour-long, ABC-funded commercial for Walt's theme park idea. He introduced viewers to the park's concept, talked about its various areas and attractions, and mixed in some cartoons.

Walt was reenergized by the news. He already had more ideas for the show—a live-action story about Davy Crockett, and plenty of new cartoons—but far more important in his mind was that money for the park was no longer a concern.

Walt's next task was to prove the skeptics wrong; skeptics he knew still included his big brother.

Burbank, California
March 10, 1955

Roy sighed. He had heard all of this before. Many times before. As polite as people were as they spoke, they were making it clear that Walt
was being a pain in the ass.

Roy had sympathy for the complainers, but he rarely let it show.
No one criticized his brother too strongly in his presence, despite
how much justification they might have had. "My brother made me a
millionaire," he would tell people when they expressed their frustra-
tions with Walt. "And you wonder why I want to do everything I can to
help him?"

Whenever he needed to find his brother, Roy would invariably have
to seek him out in Anaheim, the site of the park, where he was busy
driving everyone crazy in person. In his straw hat and ugly shirts, he
would eat hot dogs with construction workers while micromanaging
their every move: There had to be *stained* glass, not cut glass; they had
to move a tree six feet because it was too close to the entrance of Adventureland; and Walt had even insisted on a Disney University of sorts
to train all workers so that there was consistency no matter where visitors ventured. "The thing that's going to make Disneyland unique and
different is the detail," he insisted to everyone who'd listen. "If we lose
the detail, we lose it all."

Walt was also driving the park's designers crazy with his endless
demands. The other night one of them had called Roy to complain
that Walt had taken plans for an amusement park ride and redrawn
it overnight to reflect "the way it should have been." When someone
later explained that they needed to build a water tower on the site, Walt
had almost thrown him out of the office. He told them that nothing so
ugly and obstructive would ever be permitted at his park. Walt was even
feuding with Orange County building inspectors who didn't know how
to apply city ordinances and codes to something like Sleeping Beauty's
castle.

Now, Roy had just learned, the TV show itself was also blowing past
its budget—a budget they had all, *including Walt,* agreed to with ABC.
Walt wasn't one to let his imagination be limited by a lack of funds,

so he spent whatever he felt was necessary to make the show look right.

Last night's offering on ABC was another tribute to Walt's exactness and talent for excess—and it was yet another headache for Roy to manage. The program had included an expensive original film called *Man in Space,* in which Walt had somehow convinced the most famous scientists of the day to narrate their vision for the world of tomorrow. Even the former Nazi Wernher von Braun took part in it.

The show was putting forward all sorts of fanciful notions of the future: rockets lifting off into outer space; men living on board spacecraft; even satellites orbiting the earth. Another show, slated to air later that year, predicted a manned mission to the moon in the near future.

In the end, though, Roy couldn't be too upset with his brother. For all his fussing and complaining, Walt was happier than he'd ever been. Besides, the numbers didn't lie: 40 million people—*40 million!*—had watched *Man in Space* the previous night. The program was winning raves from critics. It was capturing everyone's imagination. Well, almost everyone's—Walt's wife, Lillian, was so bored by the programs that she refused to watch with him.

Four Years Later
Disneyland
Anaheim, California
June 14, 1959

Once again, Roy stood in awe of his brother. Disneyland was a smashing success, surpassing even the most optimistic projections. Five million guests were expected through the gates this year alone! Cash was flooding into the company at a rate that no one could have predicted. The Disney company's sales and net profits had risen faster than almost any company in America. The stock price was seven times what it had been before the park had opened.

Roy watched with pride as his brother debuted the park's new, clean, and practically noiseless monorail system. Walt boasted that it was the first such service in the entire Western Hemisphere.

He also watched uneasily as reporters pressed Walt about his plans for another park. "Oh, no," Walt said. "There will only be one Disneyland."

But Roy knew his brother far better than any reporter did. There was something about the way he answered that suggested he might have something even bigger in mind.

He always did.

Burbank, California
December 1, 1961

Death terrified Walt Disney. He avoided funerals at all costs and thought constantly about how time was slipping away from him.

To cheer him up on his sixtieth birthday, Hazel George, the studio's nurse, gave him a picture of herself when she had started at Disney after finishing nursing school in 1929. The photo's message was meant to be obvious, and Walt took the hint immediately: *We are all getting older. It's part of life. So suck it up.*

"You know, Hazel," Walt said, "after I die, I would hate to look down at this studio and find everything a mess."

Hazel had been attending to Walt's various ailments, including a wrenched neck after a polo accident, for years. She was also an amateur songwriter, and Walt had let her write songs for the Mickey Mouse Club and for movies like *Old Yeller* under the pseudonym "George Gil."

With her tart tongue and clever wit, Hazel was also one of the few people able to get away with teasing the temperamental Disney founder. "When you die," she replied with a smile, "what makes you think you won't be using a periscope?"

Walt smirked. "Smartass."

Jacksonville, Florida
February 12, 1964

The seventy-three-year-old man with the distinctive face and a bearing of self-assurance walked into the hotel after arriving from the airport. At the reception desk, he gave his name for the registry. It was not his real one.

From the safety of his room, Roy Disney made a long-distance call to California. "There are some large parcels of land available," he said.

On the other end of the line was his brother, waiting impatiently back in Burbank for news. Roy had decided that Walt was too recognizable to join the other Disney executives, who were currently fanning out all over Florida looking at land records and conducting discreet surveys. If anyone found out that the Disney company was trying to buy up large swaths of property, the prices would instantly skyrocket.

Within Disney itself, the initiative was code-named "Project X" and "Project Future." It was so secret that the non-Disney employees in Florida involved with the real estate transactions didn't even know their true mission or who they were really working for.

"Okay," Walt replied. "Let's go after some land."

Burbank, California
May 20, 1964

Walt listened closely as a member of Project X's clandestine team made his presentation.

Using the name "Bob Price" to avoid any ties to the Disney company, Bob Foster had linked up with a Florida lawyer to help him purchase several large parcels of land "for recreational purposes."

Foster stood beside a large map of the state, outlining possible areas for purchase in the vicinity of Daytona Beach. Walt and his team had spent years paying for surveys of land in different areas of the country for an East Coast version of Disneyland. St. Louis had been rejected. So too had the Washington, D.C.–Baltimore corridor. Only Florida had weather conditions that would allow the park to stay open all year.

But the Daytona Beach area gave Walt serious pause. He peppered his man with questions: Didn't that part of the state get too cold in winter? Would tropical vegetation survive? How close was Daytona to the typical hurricane routes? Wasn't it better—and safer—to start from scratch someplace in the middle of the state?

"But inland Florida doesn't have as much water," Foster replied.

Walt scoffed. "Then I'll build a lake."

Everyone in the room realized then that Walt had already made up his mind. Forget Daytona. Walt Disney wanted another area that had already been surveyed: Orlando.

Florida Airport Tarmac
Near Orlando, Florida
September 9, 1964

Walt had insisted on going. He couldn't *not* be there. Not for this. Even Roy couldn't talk him out of it. Walt understood the consequences if he was seen, and he swore he'd stay out of sight.

To keep him company, Walt had brought along books that he'd all but memorized—Ebenezer Howard's *Garden Cities of To-morrow* and Victor Gruen's *The Heart of Our Cities*. Both focused on the urban crisis in American cities and ways to correct them. He also had some notes for his latest film, an adaption of Rudyard Kipling's *The Jungle Book*. As usual, Walt had a particular idea for the movie, and didn't tolerate much opposition. He'd indicated as much when he'd walked up to one of his writers before he left for Florida and handed him the book. "Here's the Kipling book. The first thing I want you to do is not read it."

As their plane landed for refueling, Walt unbuckled and started to rise from his seat.

"What do you think you're doing?" Roy asked.

"I'm going into the terminal," Walt replied, looking confused. "With the rest of you."

"No way. You can't. You'll be recognized." At this point, Walt's face, voice, and mannerisms were well known to millions of people. "Walt, you promised."

Walt groused. "Well, can I at least stand out on the field for a minute?" he asked. "I need some fresh air."

Roy nodded, knowing it was useless to protest any further. As he and the other executives headed for the terminal, Walt exited the plane and stood on the tarmac. It was not long before one of the young mechanics looked at him. Then looked again. Then again.

"Excuse me, sir," the mechanic asked. "Are you Walt Disney?"

"Hell no," he replied. "I get mistaken for him all the time."

The mechanic looked bewildered.

"And if I ever run into that SOB," Walt continued, "I'm going to tell him exactly what I think of him."

Back on board, the plane took off and before long was flying low over black swamps and vast cypress groves. To Roy, the view was a sobering wake-up call: Building a park in the middle of this mess would be a Herculean task—far more difficult than it had been in Anaheim.

Walt looked through the window, as if scrutinizing every inch of the ground below. Then he looked across the aisle at his brother and smiled broadly. "This is perfect. It's going to be fine."

Walt Disney Estate
Los Angeles, California
August 14, 1965

Walt watched the scenes unfolding on his television with a pained expression. Things had gotten so bad that National Guardsmen were being sent into the neighborhood of Watts, not that far from his own home, to quell the violence.

For years, there had been growing tensions in the area as more and more African-Americans migrated to California to work in the growing defense industry. They faced discrimination in housing and employment, and there were widespread allegations of police brutality. Three days earlier, the attempted arrest of a young black man for driving while intoxicated by a white member of the California Highway Patrol had quickly escalated into a shoving match between the officer, the driver, and his mother. Fanned by rumors that the cops had attacked the mother and a pregnant woman, a mob of black residents began to form.

Nearly fifty square miles of Los Angeles had become a combat zone. Thousands of citizens were looting shops, destroying neighborhoods, and engaging in battles with police. Martial law was declared.

Walt didn't recognize his country anymore. This wasn't the United States he was seeing—it couldn't be. This looked like a riot in some banana republic.

The sixties was promising to be a decade of turbulence and uncertainty and the crisis in the inner cities was worsening by the day. Walt was thinking more and more of the children who watched his programs, and of his own young grandchildren. What kind of world would they grow up in? The inner cities were a far cry from the tranquil, carefree settings he remembered in Missouri.

The scenes of mayhem only made the Florida Project that much more urgent. Walt picked up the phone and dialed his brother. Roy knew what he was going to say before a word was ever spoken.

Cherry Plaza Hotel
Orlando, Florida
November 15, 1965

The jig was up. Earlier in the week a front-page headline in the *Orlando Sentinel* screamed the news, which they'd learned from a variety of tips:

WE SAY IT'S DISNEY.

By that point, it hardly mattered much anymore. Through dummy corporations, Walt Disney had purchased nearly twenty-eight thousand acres of swampland in the area between the cities of Orlando and Kissimmee, an area that was to be called the Reedy Creek Improvement District.

Still, Roy had been right that there would be a steep price to pay for the leak. The price of the remaining three hundred acres of land they needed had risen overnight from $183 per acre to $1,000.

Now that all of the purchasing was done, Walt and Roy appeared together before reporters to announce Disney's next great plan. Florida governor Haydon Burns was on hand to introduce them to the crush of local reporters. Burns had already given his support to a plan that would give Disney almost complete autonomy over the Reedy Creek Improvement District. The district was even slated to include a small city that would serve as a test site for urban planning. Walt was going to have his own magic kingdom—for real this time.

Walt, who had earlier acquiesced to Roy's pleas to build the Magic Kingdom part of the park in order to finance his dream of a model city, smiled before the cameras and stepped to the microphones. "This is the biggest thing we've ever tackled." Gesturing to Roy, whom the governor saluted as "Disney's financial wizard," Walt continued, "I might, for the benefit of the press, explain that my brother and I have been together in our business for forty-two years now. He's my big brother, and he's the one that, when I was a little fellow, I used to go to with some of my wild ideas. He'd either straighten me out and put me on the right path or, if he didn't agree with me, I'd work on it for years until I got him to agree with me."

The crowd laughed. Roy smiled knowingly at the truth of Walt's words, but after the smashing success of Disneyland, Roy had become a full-bore believer in his brother's dreams.

Reporters asked Walt about plans for the Florida Project and rumors about a model city. Walt acknowledged that there would be another amusement park built in Florida—an East Coast Disneyland—but that he had even higher ambitions this time around. "I would like to be part of building a model community, a City of Tomorrow, you might say," he explained.

Referred to as an Experimental Prototype Community of Tomorrow, or EPCOT for short, this was to be Walt's new obsession. He was still involved in films—the adaptation of *The Jungle Book* was proving to be a headache—but that was all going to have to play second fiddle. Now, at sixty-three years of age, Walt Disney truly believed that EPCOT was the most important thing he would ever do.

Burbank, California
October 1966

Walt outlined his plan for governing the Orlando property—which was
twice the size of Manhattan—to a local reporter. "It will be a planned,
controlled community," he explained. "A showcase for American industry and research, schools, cultural and educational opportunities. In
EPCOT there will be no slum areas because we won't let them develop.
People will rent houses instead of buying them, and at modest rates.
There will be no retirees. Everyone must be employed in something.
One of our requirements is that people who live in EPCOT must help
keep it alive."

"But what motivated you for such a project?" the reporter pressed.

"I happen to be an inquisitive guy, and when I see things I don't like,
I start thinking: 'Why do they have to be like this and how can I improve them?' City governments, for example. We pay a lot of taxes and
still have streets that aren't paved or are full of holes. And city street
cleaners and garbage collectors who don't do their jobs. And property
owners who allow dirt to accumulate and help create slums." His eyebrows raised slightly. "Why? Why is it like that?"

"Well, you seem to have enough to manage without taking on the
problems of the cities," the reporter replied.

Walt waved a hand, as if to dismiss the question. "You sound just
like my wife," he said. "When I started on Disneyland, she used to say,
'But why do you want to build an amusement park? They're so dirty.' I
told her that that was just the point. Mine wouldn't be."

Disney Studios
Burbank, California
October 27, 1966

Dressed in a light gray suit and narrow black tie, the mustachioed Walt
Disney sat on the edge of his desk, a pointer in his hand, a giant map
of his new project on the wall to his right. Looking into the camera, he

told viewers he wanted to share with them "the most exciting and challenging assignment we've ever tackled at Walt Disney Productions."

As with the ABC show he wanted to make a film that would excite viewers about what was to come. But this time around he also wanted to encourage companies to join Disney in running EPCOT and turning it into a showplace for American innovation, and to prompt companies to come up with new ideas and technologies for urban living.

"EPCOT will take its cue from the new ideas and new technologies that are now emerging from the creative centers of American industry," he told viewers. "It will be a community of tomorrow that will never be completed, but will always be introducing, and testing, and demonstrating new materials and new systems. And EPCOT will always be a showcase to the world of the ingenuity and imagination of American free enterprise."

Walt's plans for the model city were ambitious. Housed under a glass dome, the entire city would be climate-controlled. There would be no more heat and cold, no humidity, no rain. Every day would be perfect.

There would also be no cars. Pedestrians could walk and bike and browse without fear of being hit by a car or truck. Housing would be clean, spacious, and readily available at fair rates. The park's offices and laboratories would be occupied by major American corporations who would use the facilities to develop new technology for use in the EPCOT city. Guests of the theme park would be allowed to go on tours of the facility to see how it all worked. Disney hoped they would be impressed enough to bring some of the ideas to their own communities.

Disney turned back to the cameras. "Speaking for myself and the entire Disney organization, we're ready to go right now!"

Walt knew what he was saying wasn't exactly true. The Disney organization was not ready to undertake anything quite that ambitious just yet. And neither, for that matter, was he.

Several times during the taping, Walt began coughing so much that he had to stop speaking. By the end of the production he was coughing uncontrollably. The crew behind the camera shifted uncomfortably as they waited for him to stop. Roy, on the other hand, just looked worried. *For good reason,* Walt thought. He knew what the coughing meant.

But he also knew something else: He wasn't going down without a fight. EPCOT was the key to everything and Walt vowed to himself that he would speak it into existence while he was still able to work. That was why he'd rushed this film into production. He would will EPCOT into becoming a reality, even if took his last ounce of energy.

Even if it took his last breath.

Burbank, California
November 21, 1966

Walt Disney walked into his office at WED, frail, thin, and pale. His team greeted him with strained smiles. In his pocket, he carried a tattered telegram from actor John Wayne, a fellow lung cancer sufferer. WELCOME TO THE CLUB, it read.

Thoughts of death were now taunting him, dancing around his every movement, his every utterance. And he could tell by the looks on his colleagues' faces that they could see his terror.

Walt tried to ease the tension with a joke. "You'd think I was going to die or something."

Walking into the cafeteria, he shied away from his usual spot in the corner and sat with his team from WED. They looked shocked at his appearance.

"My lung was removed," he told them. "But I'm going to be fine. Just as soon as I get some rest."

It wasn't until he met his long-suffering wisecracking nurse, Hazel, in the same room where they'd teased each other and joked and laughed a million times, Walt Disney faced his harsh reality.

"There's something I want to tell you," he said quietly. He couldn't complete the thought. Hazel knew anyway. The two friends embraced each other, and they both cried.

Los Angeles, California
December 14, 1966

Walt Disney was his old self again. At least, that was how it seemed to Roy. He was smiling, animated, eager—and as impatient as always.

Bored and restless in his hospital bed, Walt looked up at the ceiling. Using it as an imaginary grid, he began sketching new designs for his EPCOT dream with his finger.

This, Roy knew, wasn't just a sick man trying to idly pass the time. Walt wanted his big brother to understand that this was the reason he had lived. Walt spoke and his voice was gravelly but firm. "You must build this when I'm gone."

"I'll do my best," Roy replied.

"No, not your best," Walt said. "You must promise me that you'll build it. Promise me that you'll see it done."

Roy could see in his dying brother's eyes that he fully believed his plans for a city of the future would change the world. Roy knew it didn't matter whether that was true—all that mattered was that Walt believed it.

Now, as he stood there watching Walt wave his finger through the air, Roy was more in awe of his younger brother than he'd ever been before. He'd stood up to their father all those years back—and he'd spent nearly every day of his life since turning that hammer from a weapon back into a tool that could be used to build, to dream, and to change the world.

"I promise," Roy said, tears streaming down his face. He started toward the door, then stopped and turned back to face his brother.

"Maybe we can still build it together."

Los Angeles, California
December 15, 1966

Roy Disney stood by the edge of his brother's bed. Walt's hands were folded across his chest. He was not moving. The official time of his death was 9:30 A.M. The cause: acute circulatory failure.

Roy had left his brother yesterday exactly the way Walt wanted Roy to remember him—cheerful, hopeful, and with a smile on his face. Now that smile was forever gone.

"Well, kid," said Roy, as tears streamed down his face and his voice choked, "this is the end, I guess."

He kissed his brother's forehead, squeezed his hand, and left Walt's side for the last time.

Orlando and Kissimmee, Florida
Spring 1967

Roy was a frequent visitor to the swamps of Orlando, watching as builders brought his brother's last wish a little closer to reality.

Roy was seventy-four years old and far past retirement age by any measure. When Walt died all the joy Roy had found in running the company was gone. *As soon as I finish Walt's dream,* he thought to himself, *I'll retire and leave it to the younger guys.*

People everywhere had begun referring to the theme park as "Disney World." And that had started to rankle Roy. "I don't care what they say, this is not going to be called Disney World," he told his executive team. That name wasn't good enough. Everyone has heard of the Ford car, but not everyone remembers that it was *Henry* Ford who started it all.

"This is going to be *Walt* Disney World. So everyone will know that this was Walt's dream."

Even as he said the words, Roy knew that the park would never really reflect the way Walt dreamed it up. Roy never really understood EPCOT the way his brother did, or its world-changing possibilities. All he could do was try his best.

Burbank, California
December 20, 1971

It had been a very long day. Exhausted, Roy undressed and readied himself for the comfort of his bed. The house was empty and quiet—

his wife and kids had gone to the Disneyland Christmas parade. His sadness over Walt's death still hovered over him like a dark cloud.

Everything inside Roy told him that it was time to retire, to finally rest and enjoy his success. But he felt a duty to carry on. At least for a little longer. There was no one else to fulfill Walt's mission. Certainly not Lilly, who'd remarried in 1969, less than three years after Walt's death. No, it was up to Roy, and Roy alone, to make Walt's last dream come true.

Two months earlier, Walt Disney World had opened to widespread acclaim and success. But Roy was not as excited. It was simply an amusement park. An impressive one, to be sure, but nothing close to the kind of model city that Walt had envisioned.

Still, Walt Disney World included some of Walt's ideas: pneumatic tubes carried garbage to a compacting plant far from the park's center; a noiseless monorail whisked people throughout the grounds; electrical circuits and other service tubes were all contained underground so there was no need for potholes and street excavations that tied up other cities in gridlock.

Overall, it was not what Walt had originally laid out in his plans, but Roy believed it was as good as he could possibly make it without his brother's personal guidance.

Roy reached for his night robe, ready to get a good night's sleep under way, and felt a sharp pain in his head.

He collapsed to the ground and, for the first time in years, Roy and Walt were reunited.

EPILOGUE

Orlando, Florida
October 1, 1982

The new EPCOT Center theme park, which would eventually be re-labeled as "Epcot," perhaps in order to take attention away from what Walt wanted those letters to stand for, was a corporate compromise.

Card Walker, Roy's successor as CEO, had made an effort a few years earlier to revive Walt's original dream. The board had voted against it.

No one, members determined, would want to live under a microscope and be watched constantly. Nothing so grandiose could ever be accomplished. Besides, nobody knew how to run such a city without Walt's guidance.

The new EPCOT contained pavilions designed to celebrate achievement and innovation. Nine other pavilions were devoted to different cultures. At the center of the park was *Spaceship Earth,* a geodesic sphere resembling a massive golf ball. But it was decidedly not the model city housed under a glass dome that Walt believed could change the world.

To all those at Disney, one thing was now clear: Walt's dream for a kind of utopian kingdom in Florida had died right along with him.

Thirty Years Later
Orlando, Florida
October 30, 2012

Robert Iger and George Lucas sat together to announce a breathtaking new deal to expand the Disney universe further. Lucasfilm, home of the Star Wars franchise, had found a new home with Disney—to the tune of $4 billion, a sum that would have likely even shocked the free-spending Walt.

The Star Wars franchise was the latest part of a vast Disney empire. With a market capitalization of $149 billion and revenue of $47 billion, the empire includes parks in Japan and Paris; hotels; the Disney Channel; live-action blockbuster films; animated smash hits; Broadway musicals; the television networks ABC and ESPN; toys and toy stores; the Animal Kingdom; a movie studio theme park; and of course, what was meant to be the biggest part of the Disney legacy of all, Epcot.

Tens of millions of people have visited Epcot since its founding. But most don't realize that it is still not even close to the EPCOT of Walt's dreams. It stands as an unambitious compromise, rather than a cutting-edge laboratory of democracy and governance.

Epcot is a theme park to honor science and culture, innovation, magic, and joy. But it's a theme park nonetheless—not the real, working city that Walt had imagined.

If, as Walt had warned his nurse, he truly was looking down on his company from above, he would undoubtedly have a lot to say.

A NOTE FROM GLENN

The 1953 Disneyland drawings done by Herb Ryman over one chaotic weekend—drawings that had been hand-colored by Walt Disney himself—were presented to bankers in an attempt to secure financing for the park. One banker who'd rejected Walt's pitch took the drawings home to show to his family the new crazy scheme that Disney had concocted.

Decades later, those weathered drawings were put up for auction by the banker's family. The Glenn Beck American History Reclamation Project purchased them in an effort to secure their preservation and place in American history.

Since one of Walt's hallmarks was his ability to speak big things into existence, I will attempt to do the same thing here: The Ryman drawings, representing Walt's entire, original, and unfinished dream (complete with the white-steepled church that he envisioned being built at the center of Main Street) will one day play an important role in my own "Independence Park." While this is still very much in the "dream stage," I don't envision this being a traditional theme park, but instead something more in line with Walt's lost dream for a new kind of city that can be a beacon of hope and courage throughout the world.

10

"Make It Great, John": How Steve Jobs and John Lasseter Changed History at Pixar

Mountain View, California
April 1, 1976

He ate only fruit, rarely wore shoes, and believed that technology should be more than efficient; it should be beautiful.

Several weeks earlier, the shaggy-haired adopted son of a car mechanic had sold his Volkswagen bus for $750. His friend had sold his HP 65 calculator for $500. As he eased back in his desk chair, he shuddered at the thought of putting his entire life's savings on the line.

He nervously twirled the pen in his hand, then gave it a few hard chomps between his front teeth. He had read the partnership agreement numerous times, but he couldn't resist flipping through its pages one final time. He finished and then signed his name on the line at the bottom of the last page.

The man who dreamed of the intersection of technology and art had just launched a computer company.

His name was Steve Jobs.

Anaheim, California
July 1, 1976

"Hello, everyone, welcome aboard Disneyland's World Famous Jungle Cruise." The man in the khaki vest and floppy hat smiled constantly as he spoke. "My name is John and I'll be your captain—unless we run into trouble."

The tourists on the boat laughed, just as John Lasseter knew they would. They'd been standing in line in the hot sun for almost an hour. They were ready for some entertainment, and their bar for humor wasn't especially high.

Lasseter felt like the luckiest guy in the world to be working at Disneyland. Like most boys growing up in the early 1960s, he had loved cartoons, but unlike his friends, his love for them had never faded. While his high school classmates played sports, he went home to watch Elmer Fudd and Mickey Mouse. When Lasseter realized in ninth grade that grown men could actually get *paid* to draw cartoons, he instantly knew what he wanted to do with his life.

"Before I came to the Jungle Cruise, I worked in an orange juice factory," he told the boat's passengers, "but I got canned because I couldn't concentrate." In truth, Lasseter had come to the Jungle Cruise after a brief stint sweeping the sidewalks of Disney's Tomorrowland. "My boss almost beat the pulp out of me," he continued, laughing along with his audience. Sure, the joke was corny, but with an easy audience and the right delivery, puns like this were part of the stock-in-trade of every Jungle Cruise guide.

Three years earlier, Lasseter had enrolled at CalArts (California Institute of the Arts), a college established by Walt Disney as a training ground for the next generation of animators. There he'd found a troupe of fellow animation junkies. In between classes taught by Disney's renowned artists and animators, John and his friends checked 16mm prints of Disney classics out of the school library and sat around watching them over and over again, like rabbis studying the Talmud.

As the boat rounded another curve, its passengers came face-to-face with animatronic jungle natives dancing in a circle. Some hopped on one foot and others thrust their spears up and down in rhythm with a beat pounded out by several drummers.

"Ladies and gentlemen," Lasseter gasped, "this is extremely rare! They're doing their 'I-Can't-Find-the-Bathroom' dance!" With that joke even the one or two grumpy dads on the boat joined in the laughter, interrupted only by Lasseter's follow-up line: "That's why they call them 'head hunters.'"

Over the course of his four years at CalArts, Lasseter learned a lot about the technical elements of writing, drawing, and production. But the lessons he learned as a Jungle Cruise guide would prove almost as valuable. His summer of making corny quips and honing his deadpan humor taught him how to time a joke, pace a story, and feel confident in front of perfect strangers. After his summer at Disneyland, Lasseter was no longer just a cartoonist.

He was also a storyteller.

San Francisco, California
December 12, 1980

Standing in the offices of a small investment bank, surrounded by his cofounder Steve Wozniak and a slew of investors, Steve Jobs—who no longer made a habit of going barefoot—raised a glass of orange juice and offered a concise, if somewhat immodest toast: "To beautiful machines. To computers that will change the world. And to an insanely great company!"

Jobs was smiling, and for very good reason: his company was going public that very day. He thought back to the moment of fear and trepidation four years ago when he signed away everything he owned in return for a sheet of paper that stipulated his ownership stake in a company called Apple.

Not that Jobs was known for lacking self-confidence. As a boy, he had once called up Bill Hewlett, the cofounder of Hewlett-Packard, at his home to ask for some spare computer parts. Now, at the age of twenty-five, Jobs was a co-owner of the most revolutionary computer company in the world, a company that endeavored to put the power of personal computers into the hands of ordinary people.

When the day began, Apple's stock was priced at $22 per share. By the time the closing bell rang its value had risen to $29. The company that Jobs had cofounded using money from the sale of his Volkswagen bus was now the most oversubscribed initial public offering since Ford Motor Company.

Anaheim, California
December 12, 1980

His office was cluttered with the classic toys he collected: a cherished tin wind-up soldier; a GI Joe; a Mr. Potato Head, all staring at him as he sketched at his drafting table. Now a junior animator at the Walt Disney Company, John Lasseter was working on the animated film *The Fox and the Hound*. It was a cute story, and everyone at Disney was fairly confident it would entertain kids and make some money—but something nagged at Lasseter. He believed it could be much more than that.

Lasseter dreamed of making movies that would become classics watched by generations of kids and treasured for decades, maybe even centuries. He thought about the animated masterpieces that had been created in the very offices where he now worked: *Pinocchio*; *Fantasia*; *Dumbo*; *Bambi*; *Cinderella*; *Alice in Wonderland*; *Peter Pan*; *Lady and the Tramp*; *Sleeping Beauty*; *One Hundred and One Dalmatians*; and *The Jungle Book*. They had been stories for the ages. But the creative geniuses behind those movies had retired years ago. In their place was a second tier of animators and executives who had risen to the top at Disney—not through talent, but through attrition. Their mission was to make movies as quickly and cheaply as possible. They seemed to care more about making big profits than making timeless movies.

As a result, the company had been making neither.

Lasseter mustered the courage to walk down the hallway and get everything off his chest. "I have a couple of ideas I'd like to run by you," he said as he walked into the office of Richard Coyle, one of Disney's more senior animators.

"Who are you?" Coyle barked.

Lasseter introduced himself, and then unleashed a slew of ideas for *The Fox and the Hound*. He believed he had come up with ways to better develop both title characters, to elevate the plot, and to make some of the key background scenery visually stunning. It would require more time and cost more money, but Lasseter thought the results would be worth it.

On the other side of the desk, Coyle's eyes narrowed. When Lasseter finally finished his pitch, Coyle stared at him in silence for what seemed like an eternity before he spoke.

"Let me tell you something, John. You are a *junior* animator. It's not your job to think big, expensive thoughts. Our audience is a bunch of kids who couldn't care less about 'character development' and 'plot strength.' Just do what you're told. And if you don't like our way, there's a line of people out the door who would be happy to take your place."

Lasseter was speechless. And crushed. In that moment he realized that his dream had never been to merely *work* at Disney; it had been to create movies like Walt himself had made. But now Lasseter was beginning to understand that when Walt had died, the magic he'd brought to the movies that bore his name had died right along with him.

Anaheim, California
September 16, 1983

In a conference room at the intersection of Mickey Avenue and Dopey Drive, John Lasseter showed his bosses at Disney Animation a pitch he'd been working on for months. His proposal was to combine computer-generated sets with traditionally animated characters for a movie based on the classic short story by Thomas M. Disch, *The Brave Little Toaster*.

Lasseter's vision for the film was based on three of his most deeply held beliefs: first, that animation could appeal to both children and adults alike by tapping into ageless themes and emotions; second, that computer animation could add unimagined visual richness to cartoons;

and third, that inanimate objects, like toasters, could be depicted to have real emotions, and that the depiction could be used not just for comic effect—as Walt Disney had done—but for dramatic effect as well.

Lasseter had first brought an inanimate object to life at CalArts when he'd made an animated short called *The Lady and Lamp*. It had generated excitement among the faculty and his peers and had won him the first of two Student Academy Awards. But now the Disney executive's reaction to his vision for animation was decidedly less encouraging.

"Tell me something, Mr. Lasseter," said Richard Coyle, after Lasseter finished his pitch. "Who told you to spend all this time and money developing a computer-animated movie?" Lasseter had all but ignored the tongue-lashing Coyle had given him three years ago.

"Well," Lasseter replied, "no one, sir."

"Right," Coyle said, "*no one*. And this computer animation—what will it mean for the artists we currently pay to draw our cartoons?"

"They'll be as important as ever," Lasseter explained. "Computers don't actually *draw* anything. They are just tools that allow artists to do more with their drawings."

"So they don't replace people?"

"Not at all."

"And I suppose that means they don't save us any money?"

"Well, no, but—"

"And I suppose they don't save us any time, either?"

"No," said Lasseter, "they don't. The point of computer animation isn't to save time and money. It's to—"

"Very well, Mr. Lasseter," said Coyle coldly. "You'll be hearing from us shortly."

Coyle was true to his word. Less than ten minutes after the meeting, Lasseter's office phone rang.

"Mr. Lasseter, this is Ed Boone and I work for Richard Coyle. It's been decided that computer animation is only useful to the extent that it's quicker and cheaper than traditional animation. Since at this time it plainly is neither quicker *nor* cheaper, your development of *The Brave Little Toaster* will cease immediately."

Lasseter gazed at the little toaster he'd placed on his office shelf for inspiration. He considered tossing it into the trash, but he couldn't bring himself to do it. Besides, the cancellation of his *Little Toaster* project wasn't much of a surprise—he'd known deep down all along that it was something of a long shot.

But if Lasseter had expected his project to be shut down, he never expected what happened next.

"Since it's not going to be made," Boone said, "your project at Disney is now complete. Your position at Disney is terminated, and your employment with Disney is now ended."

Woodside, California
May 28, 1985

When Mike Murray picked up the phone, his friend Steve Jobs could barely speak he was crying so hard. "It's over," said Jobs. Those were his only words. A moment later, Murray heard a click, and the phone went dead.

Murray immediately jumped into his car and rushed over to Jobs's house in Woodside.

Murray knocked on the front door. No answer. He looked into one of the windows. There was no sign of Jobs—or anyone else for that matter. The massive foyer was completely empty. Jobs was such a perfectionist that it was almost impossible for him to find furniture that suited his artistic sensibilities. As a result, he had failed to furnish most of the rooms in his seventeen-thousand-square-foot mansion.

Murray knocked louder. Still no answer.

Finally, he ran to the backyard and peered into one of the Spanish Colonial Revival's fourteen bedrooms. There he saw his friend lying motionless on a mattress with no bed frame in an unfurnished room.

Murray pounded on the glass door until his friend, to Murray's great relief, sat up.

Steve Jobs was still alive, but that was about the best that could be said of him. He was despondent. His reputation was in shambles. And his career appeared to be finished.

"It's over," Jobs told Murray. "They've taken away all of my operational duties. Sculley won, and I'm out." Like John Lasseter, Steve Jobs had lost his dream job.

Two years earlier, Apple's board of directors had demanded that Jobs bring in a seasoned CEO, and Jobs had immediately set his sights on recruiting Pepsi's CEO, John Sculley. Jobs had been wowed by Sculley's marketing genius, but he hadn't realized that Sculley would take a fast-and-cheap approach to product creation. Jobs, on the other hand, was a perfectionist unwilling to spare any expense in making products that he believed would not only be profitable, but would also make history.

What followed was a thunderous clash of wills. Jobs insisted on perfection; Sculley insisted on making money—preferably quickly. Jobs tried to maneuver around him but it all came to a head when Jobs tried to stage a coup and force Sculley out of Apple. Sculley rallied support for his leadership, fought off Jobs's attack, and finally, once it was clear the company wasn't big enough for both of them, kicked Apple's founder to the curb.

What had once looked like a match made in heaven—between the great Steve Jobs and the legendary John Sculley—turned out to be made in hell.

Skywalker Ranch
Woodside, California
January 30, 1986

"My people tell me you're going to buy my computer graphics division," the legendary George Lucas said over the phone to Steve Jobs.

For a second Jobs detected a note of optimism in Lucas's voice, which otherwise sounded sad and desperate. The *Star Wars* creator had been trying for a year to sell this particular part of his Lucasfilm empire. The small division of forty employees made and sold hardware and software for high-resolution, computer-generated images, but it hadn't found much of a market for its $125,000 Pixar Image Computer.

Lucas, who was going through a difficult divorce, was trying to liquidate unprofitable divisions like this one. Besides, he'd always found something troubling about the motley group of computer scientists who had built the Pixar computer: They seemed obsessed with the dream of making a computer-animated movie. Lucas was a special-effects aficionado, but he'd never cared much for cartoons.

"Yes, George," replied Jobs, "we're going to call it Pixar, after that computer your geniuses have built."

More than twenty venture capitalists had turned down Lucas's offer to sell the division, as had a long line of manufacturing companies. Siemens had considered using the Pixar Image Computer for its CAT scanners. Philips Electronics had thought about using it for MRIs. And Hallmark Cards had been interested in using it for color printing and scanning. While all of them had ultimately passed, they'd at least given the idea more thought than had Jeffrey Katzenberg, the head of Disney's Motion Pictures division. Katzenberg had bluntly told Lucas, "I can't waste my time on this stuff. We've got more important things to do."

Lucas had been only a few weeks away from simply shutting the whole operation down when Steve Jobs had offered Lucasfilm $5 million for it. That was $10 million less than Lucas had wanted, but it was $5 million more than he'd get by simply closing it down.

"Well, let me warn you, Steve," said Lucas, "you're buying a computer company run by a small group of people who don't have much interest in computers. They're only working on hardware and software so that they can use it to one day make a movie. They all want to be Steven Spielberg!

"There's an animator there named John Lasseter who's got his very own one-man animation division that is something of a sideshow. They hired him as an 'interface designer,' I guess so that I wouldn't realize there was an artist in the middle of all my computer scientists."

Jobs had met the bespectacled, Hawaiian-shirt-wearing Lasseter during his tour of Pixar, and he'd immediately warmed to the twenty-eight-year-old animator. Jobs didn't share Lasseter's smiling, childlike, huggable demeanor, but he could identify with Lasseter's perfection-ism, his love of art, and his bold, audacious dreams. Unbeknownst to George Lucas, Jobs wasn't buying Pixar in spite of the cozy relationship between their computer scientists and their creative dreamers; he was buying the company *because* of it.

"That's okay," said Jobs. "I've always been interested in combining art and technology. I think those folks share the same passion." Jobs paused and then added, almost as a confession, "I'm not buying Pixar so I can make a movie, but maybe we can make some shorts to show off the technology. Those are talented people, and I'm going to give them every chance to show me what they can do."

Three days later, Jobs found himself signing another legal document. It was longer and more complicated than the partnership agreement he signed a decade ago. But, like the previous contract, he hoped that this one would give him a new platform upon which to the change the world.

Point Richmond, California
April 5, 1988

The Pixar offices on the outskirts of Point Richmond did not occupy valuable real estate. Crime was rampant in this little pocket of California, north of San Francisco. Many of the surrounding buildings had broken windows. People said only half-jokingly that B&K Liquors, just a stone's throw away on West Cutting Boulevard, stood for "Bleed and Kill." Just past the liquor store was a Chevron refinery whose periodic explosions required frequent "shelter in place" drills at the small computer start-up Steve Jobs had bought two years ago.

Despite the surroundings, the mood of the employees at the Pixar offices was usually buoyant. The young, creative prodigies making state-of-the art computers and designing cutting-edge software felt lucky to be there. They were excited about what they were building together.

But today the mood was as bleak as the abandoned warehouses that surrounded their building. Pixar had lost millions of dollars every year since its creation, and everyone knew—or at least guessed—that there was a limit to Steve Jobs's patience.

As Jobs sat at the head of a conference table, his management team, one by one, suggested ways to save money and stop the bleeding.

Salaries would be cut. Some employees would lose their stock options. Others would lose their jobs entirely.

Jobs didn't relish inflicting pain on Pixar's team, which had swelled from forty employees to about one hundred, but today he was showing no mercy. He had bought Pixar for $5 million, immediately invested another $5 million, and, in the two years since, had spent another $10 million out of his own pocket. Less stubborn men might have already given up on Pixar, but Jobs had stuck with his team. So far.

Just before he was ready to adjourn the meeting and send his managers back to deliver the bad news to the staff, Jobs heard a soft, tentative voice speak up from the other end of the room.

"Steve, I'm almost afraid to ask this, but I'd like to make a short film," John Lasseter said. "It would show what our technology is capable of, and it could be good advertising for us. But . . . it'll cost almost three hundred thousand dollars."

Jobs sat in silence. He had always liked Lasseter. But there was no business rationale for spending $300,000 on a cartoon when his computer company was already hemorrhaging money.

While Lasseter continued to make the case for his project, Jobs thought about his adoptive father, Paul, a high-school-educated mechanic and carpenter. Paul Jobs loved to build beautiful wooden furniture in their garage. It was there that Paul had shared his passion for perfectionism with his son, teaching Steve how to make perfectly symmetrical and smooth parts for a piece of furniture, including the bottom, which would likely never be seen.

Steve Jobs had learned plenty in that garage long before he and Steve Wozniak started building their first computer in it. Now, in John Lasseter, he saw the same dreamy aspiration for beauty and perfection that his adoptive father had imparted to him.

Jobs was snapped back to the present by the silence in the room. Lasseter had finished his pitch, and everyone was looking at Jobs to see if he would scream at the animator, or perhaps even fire him. After all, it took a lot of nerve to ask for a $300,000 investment on a day when every other part of the company was making draconian budget cuts.

Finally, Jobs broke the silence. "Are there any storyboards?" There was skepticism in his voice, but with that one sentence he had opened the door just a crack.

Fifteen minutes later, Lasseter had the storyboards on the wall and was acting out the different characters. The film was about toys that have human emotions. They experience hope and fear, joy and sorrow as they strive to fulfill their greatest desire: to be played with and loved by children.

Lasseter had titled the animated short *Tin Toy* and had chosen one of his favorite vintage toys, a wind-up, one-man-band named Tinny, to play the protagonist.

By the time Lasseter had finished going through the storyboards, Jobs could see the passion in his eyes and the excitement all over his childlike, chubby face. More important, Jobs saw graceful artistry in the simple story. He saw magic in the feelings Lasseter would convey through five dialogue-free minutes of Tinny's trials and tribulations. And he saw—for the first time—the power of combining traditional storytelling techniques with Pixar's pioneering technology.

Only a handful of people in the world understood that transformative potential. For seven years, the group had included John Lasseter.

Now it included Steve Jobs as well.

"Just make it great," Jobs said to his animator. "All I ask of you, John, is to make it great."

Hollywood, California
February 15, 1989; March 29, 1989

Ten months after Jobs told Lasseter to "make it great," *Tin Toy*'s realistic emotions and breathtaking computer graphics earned it a nomination for Best Animated Short by the Academy of Motion Picture Arts and Sciences.

Six weeks later, it won an Academy Award.

Point Richmond, California
May 31, 1990

The phone rang in John Lasseter's office and Jeffrey Katzenberg, the new head of Disney Motion Pictures, was on the other end. More precisely, it was Katzenberg's secretary calling to see if Lasseter was available to talk with the studio chief.

"Hold on, just a moment." Lasseter got up to close the door of his small office at Pixar. He peered down the hallway to see if anyone was around who could listen in on his conversation. Winning the Oscar had changed little about Pixar: Its offices still felt like a summer camp; the employees still wore tennis shoes and rode through the hallways on scooters; they still slept in their offices to meet a deadline and drew on the walls to illustrate their latest ideas; and the company was still bleeding money.

The Oscar, however, was about to change things for John Lasseter. Or at least it could have.

"Yes, I can speak to Mr. Katzenberg now," Lasseter said. Katzenberg's reputation as one of Hollywood's toughest, most unpleasant bosses preceded him, but today Katzenberg was putting on the charm.

"Look, we can beat around the bush here or we can get down to business. I want you to come back to Disney. You're a breathtakingly talented storyteller and this is where you belong." He paused before adding, "And your salary will be quadruple what it is now."

The line went silent as Katzenberg's offer hung in the air. Financially, it was a tempting proposal for a man with a growing family, and it also would return him to the job he had always dreamed of as a young boy. But as he sat in his cramped Pixar office, surrounded by his vintage toys and protected by a patron who had made clear that he would keep writing checks despite the doubtful business rationale, Lasseter looked up at the ceiling and knew what he had to do.

"Jeffrey, I can go to Disney and be a director, or I can stay here and make history."

For four years, Steve Jobs had stuck with John Lasseter. And now, John Lasseter was returning the favor.

Anaheim, California
January 16, 1991

"If I had it my way," said Jeffrey Katzenberg, "we wouldn't be doing this." The already chilly atmosphere in the room at Disney Studios felt as if it had just dropped another ten degrees.

It was an odd way to begin a meeting about the movie Disney had agreed to produce with Pixar, Lasseter thought, but Katzenberg was an odd man. Balding, skinny, and nerdy, he ran Disney Animation like a dictator. His early successes with *The Little Mermaid* and *Beauty and the Beast* had caused his confidence to swell into an obnoxious arrogance.

"It's clear that the talent here is John Lasseter," Katzenberg continued. "And John, since you won't come work for me, I'm going to make it work this way."

Lasseter wondered why Katzenberg was insulting the Pixar team at his first meeting with them, but he let it go. Beggars can't be choosers, he figured, and since Pixar was broke, that would make him the beggar. The contract between the two companies gave Disney the power to shut down production at any time, which meant that if Pixar wanted its movie to be made, it would have to put up with Jeffrey Katzenberg.

True to the rumors about his management style, Katzenberg continued. "Everybody thinks I'm a tyrant. Well, I am a tyrant. But I'm usually right."

The message was clear, at least in Lasseter's mind: I am the great Jeffrey Katzenberg. This is the great Walt Disney Studios. And you people don't know what you're doing.

"So," Katzenberg said in conclusion, "do you think you can work with me, John?"

"I'd like to, Jeffrey," he said. "That's why we're all here. We have an idea for a movie, and we're awfully excited that Disney might be a part of it."

Thinking briefly about how far he'd come since the last pitch he'd made to a Disney executive, Lasseter looked around the table at his small team. These people were family to Lasseter, and the characters they had created together were like their children. He was a little nervous about sharing "his children" with Katzenberg, but he also knew he had little choice. If they were going to make a movie, it had to be with Disney.

"How would you like us to begin?" asked Lasseter.

"Well," said Katzenberg, "why don't you start with the title?"

Lasseter paused and smiled. That was an easy one.

"It's called *Toy Story*."

Anaheim, California
September 10, 1993

It was a big day for John Lasseter. He had always dreamed of making a real movie and now he was working with a real movie star: Tom Hanks, the man who would be giving voice to *Toy Story*'s main character, a cowboy named "Woody." Hanks stood in a small studio, its walls covered in foam and a lone microphone positioned above a music stand that held the script. Lasseter and the Pixar team watched from behind thick, soundproof glass. What was supposed to be one of the most memorable days of his life was quickly turning into one of the most disappointing.

"Who said your job was to think, spring-wiener?" Hanks's Woody said to Slinky Dog. "If it wasn't for me, Andy wouldn't pay attention to you at all."

Tom Hanks, almost unrecognizable from the weight he had lost for his role as an AIDS patient in *Philadelphia*, delivered the lines like a pro. In the scene they were working on, Woody throws his fellow toys out of the bed. In a later scene, Woody's jealousy of Buzz Lightyear, their owner Andy's new favorite toy, grows so intense that Woody pushes Buzz out the window, before coolly remarking, "Hey, it's a toy-eat-toy world." And in still another instance of insult "humor," Woody tells Mr. Potato Head, "You want to be Mr. *Mashed* Potato Head? You button your lip!"

In the sound studio with headphones over his ears and a microphone hanging in front him, Hanks did his best to make Woody charming, even when Woody was behaving badly. But, after a while, Hanks peered through the glass looking for Lasseter, the smile vanishing from his face. "This guy's a real jerk," Hanks said.

Lasseter grimaced as he thought back to how Woody had evolved over the last two years. He had started out as a small tin wind-up toy, then he'd become a GI Joe–style soldier, and finally he had taken on the persona of a cowboy. But Woody had evolved in other ways as well, many of which worried Lasseter. When Pixar showed the Disney team new storyboards and early footage, Katzenberg kept demanding that Lasseter make Woody more "edgy." Katzenberg issued edict after edict, tossing much of the Pixar team's vision for the story out the window and insisting on a Woody who was devious, resentful, bellicose, a little spooky, mildly violent, and sometimes downright cruel. At one point in Katzenberg's version of the story, a Slinky Dog toy asks a fellow toy, "Why is the cowboy so scary?"

Katzenberg explained to Lasseter and the team that there were two reasons for his edits. First, he believed Woody had to start out as the bad guy so that he could grow and evolve as a character. And second, he wanted a movie that appealed to adults as well as children.

Lasseter found Katzenberg's reasoning highly dubious. Woody was the main character, and if he didn't have heart, the movie wouldn't have heart. Walt Disney had once said that "adults are only kids grown up," and he'd endeavored to make movies that "create a believable world of dreams that appeals to all age groups." That's what Lasseter wanted to do with *Toy Story*. He didn't want to talk down to kids, but he didn't want to talk over their heads, either. His vision was to appeal to the child in everyone—to awaken that sometimes-sleeping, yet beautiful and universal spark of innocence and idealism.

That's not, however, how *Toy Story* was turning out. And now, as Lasseter listened to Tom Hanks record Woody's lines, he felt horrible about it. He was embarrassed by his movie, which, in reality, was no longer *his* movie.

For the second time in his life, Disney Animation had broken John Lasseter's heart.

Anaheim, California
November, 19, 1993

John Lasseter sat in the private screening room on the Disney lot, surrounded by his Pixar animation team and Disney's top executives. The
first half of *Toy Story* had been produced, and it was finally time for
Katzenberg and his deputies to screen it.

As Lasseter watched Woody in action, he was sure he was watching
one of the most loathsome protagonists in cinematic history. It wasn't
long before everyone in the room agreed. The movie lacked any sem-
blance of humor, emotion, or charm.

And, with that, it looked like *Toy Story*, and perhaps Pixar itself, were
finished.

Point Richmond, California
December 1, 1994

"Please wake me up when you arrive in the morning," Lasseter wrote
on a Post-it note he put on his secretary's desk.

It was 5 A.M., and he was planning to get a few hours of sleep on
the couch in his office, just like he had every day since Thanksgiving.
His bloodshot eyes had dark circles beneath them. He settled into the
cushions and closed his eyes. Images of toy cowboys and spacemen
raced through his mind.

Two and a half weeks earlier, after Disney had officially shut down
production on *Toy Story,* Jobs and Lasseter had visited Katzenberg and
successfully persuaded him to give Pixar one last chance. "Let us rewrite the script," Lasseter had pleaded. "Give us three more weeks. At
this point, you've got nothing to lose."

The same could not be said for Pixar. If they couldn't fix what was
broken, Pixar would be facing enormous financial pressure. Even Jobs's
deep pockets may not be able to save them any longer.

Lasseter believed he had found a solution, but it meant scrapping
Katzenberg's edits and restoring Woody's character to the Pixar team's
original vision for it. Lasseter decided to keep Woody's early resent-

ment of Andy's affections for Buzz Lightyear, but he found ways to tone down Woody's animosity and put it into better context. He started the movie with a new sequence, which was eventually set to the song "You've Got a Friend in Me," that showed the emotional bond between Woody and Andy before Buzz arrived. He removed all of Woody's insults and domineering orders to his fellow toys, and transformed him into a wise, kindhearted platoon leader of a band of brothers.

When Buzz replaces Woody as Andy's favorite toy, a musical montage pulls at viewers' heartstrings as the relationship is seen from the point of view of Woody, who has lost not just his position at the top of the toy hierarchy, but his best friend Andy as well. And, although Woody is disappointed about losing his friend, he no longer resorts to violence. Instead of Woody's pushing Buzz out a two-story window, Buzz is accidentally knocked out the window by a swinging Luxo lamp.

Lasseter felt incredible pressure to save *Toy Story*, but he also felt the joy of liberation. For years, Steve Jobs had given him unlimited creative control over movies like *Tin Toy* and *Knick Knack*, then Jeffrey Katzenberg had taken it all away. Now Lasseter had it back—and he was determined to never lose it again.

San Francisco, California
July 20, 1995

The film was being completed at a pace of about three minutes per week. One hundred and seventeen computers ran twenty-four hours a day churning out 110,000 frames that took anywhere between forty-five minutes and twenty hours to render.

During that painstakingly slow process, Jobs screened every minute of every scene—repeatedly. He loved to invite his friends over to his Woodside mansion to watch and rewatch the latest cuts. They all saw a lot of potential in the fractions of scenes they previewed, but Jobs knew that his friends didn't see what he did. They couldn't put it all together in their minds.

Not that Jobs cared. He had never spent much time worrying about what other people thought, and he was used to others being blind to possibilities that struck him as obvious.

In less than ten years, Jobs had lost $50 million on Pixar. Time and again, John Lasseter had come to him asking for another check to keep the company afloat, and time and again Jobs had given it to him. Jobs had pushed and challenged the Pixar team and sometimes lost his temper with them, but he had always supported them.

It had recently become easier for Jobs to write Pixar additional checks. It wasn't because he had more capital—he had already spent on Pixar half of the money he had earned from cashing out his Apple stock ten years ago—but because Jobs now knew, without a shadow of a doubt, that *Toy Story* would save Pixar. The last screening had even warmed Katzenberg's ice-cold heart.

It was Jobs's faith in *Toy Story* that eventually led to this visit to his longtime lawyer, Larry Sonsini, in San Francisco. Sonsini had been an unlikely choice to help Jobs take Apple public back in 1980, but the success of that IPO had propelled Sonsini into the top ranks of West Coast securities lawyers. Now Jobs was back with another proposal.

"I want to take Pixar public a week after *Toy Story* premieres in November," Jobs told Sonsini.

"Are you crazy? Who's going to buy stock in a company that's never made a profit?"

"I've been called crazy many times before," said Jobs. "And maybe sometimes I was a little crazy. But it takes a bit of insanity to change the world."

There was more to Jobs's impatience than a simple penchant for risk. He was already thinking beyond *Toy Story*, and he didn't want Pixar to be financially dependent on Disney any longer. He refused to allow Katzenberg, or anyone else, to interfere with John Lasseter's work ever again. But that kind of leverage would require a lot of money.

The kind of money that even Steve Jobs didn't have.

The kind of money that could only be raised with a successful IPO.

Sonsini pleaded with Jobs. The company had lost $8 million last year; what kind of a crazy person would think investors would buy stock in a company like that?

Jobs looked Sonsini in the eye and pointed his thumb at his chest, "This kind."

Offices of Robertson, Stephens & Company
San Francisco, California
November 29, 1995

Steve Jobs looked out the window at San Francisco Bay, raised a glass of Odwalla carrot juice, and toasted Pixar's imminent IPO with the underwriters who had initially shared Larry Sonsini's skepticism over Pixar going public,

"To beautiful movies," he said. "To people and computers that will change the world. And to another insanely great company!" It was almost the same toast he had given when Apple went public.

Ten days earlier, *Toy Story* had premiered at Los Angeles's historic El Capitan Theatre. The *Washington Post*'s film critic wrote that "to find a movie worthy of comparison you have to reach all the way back to 1939, when the world went gaga over Oz." *Newsweek* called it a "marvel" that "harnesses its flashy technology" with "rich characters" and "a very human wit." A reviewer for *Entertainment Weekly* gushed, "I can hardly imagine having more fun at the movies than I did at *Toy Story*."

In an almost unprecedented consensus for a feature film, not a single movie critic gave *Toy Story* anything less than a glowing review. And the public agreed: *Toy Story* enjoyed the most successful Thanksgiving weekend in box-office history.

The only group left to weigh in was investors who were about to have an opportunity to buy Pixar stock. The shares started trading at $22, the exact price Jobs had insisted on when his underwriters had recommended $14. Ultimately, it didn't matter where the share price started; it only mattered where it finished.

As soon as Pixar went on sale, the price of the shares began to rise. And rise. And rise some more. After just thirty minutes, Pixar's price had more than doubled, and by the end of the first hour, it was approaching $50 per share. The quantity of purchase orders throughout the day was so great that trading frequently had to be paused.

When the closing bell finally sounded, the stock had settled at $39 per share—nearly 80 percent higher than where it had been when trading commenced. Steve Jobs was no longer a multimillionaire.

He was now a billionaire.

Far more important to Jobs than the money was the leverage Pixar would now enjoy over Disney and Jeffrey Katzenberg. "Right now," Jobs said to Lasseter as they sipped their glasses of juice, "there are only two significant brands in the film industry—'Disney' and 'Steven Spielberg.' I want to establish 'Pixar' as the third."

Lasseter smiled. "You know, Steve," he said, "you only gave me one order when you signed off on producing *Tin Toy*. Do you remember what it was?"

"'Make it great, John,'" Jobs recalled. "'All I ask is that you make it great.'"

Lasseter put his arm around Jobs and, with a twinkle in his eyes and a smile on his boyish face, the most talented animator since Walt Disney told the most innovative entrepreneur of Silicon Valley, "We're not going to stop now."

EPILOGUE

In 1997, Steve Jobs accepted an invitation from Apple Computer to return as its CEO. The year before, Apple had lost more than a billion dollars. In 2012, it became the most highly valued public company in the history of the world.

Around the same time Jobs returned to Apple, Disney Animation began to produce a string of forgettable animated duds, from *Treasure Planet* to *Brother Bear*. The enormity of Disney's troubles dawned on its CEO, Bob Iger, in 2005 when he watched a parade through Hong Kong Disneyland and realized that not a single character marching in the parade had appeared in a film made in the last ten years. The only exceptions were the characters from Disney's partnership with Pixar.

Market analysts had previously wondered how Disney would survive after Steve Jobs cut off contract talks for a new partnership between the two studios. Now, watching Woody and Buzz parade through Hong Kong Disneyland, Bob Iger was asking himself the same question.

By 2005, Pixar had made *Toy Story*, *A Bug's Life*, *Toy Story 2*, *Monsters Inc.*, *Finding Nemo*, and *The Incredibles*. Each film had been critically acclaimed and had taken computer animation technology to a new level. Not incidentally, each film also took in more than $500 million at the box office. Polls reported that mothers of young children trusted the Pixar brand even more than Disney's.

When Iger returned from Hong Kong, he called Steve Jobs and offered to buy Pixar, lock, stock, and barrel. His thinking was simple: The Walt Disney Company's empire couldn't survive without beloved new characters coming out of its animation division, and the animation division couldn't survive without Pixar.

After relatively brief negotiations between Jobs and Iger—whom Jobs found much easier to deal with than the previous head of Disney, Michael Eisner—Disney bought Pixar for $7.4 billion. At Disney's insistence, the deal required that only one Pixar employee join Disney: John Lasseter. Three decades after Lasseter had tried to return Disney animation to its glory days, Disney paid Pixar 10 percent of their market capitalization largely for the privilege of bringing Lasseter aboard to do exactly that.

"You know, John," Steve Jobs had told his friend over dinner during one of the most exhausting and trying days of producing *Toy Story*, "when I make a computer for Apple, it has a life span of three years. In five years, it's literally a doorstop. But if you do your job right then what you're creating can last forever."

Today, the original Pixar Image Computer can only be found at the Computer History Museum in Mountain View, California, but the characters created by the artists who worked with it and its progeny will be a part of our memories, our imaginations, and our culture to infinity . . . and beyond.

Appendix

UPTON SINCLAIR
STATION A
PASADENA, CALIFORNIA

August 29, 1929

John Beardsley
610 Rowan Bldg.,
Los Angeles, Calif.

Dear John:

I will write you a few notes about the matter concerning which we were talking last night.

When I went to Boston the last time in October 1928 I was completely naïve about the Sacco-Vanzetti case, having accepted the defense propaganda entirely. But I very quickly began to sense something wrong in the situation. There was an air of mystery about the Boston anarchists, and I saw they had something to conceal. Then in Sacco's cross examination I detected what to seemed to be a slip in his alibi. I began asking catch questions, and ultimately I got the admission from one of the leading defense witnesses that his testimony had been framed. I got a virtual admission of the same thing from another witness. It became certain to me that Sacco at least had been concerned in the dynamitings which had occurred in New England just after the war, and I supposed that this was what was being hidden from me. I remained of the opinion that both men had been unquestionably innocent of the crime of which they

*were accused. Their trial had manifestly not been a fair one, and on that
basis I was prepared to defend their right to a new trial. That was my
state if mind at the time that I agreed with The Bookman for the serial
publication of "Boston."*

*But on my way to Denver, where I had arranged by telegraph to meet
Fred Moore, I turned the matter over in my own mind, and doubts began
to assail me. Alone in a hotel room with Fred I begged him to tell me the
full truth. His reply was, "first tell me what you have got." I decided
to take a chance at the worst, and I told him that I knew that the men
were not merely terrorists, but that they were guilty of the holdup. His
reply was, "Since you have got the whole story there is no use my holding
anything back," and he then told me that the men were guilty, and he
told me in every detail how he had framed a set of alibis for them. He
said that there were quite a group of terrorist anarchists who had been
supporting the movement by various kinds of pay-roll holdups, and that all
the practises were well known to Carlo Trsca and Gurley Flynn.*

*This naturally sent me into a panic. I telegraphed Seward Collins of
The Bookman saying that I could not write the book, and I cabled half a
dozen translators and publishers abroad canceling arrangements which I
made for serial publication. But on my way to Los Angeles I thought the
matter over, and I realized certain facts about Fred Moore. I had heard
that he was using drugs. I knew that he had parted from the defense
committee after the bitterest of quarrels. Sacco in a letter had addressed
him as, "your implacable enemy." Moore admitted to me that the men,
themselves, had never admitted their guilt to him; and I began to wonder
whether his present attitude and conclusions might not be the result of his
broodings on his wrongs. This first thing I did when I got to Los Angeles
was to see Lola Moore, Fred's former wife, who had divorced him.
She had been all through the four or five years of the case with him, and
she expressed the greatest surprise, when I told her of Fred's conclusion,
saying that he had most positively not been of that opinion when had
dropped the case and left Boston.*

*I faced the most difficult ethical problem of my life at this point. I had
come to Boston with the announcement that I was going to write the truth
about the case. If I had dropped the project it would have been universally
said and believed that it was because I had decided the men were guilty.*

I had, of course, no first hand knowledge of the framing of their guilt, but I did have first hand knowledge of the framing of testimony. I decided that I would write the story on the basis of telling exactly what I knew. I could portray all sides, and show all the different groups and individuals telling what they knew and what they believed. I would take my stand on the point that the men had not been proved guilty, and that their trial had not been fair. That was all that the law required in order to prevent the execution, and it was all that my thesis required.

I put the problem up to Floyd Dell who happened to come out here, and he read the chapters which I had so far completed, and said that what I was doing was exactly correct. Of course, word spread among the committee in Boston what I was doing, and they flew into a panic, and I had a long string of horrified and indignant letters and telegrams. They strenuously denied that there had ever been any perjury in the case—which, of course, I knew to be perfectly absurd. They also denied that Sacco had ever been a terrorist—though on this point I was finally able to back Gardner Jackson down. I saw him in New York before the book went to press, and we went all over various scenes line by line, and argued for hours. Gardner admitted that I was all right about Sacco, but he claimed that I was doing Vanzetti an injustice. Charles Boni had listened to our discussion. I asked him his opinion, and he said that Gardner had admitted everything that I was claiming, and a little more. Vanzetti as a pacifist was a perfect absurdity, because I talked with a Socialist whom he had chased with a revolver, and young Brini told me of having witnessed a similar scene as a child in his home.

The rumors of Sacco's guilt were very general in the Italian colonies in Boston, and there is no possible question that these rumors, brought to Thayer and Fuller and Lowell in a thousand forms by the police, were the real reason for the execution. When I was in New York last fall I made another effort to satisfy my own mind about the problem. I asked Roger Baldwin, who is, himself, an anarchist, and knows the whole crowd. He told me there was no possible doubt of the guilt of Sacco and Vanzetti, and that the militant anarchists had financed themselves that way for years, both here and abroad. They never took the money for themselves, but only for the movement, and this constituted them idealists and heroes from the point of view of extreme class war theories.

I then took this proposition to Robert Minor, who was an anarchist up to the time of the Russian revolution, and who knows the whole movement. Bob said that he had heard these rumors from the beginning, and had investigated them carefully, and was convinced that they were not true about Sacco and Vanzetti. He said he has never known a class war case of this sort in which there were not similar rumors, and people who will tell you all about it from the "inside." Sometimes they are started by police agents and sometimes by a certain type of weak mined person who takes a pleasure in having the real inside story about a sensational mystery.

So you see that in the end I don't really know any more about the thing than I did in the beginning, and can only take my stand as I did in "Boston," upon the thesis that men should not be executed upon anybody's rumors.

This letter is for yourself alone. Stick it away in your safe, and some time in the far distant future the world may know the real truth about the matter. I am here trying to make plain my own part in the story, and the basis of my seemingly contradictory moods and decisions.

Sincerely,
Upton Sinclair

About the Writing of This Book

This is a work of historical fiction—meaning that we've combined real history with fictional scenes to create compelling, readable stories that hopefully help readers connect with key facts and understand the characters as more than simply names from history books.

Our research process involved teams of people combing through books, oral accounts, court transcripts, biographies, and interviews. It probably won't come as much of a surprise that many of these accounts differ from each other. Our job was to review all the evidence and decide what was most likely to be true. I am certain that we probably got it wrong in some instances, and it's possible that relatives or friends of those depicted in these stories may have compelling evidence that disputes some of our narrative.

This section is meant to help you better understand the research and writing process for each story, including any key decisions we made regarding major facts, characters, or scenes. A chapter-by-chapter accounting is below, but there are also a few things that apply to the entire book that I want to point out.

1. We sometimes modified quotations for clarity, especially if we felt that they left the reader confused. We tried to be as delicate as possible and we never changed the meaning of any direct quotations.
2. In some cases we imagined characters and scenes in order to tell the story in a new way. Whenever we did this we were careful to ensure that nothing we created would contradict anything that we knew to be true from the record.
3. Dialogue and character thoughts were often imagined based on the historical record. None of this dialogue contradicts anything about the characters or story that we know to be true.
4. Specific dates were occasionally imagined if they were not available from the record.

Chapter 1: Grover Cleveland: The Mysterious Case of the Disappearing President

Most of the facts used to create this story came from the following source:

Algeo, Matthew. *The President Is a Sick Man.* Chicago Review Press, 2011.

Much of the dialogue in this chapter was imagined, but the following quotations were taken in whole or in part from the historical record.

- "A dark chapter in a public man's history." (Algeo, 35)
- "Write this down, and send it to all my friends . . ." (Algeo, 35)
- "He is an honest man." (Algeo, 136–37)
- "The falsehoods daily spread before the people . . ." (Algeo, 48)
- "The enormous power of the modern newspaper . . ." (Algeo, 48)
- "I have nothing to say for publication." (Algeo, 84)
- "What does Holland say today?" (Algeo, 139)
- "A delegation of starving miners." (Algeo, 141)
- "Mr. Benedict says that Mr. Cleveland is as impatient . . ." (Algeo, 141)
- "If you hit a rock . . ." (Algeo, 89)
- "Inasmuch as the boat has not been reported . . ." (Algeo, 97)
- "No Sign of the Oneida." *New York Times,* July 4, 1893.
- "He was suffering from a slight attack of rheumatism." (Algeo, 105)
- "That is all." (Algeo, 106–7)
- "The president is absolutely free from cancer." (Algeo, 107)
- " 'Incurable' disease." (Algeo, 42)
- "To Walter Q. Gresham . . ." (Algeo, 109)
- "Likely to recover in a few days." (Algeo, 112)
- "The assertion that President Cleveland . . ." (Algeo, 112–13)
- "The persistent attempts to misrepresent . . ." (Algeo, 113)
- "A pity if a president cannot have a 'touch of rhoumatix' " (Algeo, 113)
- "Some of the physicians who were aboard the yacht must have." (Algeo, 143)
- "Mr. Cleveland recovered from the shock . . ." (Algeo, 145–48)
- "The very depth of despicable journalism." (Algeo, 159–61)
- "The only element of truth in the latest story of President Cleveland's illness." (Algeo, 159–60)
- "There was no question of cancer or of sarcoma." (Algeo, 160)
- "Tumor—Specimen removed . . ." (Algeo, 223)
- "Was substantially correct . . ." (Algeo, 214)

Some scenes in this chapter were imagined or expanded beyond the basic historical record, including:

- The scene in Albany on July 21, 1884, is imagined. The quotations from the newspaper are from the historical record. Cleveland's command to his friends to "tell the truth" is from the record.
- In the scene in New York on July 1, 1893, there is no record of Elisha Jay Edwards being on the ferry with Cleveland.
- In the scene on the *Oneida* at 12:05 P.M. on July 2, 1893, the dialogue is imagined.
- In the scene in New York on July 3, 1893, the opening sentence says that Elisha Jay Edwards was midway through the *New York Times* when he noticed a dispatch. This is imagined, although the words of the dispatch are real.
- The scene in New York on July 4, 1893, is imagined.
- In the scene in New York on July 7, 1893, E. J. Edwards's thoughts are imagined. The quotations of Lamont and the United Press interview with Bryant are from the historical record.
- In the scene at Gray Gables on July 7, 1893, much of the dialogue is imagined, although it is inspired by the historical record of Lamont's press conference. See Algeo, 108–9 for more.
- In the scene in New York on July 8, 1893, E. J. Edwards's actions and thoughts are imagined.
- In the scene in Greenwich on August 27, 1893, the dialogue is imagined.
- In the two scenes in New York on August 28, 1893, much of the dialogue and some of the details are imagined. The text from the article Edwards dictated is, however, from the record.

Chapter 2: "I Did Not Kill Armstrong": The War of Wills in the Early Days of Radio

It's said that history is written by the winners, and at least while he was alive, Edwin Howard Armstrong didn't win. Consequently, a number of credible but conflicting accounts exist and describe the battle between Armstrong, de Forest, and Sarnoff from differing points of view.

For the foundation of this story, we chose an excellent, meticulously researched book:

Lewis, Tom. *Empire of the Air: The Men Who Made Radio.* Edward Burlingame Books, 1991.

Additional material was derived from:

Lessing, Tom. *Man of High Fidelity: Edwin Howard Armstrong, a Biography.* J. B. Lippincott, 1956.

Even before the United States entered World War I, there was an effort by the Wilson administration to establish significant regulation, and possibly even total government control, over radio technology and broadcast content. Many thought leaders in the private sector—including a young David Sarnoff, representing Marconi—vehemently opposed this idea of control of broadcast media by the government. More reading on this subject can be found at http://bit.ly/1tj5UdJ.

Among other great advances, Howard Armstrong's work led to the trouble-free, one-touch controls of later consumer-friendly radio receivers. The terms "tune in" and "stay tuned" are still used today in radio and TV promos, but much like the idea of "dialing" a telephone number, the original context is lost on many people today. Tuning in a radio station was once quite an involved process, and to "stay tuned" required frequent adjustments of multiple knobs and controls. For more on how complicated even these early sets were to use, read this great Wikipedia article: http://bit.ly/1tj644L.

As a wedding present to Marion MacInnes, Armstrong built her the first portable superheterodyne receiver. Historic though it was, this set was "portable" only in the sense that a strong man could manage to carry it for a short distance before resting. A photograph of this receiver with the happy couple on their honeymoon can be found here: http://bit.ly/1tj69W5.

The tale of Howard Armstrong, John Shepard III, and the turbulent founding of the first FM radio network (the Yankee Network) is a story unto itself. To read more about the Yankee Network, visit http://bit.ly/1tj6Dvp.

The essence of David Sarnoff's court testimony in Armstrong's FM patent suit has been paraphrased for dramatic purposes. On the subject of who invented FM, Sarnoff stated that "[RCA] and [NBC] have done more to develop FM than anybody in this country, including Armstrong."

If this story has motivated you to take a more hands-on approach to learning about the work and legacy of Edwin Howard Armstrong, there's a kit available that allows you to build your own one-tube, Armstrong-inspired regenerative receiver. See http://bit.ly/1tj7egv.

There is a wealth of resources available for further reading on David Sarnoff, Lee de Forest, and Edwin Howard Armstrong. As a starting point for more in-depth reading on these men, see:

de Forest: http://fla.st/1tj7BI0
Sarnoff: http://bit.ly/1tj7Dzy
Armstrong: http://bit.ly/1tj7Hzk

Chapter 3 : Woodrow Wilson: A Masterful Stroke of Deception
Most of the facts used to create this story came from the following sources:

Berg, Scott. *Wilson.* Putnam Adult, 2013.
Chandler, Michael. "A President's Illness Kept Under Wraps." *Washington Post,*
     February 3, 2007.

Cooper, John. *Breaking the Heart of the World: Woodrow Wilson and the Fight for the League of Nations.* Cambridge University Press, 2010.

Deppisch, Ludwig. *The White House Physician: A History from Washington to George W. Bush.* McFarland, 2007.

Grayson, Cary T. *Woodrow Wilson: An Intimate Memoir.* Holt, Rinehart & Winston, 1960.

Levin, Phyllis Lee. *Edith and Woodrow: The Wilson White House.* Scribner, 2001.

Pestritto, Ronald J. *Woodrow Wilson and the Roots of Modern Liberalism.* Rowman & Littlefield, 2005.

Most of the dialogue in this chapter was imagined, but the following quotations were taken in whole or in part from the historical record.

- "I should regard it as my duty . . ." (Berg)
- "You know him and he is devoted to you . . ." (Deppisch)
- "President Wilson is a great man with his heart torn out." (Levin, 49)
- ". . . Easily outrank any other American that has yet lived." (Levin, 119)
- "Omnipotence might be her middle name." (Levin, 165)
- "Use this." (Levin, 179)
- "Universal suffrage is at the foundation of every evil . . ." (Pestritto)
- "I have my own diagnosis for my ailment . . ." (Levin, 277)
- "He's got the servants acting as spies . . ." (Levin, 295–96)
- ". . . I have caught the imagination of the people. They are eager to hear what the League stands for . . ." (Berg)
- "If you feel that way about it, I will surrender." (Levin, 331)
- "Please convey our sympathy to the president . . ." (Levin, 348–49)
- ". . . Must have information that I do not possess." (Levin, 354)
- "I thought it wise to record this interview . . ." Kati Marton, *Hidden Power: Presidential Marriages That Shaped Our Recent History,* Pantheon, 2001, 40.
- "Edith emerges as the master of the cover-up." (Levin, 13)

Notes on specific scenes, facts, and characters:

- Grayson had recommended the president take long walks and horseback rides. (Chandler)
- Edith Galt had a severe preoccupation about her shoes. (Levin, 50)
- They bonded over their mutual status. (Levin, 57)
- The lawyer told her that it was her destiny to hold in the palm of her hand the weal or woe of a country. (Levin, 57)
- A sign of Edith's utter devotion: Official Report of the Second Inauguration of Woodrow Wilson, March 5, 1917.

- Grayson agreed with the president's vision for the League of Nations and believed it would be an historic effort to end all wars: "The Anosognosic's Dilemma: Something's Wrong but You'll Never Know What It Is (Part 3)," August 19, 2014, http://nyti.ms/1tjdqoJ.
- It was Edith who managed his workflow. (Levin, 351–52)
- She had written every word. (Levin, 353–554)
- Nobody expected the president to agree to see them. James McCallops, *Edith Bolling Galt Wilson: The Unintended President,* Nova Science, 2003.
- The two men discussed taking a wheelchair to the Capitol so that Wilson could announce his decision to the Congress in person. (Cooper, 319)
- Quitting now was out of the question. (Levin, 420–21)
- Her list had reached a total of fifty-four names. (Cooper, 319)
- His cane appeared to have been erased. (Chandler)

Some scenes in this chapter were imagined or expanded beyond the basic historical record, including:

- The scene of Woodrow and Ellen Wilson with their daughters is invented. Wilson's animus toward women is well documented in the historical record.
- Wilson's conversation with Colonel George Harvey is invented, as are details of the dinner with Ellen Wilson.
- Cary Grayson's encounter with Taft and Wilson is partially imagined, but otherwise based on Grayson's own memoir, *Woodrow Wilson: An Intimate Memoir.*
- Wilson's conversation with Grayson over the care of his sister is imagined, though it is based on Grayson's own recollections and other published accounts.
- Grayson's care of Ellen Wilson and their conversation is partially invented. It was Wilson who has been widely quoted as saying there was nothing "organically wrong" with his wife, an opinion shared or reinforced by his doctor.
- Edith Wilson's first encounter with Woodrow Wilson is partially imagined, but based on her own memoir, Grayson's memoir, and other historical sources.
- Wilson's proposal to Edith is partially invented, but based on her own recollections in her memoir.
- The dialogue included in the scene describing Edith's encounter with Colonel House is partially invented.
- The scene involving the arrest of women's suffragists is partially imagined, but based on real events.
- Grayson's care for Wilson is pieced together from various historical ac-

counts, and the text of his letter warning of Wilson's precarious health is found at the Woodrow Wilson library website: http://bit.ly/1niL9tK.

- Wilson's conversations with Grayson and Edith on the train are partially imagined, but based on sources, including Phyllis Lee Levin's book, as well as Cary Grayson's and Edith Wilson's memoirs.
- Details of Wilson's stroke in the White House are taken from Edith Wilson's "My Memoir." There was also a play that reenacted the scene, *Woodrow Wilson Suffers a Stroke,* found here: http://bit.ly/1zc7Q8x.
- Grayson's poststroke conversations with Edith Wilson are imagined, but based on Grayson's memoir.
- The scene detailing Wilson's consideration of resignation is imagined, though largely based on the historical record.

Chapter 4 : Streets of Gold : Charles Ponzi and the American Scheme
Most of the facts used to create this story came from the following sources:

Blumenthal, Ralph. "Lost Manuscript Unmasks Details of Original Ponzi." *New York Times,* May 2009.

Darby, Mary. "In Ponzi We Trust." *Smithsonian,* December 1998.

Dunn, Donald. *Ponzi: The Incredible True Story of the King of Financial Cons.* Broadway Books, 2004.

Zuckoff, Mitchell. *Ponzi's Scheme: The True Story of a Financial Legend.* Random House Trade Paperbacks, 2006.

Most of the dialogue in this chapter was imagined, but the following quotations were taken in whole or in part from the historical record.

- "Student." (Zuckoff, 24)
- "Dearest Mother, your son has at last stumbled . . ." (Dunn, 28)
- "Your account is more of a bother to us than a benefit." (Zuckoff, 89)
- "Our returns have been enormous already!" (Zuckoff, 115–16)
- "I can think of no more worthy cause . . ." (Zuckoff, 119)
- "A little dollar could start on a journey across the ocean . . ." (Zuckoff, 121–22)
- "She's worried about my hat!" (Dunn, 154–55)
- "Tell me, can you come down to our offices?" (Dunn, 179)
- "I'm the man! I'm doing it!" (Dunn, 234)
- "I've given back more than two million." (Dunn, 279)
- "Declares Ponzi is now hopelessly insolvent." (Blumenthal)
- "How are your newspapers selling?" (Zuckoff, 236–37)
- "I might have." (Zuckoff, 256)
- "After I am proved on the level . . ." (Zuckoff, 258)

- "Yes, I have agreed." (Zuckoff, 280–81)
- "The man's nerve is iron." (Darby)
- "No man is ever licked" (Zuckoff, 281)
- "I do not anticipate that another Charles Ponzi will ever appear in the financial world." (Blumenthal)

Notes on sourcing of specific facts, scenes, and characters:

- Satisfied with his letter to his mother, Carlo had a few more drinks. (Zuckoff, 21)
- He was impressed by the man's skill. (Dunn, 11)
- Banco Zarossi became one of the fastest-growing financial institutions. (Dunn, 24)
- Mattress made from a sack of corncobs and husks. (Zuckoff, 30)
- He'd hinted that he'd worked for the Italian government. (Zuckoff, 79–81)
- Ponzi had already rented a large office and hired two stenographers. (Zuckoff, 88)
- The wife took fifteen dollars from her purse and handed it to Ponzi. (Zuckoff, 121–22)
- Ponzi told them that such information was a trade secret. (Darby)
- Ponzi thought he and Columbus were similar in many ways. (Zuckoff, 135)
- Ponzi concluded that the story could not have been better. (Darby)
- Ponzi was infuriated by the accusations. (Dunn, 246)
- The story included photos of his mug shot. (Darby)
- Sixty years old, nearly blind, and partially paralyzed from stroke. (Dunn, 337)

Some scenes in this chapter were imagined or expanded beyond the basic historical record, including:

- Ponzi's conversation with William H. McMasters is imagined, but is primarily based on Donald Dunn's *Ponzi: The Incredible True Story of the King of Financial Cons.*
- Young Ponzi's letter to his mother and his college exploits are partially imagined, but based on Mitchell Zuckoff's *Ponzi Scheme: The True Story of a Financial Legend.*
- Ponzi's conversation with his uncle is partially imagined. His uncle's declaration that the streets of America "are literally paved with gold" is, however, taken directly from Zuckoff's book.
- Why Ponzi briefly changed his name to Bianchi is an educated supposition.

- Most of the details surrounding Ponzi's involvement with the Banco Zarossi are taken from Dunn's book, though parts of the conversation are imagined.
- Ponzi's letter from prison to his mother appears in Donald Dunn's biography, though his motivations for the letter are partially theorized.
- The details of Ponzi's encounter with Detective McCall are taken from the Zuckoff biography.
- The conversations with Ponzi and the immigration official at the New York border are partially imagined and partially taken from Donald Dunn's biography, 32–34.
- The details of Ponzi's encounters with Charles Morse come from Donald Dunn's biography, including Morse's quote about "it's all a matter of keeping your sights high." (Dunn, 42)
- Ponzi's conversations with Rose are imagined and based on the Dunn and Zuckoff biographies, as well as other sources.
- Ponzi's conversations with potential investor Gilberti are partially imagined and partially taken from the Dunn and Zuckoff biographies.
- William McMaster's views and conversations with Ponzi are partly imagined but also influenced by McMaster's lost manuscript, which was detailed in the *New York Times* on May 4, 2009: http://nyti.ms/1rq97KN.
- Accounts differ as to whether Ponzi compared his exploits as being bigger than the landing of the Pilgrims or if he instead referred to the *Mayflower.*

Chapter 5 : He Loved Lucy : The Tragic Genius of Desi Arnaz, the Inventor of the Rerun

Most of the facts used to create this story came from the following sources:

Arnaz, Desi. *A Book.* Morrow, 1976. http://bit.ly/1rpZThD.

Edwards, Elisabeth. *I Love Lucy: Inside the World of Television's First Great Sitcom.* Running Press, 2011. http://bit.ly/1w9TCZJ.

FBI Records on Desi Arnaz. Part 3 of 7. http://1.usa.gov/1w9RTU2.

Folkart, Burt A. "Desi Arnaz, TV Lucy's Loving Co-Star, Dies." *Los Angeles Times,* December 3, 1986. http://lat.ms/1w9Wo0N.

Harris, Warren G. *Lucy & Desi: The Legendary Love Story of Television's Most Famous Couple.* Simon & Schuster, 1991.

Kanfer, Stefan. *Ball of Fire: The Tumultuous Life and Comic Art of Lucille Ball.* Knopf Doubleday, 2007.

McGrath, Douglas. "Television/Radio: The Good, the Bad, the Lucy: A Legacy of Laughs; The Man Behind the Throne: Making the Case for Desi." *New York Times,* October 14, 2001. http://nyti.ms/1w9QfSq.

Sanders, Coyne S., and Tom Gilbert. *Desilu: The Story of Lucille Ball and Desi Arnaz.* HarperCollins, 1994.

Schindehette, Susan. "The Real Story of Desi and Lucy." *People,* February 18, 1991. http://bit.ly/1w9PYPx.

Most of the dialogue in this chapter was imagined, but the following quotations were taken in whole or in part from the historical record.

- "Instead of divorce lawyers profiting from our mistakes . . ." (Desilu, 29)
- "Oh, Desi, It just isn't the same, is it?" Bart Andrews, "Last Five Years Were Rocky for Lucy & Desi," *Philadelphia Inquirer,* May 3, 1989.
- "Dios mio! What is happening?" (Arnaz, 26)
- "Especially you, Desi. You're a young boy . . ." (Arnaz, 31)
- "I am very sorry I couldn't have you join me here sooner . . ." (Arnaz, 32)
- "That's silly, Dad. We'll be more comfortable here." (Arnaz, 37)
- "No way my son is going to be a musician." (Arnaz, 43)
- "Why don't you call me Lucille, and I'll call you Dizzy." (Kanfer, 75)
- "Wouldya like me to teach you? It may come in handy for your part." (Arnaz, 109)
- "Now, Desi, I want you to sweep Lana into your arms and kiss her passionately." (Arnaz, 141)
- "You can't have children over the telephone." (Desilu, 22)
- "If no one will give us a job together, then we'll give ourselves one." Bart Andrews, "Lucy's 'Favorite Husband' for Years, She Tried Her Best to Make the Marriage Work," *Philadelphia Inquirer,* April 27, 1989.
- "Why are they so unhappy about *Look* magazine? Who's going to care about that?" (Arnaz, 205)
- "Five thousand an episode." (Arnaz, 72)
- "Well, that's no problem. Tell the ladies to be my guest." (Arnaz, 225)
- "How ya doing, you gorgeous Cuban?" (Kanfer, 137)
- "Thank you, America." "Lucille Ball & Desi Arnaz—Toast of the Town October 3, 1954," YouTube. http://bit.ly/1rqd4PN.
- "Oh, hell. I could tell them worse than that." (Schindehette)
- "Maybe I'm a romantic, but there was a great, great love there." (Schindehette)
- "We certainly did have everything. Worked very hard to get it . . ." "Lucille Ball & Barbara Walters: An Interview of a LifeTime (FULL)," YouTube. http://bit.ly/1rqdaa6.
- "Give Lucy ninety percent of the credit—divide the other ten percent among the rest of us . . ." (Sanders, 357)
- ". . . Every evening we spend watching television, we are exposed to his influence." (Folkart)

Notes on specific scenes, facts, and characters:

- Desi Arnaz's initials were etched in gold paint on his black Buick Roadmaster. (Sanders, 13)
- Desi could not believe that Lucille Ball was the same woman he had spotted on set yesterday. (Arnaz, 109)
- Desi was not angry that Lucy had signed a contract with MGM; he was mad that she signed it with help from Pandro Berman—her former lover. (Harris, 322)
- Although Desi did not want any visitors, Lucy was determined to see him and insisted on being let into his room. (Harris, 322)

Some scenes in this chapter were imagined or expanded beyond the basic historical record, including:

- The details of Desi Arnaz's childhood in Cuba, including his flight from his home, as well as some of the direct quotes, are taken from Desi's autobiography, *A Book.*
- Most of the details and conversations with Desi's father after he arrived in America are also taken from the Arnaz autobiography, as well as from numerous articles and interviews.
- Desi and Lucy's first meeting and their conversation are based on details in both of their autobiographies. Lucy's was titled *Love, Lucy* and was published posthumously by their daughter. Other sources for this scene include Coyne and Gilbert, *Desilu.*
- Desi's performance at the Roney Plaza Hotel is partly imagined but based on his autobiography.
- The scene with Desi in Louis B. Mayer's office at MGM is partially imagined, but most of the details come from Arnaz's memoir.
- The meeting with CBS executives and Lucille Ball is largely invented, though it does reflect actual conversations that Lucille recounts in her memoir.
- Desi's conversations with his agent are imagined.
- Lucille's decision-making process to green-light *Star Trek* is largely imagined, but is based on details included in several sources.
- The scene where Lucy and Desi play with their grandson is based on a real home movie taken by their daughter, Lucie Arnaz.
- Desi's deathbed conversation with his nurse is invented. The words from Desi's speech are from the historical record. See the video at http://bit.ly/1rq25FV.

Chapter 6 : The Muckraker: How a Lost Letter Revealed Upton
Sinclair's Deception

Most of the facts used to create this story came from the following sources:

Alexander, Michael. *Jazz Age Jews.* Princeton University Press, 2001.
Arthur, Anthony. *Radical Innocent: Upton Sinclair.* Random House, 2007.
Literary Digest Magazine. Vol. 61, no. 11, June 14, 1919.
Summation of Fred Moore for the Defense. Dedham, Mass., July 13, 1921.
     Court transcript available online: http://bit.ly/1tjgPUs.
Watson, Bruce. *Sacco and Vanzetti: The Men, The Murders, and the Judgment of
     Mankind.* Penguin, 2007.
Whitman, Alden. "Upton Sinclair, Author, Dead; Crusader for Social Justice,
     90." *New York Times,* November 26, 1968.

*Most of the dialogue in this chapter was imagined, but the following quotations were
taken in whole or in part from the historical record.*

- "In the course of the arguments had in this case, attention will be di-
  rected . . ." (Moore)
- ". . . The will find two words there—'Social Justice' for that is what I
  believe I fought for." (Whitman)
- "Long live anarchy!" "Sacco and Vanzetti Put to Death Early This
  Morning," *New York Times,* August 24, 1927. http://nyti.ms/1lbXHrf.
- "I wish to tell you that I am innocent, and that I never committed any
  crime but sometimes some sin. I am innocent of all crime, not only of
  this, but all. I am an innocent man." (Ibid.)
- "What is your full name. . . . The fellow on the right here." Testimony
  of Prosecution Witness Lewis Pelser, Courtroom Transcript. http://bit
  .ly/1lbXXXc.
- "Perhaps a thousand times as many people will read my novel as will
  ever look at the official record." (Arthur)
- "To a hundred million groping, and ten times as many still in slumber,
  the names of Sacco and Vanzetti would be the eternal symbols of a
  dream, identical with civilization itself, of a human society in which
  wealth belongs to the producers of wealth, and the rewards of labor are
  to the laborers." Upton Sinclair, *Boston: A Novel,* Scholarly Press, 1970.

*Some scenes in this chapter were imagined or expanded beyond the basic historical record,
including:*

- The scene that takes place in Boston on August 23, 1927, is imagined.
  Upton Sinclair spent a great deal of time in Boston in 1926 and 1927

researching his book on Sacco and Vanzetti, but there is nothing that explicitly says he was there on the night they were executed.

- "To the workers of the whole world, it is a warning to get organized and check the bloodlust of capitalism." Upton Sinclair as quoted in Paul Avrich, *Sacco and Vanzetti: The Anarchist Background,* Princeton University Press, 1996, 161.
- "What an ironic twist of fate," Sinclair, *Boston,* Bentley, 1978, 262.
- The scenes that occur on June 30 and August 4, 1901, are imagined, but according to Sinclair biographers, Meta Sinclair did try to abort her child. See, for example, Arthur, *Radical Innocent.*
- Teddy Roosevelt and Upton Sinclair did meet in the White House, but the dialogue is imagined. The last quote summing up Roosevelt's view of Sinclair is taken from a private letter he wrote to a friend: Roosevelt to William Allen White, July 31, 1906, in Elting E. Morison and John M. Blum, eds., *The Letters of Theodore Roosevelt,* 8 vols., Harvard University Press, 1951–54, vol. 5, 340.
- Most of the details of Carlo Valdinoci's attack on Attorney General Palmer are taken from Alexander, *Jazz Age Jews.*
- The July 13, 1921, courtroom scene is taken directly from the stenographer's record. The court transcript is available online: http://bit.ly/1tjgPUs.
- Stalin was an admirer of Sacco and Vanzetti. More details are available in Watson, *Sacco and Vanzetti.*
- Sinclair and Moore met in Denver in 1928, though exactly what was said is unknown. We do know from Sinclair's letter that Moore clearly admitted to his belief that Sacco was not innocent of the murders.

Chapter 7: Alan Turing: How the Father of the Computer Saved the World for Democracy

Most of the facts used to create this story came from the following sources:

Copeland, Jack. *Turing.* Oxford University Press, 2013.

Duffus, Kevin. *War Zone: World War II Off the North Carolina Coast.* Looking Glass Productions, 2013.

Dyson, George. *Turing's Cathedral.* Vintage, 2012.

Hodges, Andrew. *Alan Turing: The Enigma.* Centenary ed. Princeton University Press, 2012.

Hold, Jim. *Code-Breaker: The Life and Death of Alan Turing. The New Yorker,* 2006.

Leavitt, David. *The Man Who Knew Too Much.* Norton, 2006.

Whitemore, Hugh. *Breaking the Code.* Fireside Theatre, 1987.

Most of the dialogue in this chapter was imagined, but the following quotations were taken in whole or in part from the historical record.

- "White man's burden." (Hodges, 23)
- "From cover to cover, it made science approachable . . ." (Hodges, 12)
- "The life of any creature—man, animal, or plant—is . . ." (Hodges, 17)
- "The body is a machine." (Hodges, 13)
- "Look at the skin: a symbol of what lies within . . ." (Leavitt, 140)
- "When she breaks the tender peel . . ." (Leavitt, 140)
- "The life of any creature, is one long fight" (Hodges, 17)
- "The victim of the sleeping death . . ." (Leavitt, 280)
- "Dip the apple in the brew. Let the sleeping death seep through." (Leavitt, 140)
- "The British Ambassador in Berlin handed . . ." The transcript of Neville Chamberlain's declaration of war is at http://bbc.in/1tjkRwn.
- "I have to tell you now that no such undertaking . . ." (Chamberlain)
- "You can imagine what a bitter blow it is to me . . ." (Chamberlain)
- "You may be taking your part in the fighting services . . ." (Chamberlain)
- "Now may God bless you all . . ." (Chamberlain)
- "Simplicity is the ultimate sophistication." Walter Isaacson, *Steve Jobs,* A&C Black, 2012, 90.
- "There were 17,576 possible states of rotors." (Hodges, 167)
- "There were 150,738,274,937,250 possible ways of connecting ten pairs of letters." (Hodges, 178)
- "Hitler's fate was sealed." "Arsenal of Democracy—Chicago's Industrial Might Quickly Mobilized for WWII," *Chicago Tribune,* March 24, 2013, http://trib.in/1tjldTF.
- "Communications Supplementary Activities . . ." (Hodges, 243)
- "You are about to embark upon a great crusade . . ." Messages from General Dwight D. Eisenhower prior to Normandy invasion, http://bit .ly/1tjloy7.

Some scenes in this chapter were imagined or expanded beyond the basic historical record, including:

- The scene that takes place on April 9, 1919, is imagined. It does, however, incorporate elements of Turing's childhood that are in the historical record, including examining the flight paths of bees.
- Details included in the scene that takes place on December 25, 1924, are imagined. It does, however, incorporate documented elements

from Turing's childhood, like Brewster's book and Turing's receiving a chemistry set for Christmas.

- Details included in the scene that takes place on March 15, 1935, are all imagined.
- Details of the scene that takes place on October 28, 1938, are imagined, although Turing did see, and become a huge fan of, *Snow White and the Seven Dwarfs.*
- Turing's listening to Chamberlain's speech in the scene on September 3, 1939, is imagined, although Chamberlain's words are from the historical record.
- In the scene on September 4, 1939, the dialogue and some details are imagined.
- The scene that takes place on October 26, 1940, is imagined, including the dialogue. It is known that Turing and Denniston did not always see eye to eye, but it is unknown if they had the substantive disagreement described in this scene. Accounts conflict, but it is possible that Denniston's beliefs do not perfectly align with the way we've described them.
- The scene on January 7, 1941, is imagined, including the dialogue. Many of the dates in this chapter are educated guesses. It is possible that, by this date, Turing would have already been using cribs, and it is also possible that Denniston would have been familiar with the concept of cribs.
- In the scene from November 13, 1942, to March 23, 1943, Alan's first day at Bell Labs is imagined, including the dialogue. Frank Cohen is not a person from the historical record.
- In the scene on February 7, 1952, the dialogue is imagined.
- The scene on June 7, 1954, describes Turing's suicide. There were no witnesses, so details and his internal monologue are imagined, as are his final words. In his play *Breaking the Code,* Hugh Whitemore imagines Turing saying the same words when he eats the poisonous apple. In the biography of Turing by David Leavitt, Leavitt also quotes this couplet from *Snow White* on the last page of the biography, which discusses what Turing was thinking when he bit into the poisoned apple. The historical record shows that these words were among Turing's favorite from *Snow White,* and he frequently recited them after seeing the movie.
- There is plenty of debate about whether the Apple logo has anything to do with Alan Turing. Apple itself has never officially denied or confirmed it, but the man who drew the original logo says he was unfamiliar with Turing at the time. See, for example, http://cnn.it/1qxJ6mm.

Chapter 8 : The Spy Who Turned to a Pumpkin : Alger Hiss and the Liberal Establishment That Defended a Traitor

Most of the facts used to create this story came from the following sources:

Ambrose, Stephen. *Nixon.* Simon & Schuster, 1988.

Kennedy, David M. *Freedom from Fear: The American People in Depression and War, 1929–1945.* Oxford University Press, 1999.

Shelton, Christina. *Alger Hiss: Why He Chose Treason.* Threshold Editions, 2012.

Tanenhaus, Sam. *Whittaker Chambers: A Biography.* Modern Library, 1998.

Weinstein, Allen. *Perjury: The Hiss-Chambers Case.* Random House, 1997.

White, Edward G. *Alger Hiss's Looking-Glass Wars: The Covert Life of a Soviet Spy.* Oxford University Press, 2005.

Most of the dialogue in this chapter was imagined, but the following quotations were taken in whole or in part from the historical record.

- "These are among the most important days that any of us shall live." (Dallas, 408)
- "For the Russian people, the question of Poland is not a question of honor . . ." "Yalta Conference," *New World Encyclopedia,* July 31, 2013, 13:48, http://bit.ly/1mN4ovj.
- "the truth, the whole truth and nothing but the truth." Douglas Linder, "The Alger Hiss Trial," University of Missouri-Kansas City School of Law, 2003. http://bit.ly/1ltUqnK.
- "So help me God." (Weinstein, 10)
- "I am not and never have been a member of the Communist Party." (Ambrose, 171)
- "We're ruined." Lance Morrow, *The Best Year of Their Lives: Kennedy, Johnson, Nixon in 1948,* Basic Books, 2005, 242.
- "In view of the facts Chambers has testified to . . ." (Tanenhaus, 241–42)
- "On the Potomac" (Ambrose, 181)
- ". . . I challenge you to do it, and hope you will do it damned quickly." Robert G. Whalen, "Hiss and Chambers: Strange Story of Two Men," *New York Times,* December 12, 1948.
- "You knew this man . . ." (Weinstein, 44)
- "We are caught in the tragedy of history . . ." (Weinstein, 45)
- "I have other documents. Important ones . . ." (Ambrose)
- "Here is what you're looking for." (Tanenhaus, 302)
- "Until the day I die, I shall wonder how Whittaker Chambers got into my house to use my typewriter." (Ambrose, 195; Weinstein, 266)

- "When you get to Lewisburg, ask for Mike M." (White and Minor, 84)
- "None of what went on was justified. It was all hyped up for political purposes . . ." Frederick N. Rasmussen, "Alger Hiss Spoke of His Innocence in Spy Case During 1974 Hopkins Talk." *Baltimore Sun,* June 11, 2011, http://bit.ly/1nxX3Qz.
- "If Mr. Ford is so handy with pardons, I'd be glad to gone one . . ." "Nixon's Watergate Resurrects Alger Hiss' Image," *Pittsburgh Press,* October 9, 1975, http://bit.ly/1tFG5o7.
- "Alger defended himself . . . with great intelligence. He had been trained as a lawyer . . ." Sam Tanenhaus, "Hiss Case 'Smoking Gun'?" *New York Times,* October 14, 1993, http://nyti.ms/1BYPDiM.
- "Hiss considered vindication a declaration by a Russian General . . ." Wes Vernon, "AIM Report: Media Won't Give Up on Red Spy Alger Hiss—July B," Accuracy In Media, July 2007, http://bit.ly/1qeHd0G.

Notes on sourcing for specific scenes, facts, and characters:

- Alger sold spring water from a little wagon to earn money when he was a boy. (Tanenhaus, 237)
- Hiss had been introduced to Professor Frankfurter. (Shelton, 24–25)
- Holmes soon relented and Hiss read to him every day. (White, 419–26)
- Roosevelt attended Yalta on the Crimean Sea. (Kennedy, 799)
- Hiss wasn't concerned about the Soviet Union. (Weinstein, 313)
- Hiss had been tasked with preparing all of the background material to be used at the Yalta Conference. (Weinstein, 315)
- Richard Nixon's appearance. (Ambrose, 119)
- Elizabeth Bentley's testimony put Harry S. Truman on the defense. (Weinstein, 13)
- Chambers explained how Hiss became a part of Ware's Communist Party. (White, 703)
- Hiss's request to sit before a committee was granted. (Weinstein, 9)
- Hiss was dressed in a gray suit and dark tie. Digital image, http://bit.ly/1rxqc5I.
- Hiss's credentials walking into the courtroom. CIA, Center for the Study of Intelligence, *The Alger Hiss Case,* n.p., n.d. *Studies of Archives Indexes,* http://1.usa.gov/OUIxrd.
- Hiss could be a future candidate for secretary of state. (White, 179)
- Hiss's voice was assured, confident, and resolute. (Linder)
- Truman's White House counsel already had a bill in his desk drawer to abolish the committee. (White, 926)
- Theories stated that communist advisors manipulated the sickly president. (Kennedy, 800–806)

- Nixon knew that no one cared about throwing him to the wolves. (Tanenhaus, 241–42)
- How the Commodore Hotel was stocked: "The Hotel Commodore, New York," *Architectural Review,* January 1919, http://bit.ly/1qeIy7E.
- Hiss acknowledged that he knew Chambers, but only as George Crosley. (Tanenhaus, 259)
- Hiss could not hide his disdain. (Tanenhaus, 266)
- Hiss's defense rested chiefly on the opinions of others. (Tanenhaus, 271–72)
- The photo had been staged. (Ambrose, 193)
- He showed little emotion as federal marshals placed handcuffs on him. (Weinstein, 446)
- Hiss planned to maintain his complete and total innocence. (White, 1359)
- After prison Hiss knew his wife wanted them to move away. (White, 1873)
- All materials from the scene at Princeton University, April 26, 1956, come from Edward White's book.
- As the *Wall Street Journal* noted, after Verona, the only people still proclaiming Hiss's innocence . . . (White, 3520)

Some scenes in this chapter were imagined or expanded beyond the basic historical record, including:

- The scene involving Hiss's arrival at Lavadia Palace is imagined.
- Hiss's graduation scene at Harvard is imagined, based on details of his family life in a number of biographical accounts.
- Hiss's conversation with Justice Oliver Wendell Holmes is imagined, but is based on historical accounts.
- Hiss's trip aboard the *Ferdinand Magellan* with FDR and the American delegation was re-created and imagined based on the historical record.
- Alger Hiss's scene in his office responding to accusations from Whittaker Chambers was imagined based on a variety of sources. The defense of Hiss by Eleanor Roosevelt, Felix Frankfurter, Dean Acheson, and others is attested to in a number of articles. See, for example, Sam Tanenhaus, "The Hiss Case Isn't Over Yet," *New York Times,* October 31, 1992, http://nyti.ms/1wtvFN5.
- The scene with Richard Nixon and HUAC behind the scenes is imagined based on a variety of historical sources.
- The scene with Nixon and Dulles has been re-created with quotes taken from cited sources.

- Nixon's interrogation of Hiss was imagined based on sources.
- The scenes involving Nixon, Stripling, and the confrontations with Chambers and his lawyer were imagined based on various sources. Some of the details came from Ambrose's *Nixon*.

Chapter 9 : The City of Tomorrow : Walt Disney's Last and Lost Dream

Most of the facts used to create this story came from the following sources:

Broggie, Michael. *Walt Disney's Railroad Story.* Pentrex, 1997.
Gabler, Neal. *Walt Disney: The Triumph of the American Imagination.* Knopf, 2006.
Thomas, Bob. *Walt Disney: An American Original.* Simon & Schuster, 1976.

Most of the dialogue in this chapter was imagined, but the following quotations were taken in whole or in part from the historical record.

- "It's unique. I know, because I've looked everywhere for something like it . . ." (Thomas, 245)
- "Walt, if you are going to look at more zoos, I am not going with you!" (Thomas, 241)
- "I want you to work on Disneyland, and you're going to like it!" (Gabler, 494)
- "You're going to make it" (Thomas, 196)
- "You're the only one who can do it. I'll stay here with you and we'll do it together." (Broggie, 208)
- "Sometime in 1955 Walt Disney will present for the people of the world . . ." (Thomas, 247)
- "If we lose the detail, we lose it all." (Gabler, 527)
- "the way it should have been." (Gabler, 496)
- "Okay, let's go after some land." (Thomas, 335)
- "This is perfect. It's going to be fine." (Thomas, 336)
- "A showcase for American industry and research . . ." (Thomas, 349)

Notes on specific scenes, facts, and characters:

- Elias wasn't interested in anything new or novel; this was the type of thing that set off his temper. (Thomas, 35)
- Elias Disney started to cry after hitting his son. (Gabler, 24)
- The neighbors' judgment of his father embracing socialism was painful for Walt. (Gabler, 17)
- Roy managed to get ABC to agree with a deal in principle. (Thomas, 249)
- During the *Disneyland* show Walt introduced viewers to the park's concept. (Gabler, 510)
- Walt was feuding with Orange County building inspectors over applying city ordinances and codes to Sleeping Beauty's castle. (Thomas, 263)

- Walt knew what Hazel was hinting—we are all getting older. (Thomas, 299)

Some scenes in this chapter were imagined or expanded beyond the basic historical record, including:

- The scene involving Walt and the unlucky opening of Disneyland is invented, though many of the details are taken from various biographies. The story about heels of women sinking into the freshly laid pavement, for example, appears in a number of books.
- The scene with Walt, his brother Roy, and their father is invented, based on details in various sources, including Gabler's *Walt Disney*.
- Roy Disney's meeting with the Disney board of directors is imagined.
- Roy's encounter with employees exasperated with his brother is imagined, but is based on well-chronicled details about Walt Disney's management style.
- The scene describing Roy's clandestine arrival in Florida to survey the plans to buy land in Orlando was invented based on historical evidence.
- Walt's viewing of the riots in Los Angeles is imagined, though it was well known that one of the primary motivations for EPCOT was his concern about the safety and quality of life of American cities for his grandchildren.
- Walt's announcement of plans to build Disney World in Orlando can be seen here: http://bit.ly/1rqaadF.
- Walt Disney's televised presentation on his plans for Disney World can be viewed here: http://bit.ly/1rqaglK.
- Walt's conversation with his employees and his friend, Hazel, after his hospitalization is based on various biographies, including Gabler, 628.
- Roy's hospital visits with his brother are partially invented. It is well chronicled that Walt talked to Roy about finishing EPCOT and sketched out the plans for it on a grid in the ceiling tile above his bed. See, for example, Gabler, 630–32.
- The scene of Roy Disney's collapse is imagined.

Chapter 10 : "Make It Great, John": How Steve Jobs and John Lasseter Changed History at Pixar
Most of the facts used to create this story came from the following sources:

Isaacson, Walter. *Steve Jobs*. A&C Black, 2012.
The Pixar Story. Dir. Leslie Iwerks. Disney/Pixar, 2007. Documentary.
Price, David A. *The Pixar Touch: The Making of a Company*. Knopf, 2008.

Most of the dialogue in this chapter was imagined, but the following quotations were taken in whole or part from the historical record.

- "That's why they call them head hunters." (See video of an interview with Lasseter: http://bit.ly/1uWRjYk)
- "It's over." (Isaacson, 206)
- "I can't waste my time on this stuff . . ." (Price, 71)
- "All I ask of you, John, is to make it great." (Isaacson, 247)
- "I can go to Disney and be a director, or I can stay here." (Isaacson, 248)
- "If it wasn't for me, Andy wouldn't pay attention to you at all." (Price, 131)
- "Toy-eat-toy world." (Price, 131)
- "You want to be Mr. Mashed Potato Head?" (Price, 131)
- "This guy's a real jerk." (Isaacson, 287)
- "Adults are only kids grown up." Disney Book Group, *The Quotable Walt Disney,* Disney Editions, 2001, 136.
- "Create a believable world of dreams that appeals to all age groups." (Disney, 139)
- "To find a movie worthy of comparison you have to." (Price, 152)
- "A very human wit." (Price, 152)
- "I can hardly imagine having more fun at the movies." (Price, 152)
- "I would like to establish Pixar as the third." (Price, 164)

Some scenes in this chapter were imagined or expanded beyond the basic historical record, including:

- Many of the exact dates of the scenes are imagined, although we tried to make educated guesses based on the record.
- Some details in the scene that takes place on April 1, 1976, are imagined.
- The scene on July 1, 1976, is imagined. Lasseter did work as a guide on the Jungle Cruise, and his jokes in this scene are taken from an interview with him, as well as from jokes traditionally told by Jungle Cruise guides.
- In the scene that takes place on December 12, 1980, in San Francisco, the dialogue and some of the details are imagined.
- In the scene on December 12, 1980, in Anaheim, some of the dialogue is imagined, as are some of the details. Richard Coyle is an imagined name and is based on a person—whose name is unknown—that Lasseter said told him, "Just do what you're told. If you don't want to do it, there's a line of people out the door who will take your place."
- Ed Boone is imagined.
- In the scene that takes place on September 16, 1983, many of the

details are imagined, as is most of the dialogue, including all of Ron Miller's dialogue. There are many different perspectives about the pros and cons of Disney's strategy during the 1980s. We have told the story from the perspective of John Lasseter. Others involved might believe that Lasseter oversimplified what he saw as problems at Disney.

- In the scene that takes place on May 28, 1985, the dialogue is imagined and the characterization of the differences between Jobs and Sculley has been greatly simplified. Sculley was undoubtedly right about some things, and Jobs was undoubtedly wrong about some things—but this scene is meant to portray their differences from Jobs's perspective.
- The scene that takes place on January 30, 1986, is imagined, including the dialogue and some details.
- In the scene on April 5, 1988, some details and most of the dialogue are imagined, although the final quote ("Make it great, John") is from the historical record.
- The scene on May 31, 1990, is imagined, including the dialogue. Unless otherwise noted in the sourcing above, Katzenberg's dialogue in this chapter is imagined.
- In the scene that takes place on January 16, 1991, some details are imagined.
- In the scene that occurs on September 10, 1993, some details and some dialogue are imagined.
- The scene that takes place on December 1, 1994, is imagined, including the dialogue.
- Details included in the scene that occurs on July 20, 1995, are imagined. Some dialogue is imagined, while some is based on a statement Sonsini made in a meeting with Pixar executives, as reported in David Price's *The Pixar Touch*. Sonsini said, "Look, Steve is not going to take this company public. . . . He cannot take this company public. This company is fifty million dollars in deficit and has no revenue" (Price, 148). Some dialogue by Sonsini in this scene is imagined.
- In the scene that takes place on November 29, 1995, the dialogue is imagined, though some of it is based on statements Jobs made on other occasions. Some details are also imagined, including the initial skepticism of these particular underwriters about going public. The characterization of their skepticism is based on Price's statement: "One financial adviser after another told him to forget about it. At the time, the notion of a public stock offering for a company that had never even turned a profit was alien to the thinking of serious investors" (Price, 143).